WITHDRAWN FROM STOCK

KT-133-652

on
Irish Industry

Jim Fitzpatrick and John H. Kelly
(Editors)

Irish Management Institute

IRISH MANAGEMENT INSTITUTE
DUBLIN

First published 1985

All rights reserved. No part of this publication may be reproduced, stored in a retrieval system, or transmitted in any form or by any means, electronic, mechanical, photocopying, recording, or otherwise, except for normal review purposes, without the prior permission of the copyright holders.

© Irish Management Institute.

ISBN 0 903352 43 5 (Hard Cover)
     0 903352 44 3 (Soft Cover)

Printed in Ireland by Mount Salus Press Limited, Dublin.

Contents

List of Tables

INTRODUCTION

CHAPTER 1

CHAPTER 2

CHAPTER 3

CHAPTER 4

CHAPTER 5

CHAPTER 6

Editors

Jim Fitzpatrick   Jim Fitzpatrick and Associates

John H. Kelly   Central Bank of Ireland

Other Contributors

Alan W. Gray   Craig Gardner and Co.

Tom Healy   Economic and Social Research Institute

Kieran A. Kennedy   Economic and Social Research Institute

Ronan O'Brien   Science Policy Research Centre, UCD.

Eoin O'Malley   Economic and Social Research Institute

James Stewart   Trinity College Dublin

Foreword

Brendan M. Walsh

Industrial policy is the subject of a lively current debate among economists. Quite sharp divisions have emerged between those who favour active state intervention in stimulating and guiding industrial development and those who feel that such a policy is unlikely to raise economic welfare. Although expressed in a new language, the ideas and ideologies would not be unfamiliar to a student whose knowledge of economics was limited to the writers of the eighteenth and nineteenth centuries.

The champions of industrial policy in America argue that it is essential to have a coherent strategy towards industry. The existing patchwork quilt of incentives and grants, penalties and obstacles, constitutes a *de facto* industrial policy that is proving inadequate in meeting the challenges facing America today. Failure to respond to these challenges in a more effective manner will lead to the decline of America from its pre-eminence as an industrial nation, to be replaced by Japan, the country that is inevitably held up as the paragon of policy relating to industrial development.[1]

To others — and outside Ireland they are probably in the majority among economists — the idea of a formal industrial policy is a Trojan horse in whose hollow entrails lurks an unholy alliance of businessmen, lobbyists, planners and politicians ready to continue their conspiracy to transfer taxpayers' money into their own pockets under the guise of helping the national economy. In America it has been argued that any extension of government in the industrial area would further politicize the country's business community and divert politicians' attention from the pressing problem of the Federal budget deficit.[2]

In Ireland we have a long experience with industrial policy, although the term is relatively novel. In the 1930s we relied on protectionism and a guaranteed domestic market to foster industrial growth and employment. The limits of this approach became apparent early in the post-war era. A detailed study of the economic costs and benefits of this experiment has yet to be written.

There was a fairly abrupt change from our attempts at autarky to an outward-looking set of policies during the 1950s. Restrictions on foreign investment in Ireland were replaced by tax incentives, fixed asset grants and a favourable climate for firms offering the promise of export-led growth. The new approach was credited with much of the improvement in Ireland's economic performance during the 1960s and into the 1970s. In recent years, however, there has been a growing disillusionment with these policies, mainly because of the stagnation of industrial employment. But just as it is far from clear how much of the growth of the 1960s and 1970s should be ascribed to the industrial policies pursued during those years, it is also not clear whether an alternative set of policies is available to help us over our present difficulties.

A long re-evaluation of industrial policy has been taking place in Ireland, culminating in the publication of the government White Paper in July 1984.[3] It is understandable that some of the input to this debate should have come from participants in the US debate on industrial policy, but less so that only those identified as proponents of an active industrial policy should be invited to contribute to our deliberations. It tends to be taken for granted in Ireland that we should have an industrial policy: the debate is confined to what form this policy should take. One of the topics that has not received adequate attention is whether politicians, civil servants and economic experts are more or less effective in guiding the allocation of resources than the impersonal forces of the market place. Or, since economic decisions should be taken at the margin, whether the economy would benefit from less, rather than simply a different type of, intervention.

The Irish experience since the 1930s offers a valuable case history for the student of industrial policy. A critical examination of past experience is likely to be helpful in identifying the policies that are likely to prove effective in the future. An uncritical frame of mind leads to the extension of policy into areas such as the distribution of investment by sector, by region of the country, size of enterprise and even sex-ratio of labour force. What planners regard as desirble is all too readily confused with what is attainable. The availability of effective instruments receives less attention than the properties of the desired outcome.

It is, of course, inescapable that the activities of the state affect the incentives to work and invest. However, it would be helpful, in my view, if the assumptions were that neutrality between sectors is to be preferred, and departures from this ideal kept to a minimum. Even the priority that should be assigned to industry, relative to agriculture and services, should be decided by technology, consumers' preference and producers' work habits, rather than by politicians acting on the advice of experts and subject to pressure from lobbyists.

Journalists and commentators occasionally complain about the volume of literature generated by the debate on industrial policy. It is, however, important to view the resources that have been devoted to analysis and evaluation in relation to the amount of money that has been spent on the policy. The essays that make up the present book explore individual topics that occur and recur in the debate on Irish industrial policy. They represent valuable contributions to this debate. Policy-makers, industrialists and students will benefit greatly from their availability.

Department of Political Economy, University College, Dublin
June 1984

---

1. See Ira Magaziner and Robert Reich, *Minding America's Business* (New York: Harcourt Brace Jovanovich), 1982.
2. See Charles L. Schulze, 'Industrial Policy: A Dissent', *The Brookings Review* (Fall 1983).
3. White Paper on Industrial Policy (Dublin: Stationery Office, 1984).

Introduction

Industry in Ireland:
Policies, Performance and Problems

Jim Fitzpatrick and John H. Kelly

Future Irish economic historians are likely to view the late 1970s and early 1980s as a period of change in Ireland's industrial policy. It will rank alongside the early years of the 1930s and the last years of the 1950s as a time when Irish industrial policy took a distinct shift in direction. The events surrounding these earlier periods of change are well known.[1] With the coming to power of Mr. de Valera in 1932 a switch took place from the immediate post-independence laissez-faire approach to one of autarkical import-substituting industrial development behind high tariff barriers. The late 1950s and early 1960s, a period generally centred on 1958, saw the final abandonment of this approach under Seán Lemass. An outward-looking industrial policy and the attraction of foreign investment were initiated, the policy direction which has remained largely intact up to the present day.

POLICY TOWARDS INDUSTRY — A LOOK BACKWARDS

In 1932, the combination of internal policy goals and external economic circumstances lead to the then new Fianna Fáil government's policy of self-sufficiency, of industrialisation behind high tariff barriers. This policy achieved some impressive results in its early years. For example, between 1931 and 1936 the number of people employed in manufacturing industry in Ireland rose from 61,000 and 98,000. The international protectionism of the 1930s was followed by the enforced economic isolation of the war years and the import substitution policy continued broadly unchanged up to the late 1950s. Chinks in the armour were, however, evident in earlier years; for example, the establishment of Shannon Free Airport in 1947, the Industrial Development Authority in 1949 and Córas Tráchtála in 1951.

The major impetus for a change in policy came in 1958 with the publication of the Government report "Economic Development". Set against the recession and emigration of the 1950s, this report concluded that "policies hitherto followed, though given a fair trial, have not resulted in a viable economy." It heralded the switch to an outward looking policy based on export-led growth. The main elements of this policy still remain in place:

— attraction of foreign investment;
— corporation profit tax concessions initially to exporting and later to all manufacturing firms;
— capital and other grants to new and expanding firms;
— absence of controls on foreign ownership of firms or on profit repatriation;
— free trade with Europe.

The experience of the 1960s and 1970s was, by most standards, highly successful. These were years of unprecedented and sustained economic and industrial growth. Between 1963 and 1973, manufacturing employment in Ireland rose at an average annual rate of 1.7 per cent, almost three times the OECD average. During the 1970s, Ireland had the highest rate of GDP growth in the European Community. Manufacturing industry was to the fore in this performance. Manufactured exports, for example, grew twice as rapidly as merchandise exports as a whole, while exports of manufactures (excluding food and drink) constituted 62 per cent of merchandise exports in 1981 as against 22 per cent in 1960. Government policy was not solely responsible for these achievements, of course. The favourable international economic environment up to the oil crises was an essential backdrop.

With the benefit of hindsight, we now know that the period was not one of unmitigated success. Current problems in the major macroeconomic balances of external payments and government finances are the central indicators of this. Clearly, these involve policies outside the domain of industry and industrial policy. Macroeconomic and industrial policies are, however, interrelated. Basically, Ireland's industrial success over the 1970s did not allow it to either avoid or overcome present economic difficulties.

This is most clearly evident in looking at unemployment, the longstanding central consideration in Irish economic policy. Over the 1970s, manufacturing industry, despite high growth in output, failed to "deliver the goods" in job terms. As the structure of industry in Ireland has changed, job gains in new firms have been outpaced by job losses in older firms. Over the eleven years 1973-1984, the output of manufacturing industry in Ireland rose in all but three years — 1975, 1980 and 1982. Yet only in one year, namely 1979, did employment in manufacturing exceed its 1973 level.

THE CHANGING STRUCTURE OF IRISH INDUSTRY

One of the consequences of the outward-looking policies of the 1960s and 1970s is that today the Irish economy is highly open to international trade, both exports and imports. This is particularly true in manufacturing industry. Half of the output of manufacturing firms in Ireland is sold overseas, and this proportion is much higher in the newer growth industries such as electronics and pharmaceuticals.

Table 1: Growth of Output and Employment in Manufacturing Industry in Ireland (Index 1973 = 100)

Year	1973	1974	1975	1976	1977	1978	1979	1980	1981	1982	1983	1984	Average Annual Change %
Output[1]	100	103	98	108	118	127	135	134	138	137	147	167	+4.7
Employment[2]	100	99	93	95	97	100	105	100	98	93	88	87	−1.3

[1] Yearly average.
[2] December each year.
Source: Central Statistics Office, *Industrial Production Index* and *Industrial Employment, Earnings and Hours Worked* series, various issues.

Together with this increase in openness, the past two decades have witnessed important structural changes in the industrial sector. Older established, traditional industries have declined in importance. Industries such as textiles, clothing and footwear, and leather have been particularly affected, with employment in these industries declining by almost 40 per cent over the decade 1973 to 1982. At the same time, employment in newly-established foreign-owned firms has shown a marked increase. These new foreign firms have increasingly tended to concentrate in the electronics and chemicals sectors, which together accounted for 90 per cent of IDA-approved new foreign investment in 1982.[2] The growth of the electronics sector is an outstanding example of the structural changes which have taken place. From 7,750 employees in 36 firms as recently as 1973, this sector had grown to over 16,000 employees in about 200 firms by 1983,[3] with by far the major proportion of this growth coming from subsidiaries of multinational firms.

The overall pattern of structural change in manufacturing industry during the 1973 to 1983 period is summarised in Table 2. Most notably, employment in foreign-owned firms in the metals and engineering and chemicals sectors increased by more than 80 per cent during this period, while there was a very substantial 37 per cent increase in total employment in foreign-owned firms. As against this, total manufacturing employment in indigenous firms fell by almost 11 per cent.

The emergence of Ireland as a base for export-oriented foreign-owned firms, attracted by extensive financial and fiscal incentives as well as by free access to the EEC market, is reflected in this structural transformation of Irish manufacturing industry. However, although the employment contribution has been striking, there are a number of drawbacks associated with this kind of industrial development. First, while producing a sophisticated product, a proportion of foreign-owned firms use their Irish plant for only one stage in the manufacturing process. More generally, even when the entire

Table 2: Structural Change in Manufacturing Industry in Ireland, 1973-83

	Industrial Production	Employment			Foreign Employment			Domestic Employment
	1983/1973 % Change	1973	1983	1983/1973 % Change	% Share 1973	% Share 1983	1983/1973 % Change	1983/1973 % Change
Total manufacturing of which:	44.9	217,292	216,420	−0.4	27	37	36.6	−10.8
Chemicals	160.6	11,253	13,610	20.9	52	65	50.2	−11.3
Metals and engineering	88.4	42,513	64,970	52.8	47	58	90.4	20.2
Food	38.4	46,856	45,560	−2.8	15	14	−9.8	−1.6
Drink and tobacco	20.4	10,790	10,230	−5.2	39	37	−9.5	−2.5
Textile industry	−15.6	23,003	11,830	−48.6	23	42	−8.5	−60.8
Clothing, footwear	−28.4	24,769	18,850	−23.9	21	35	24.0	−36.8
Timber, wooden furniture	−14.2	10,771	11,750	9.1	7	6	−7.5	10.3
Paper and printing	−7.6	14,503	14,100	−2.8	12	12	−7.7	−2.1
Non-metallic production	11.8	17,282	15,190	47.7	50	18	1.4	93.0
Miscellaneous	53.1		10,330			58		

Source: OECD Economic Surveys, Ireland, April 1985.

product is manufactured in Ireland the key functions of marketing and of research and development are usually retained by the parent company. Second, a large proportion of profits earned by foreign subsidiaries in Ireland may be repatriated by the parent firm, rather than invested in further expansion in this country. Until quite recently profit repatriation was not thought to be a serious problem[4]. However, the revisions to the balance of payments published by the CSO in May 1984 reveal an increasing outflow from this source, making the deficit on the current account of the balance of payments progressively higher than originally estimated in the years 1980 to 1983.[5] Third, foreign firms have tended to source most of their raw materials and intermediate inputs abroad.[6] This leads to low linkages between foreign and domestic firms. Consequently, the potential spin-off contribution of multinational subsidiaries to the Irish economy is not maximised.

In addition to the above difficulties, which are common to most countries pursuing industrial policies based on the attraction of direct foreign investment, two major problems for policy in Ireland have become increasingly obvious in recent years. The first is an apparent decline in Ireland's relative attractiveness as a location for foreign industry. The failure of foreign industry to develop strong ties with the domestic economy means that further employment increases depend on continuing high levels of new direct foreign investment. Recent trends suggest that these will be harder to maintain in the future. While some of the decline in investment inflows in the early 1980s is undoubtedly linked to the international recession, and a reduced volume of internationally mobile investment, there are also some signs that a more competitive environment among potential host countries has had a detrimental effect on inflows to Ireland. Between 1979 and 1982, Ireland's share of new US overseas investment in Europe declined from 2.3 per cent to 1.5 per cent, at the same time as Italy's share increased from 7.3 per cent to 8.3 per cent,

Holland's increased from 7.2 per cent to 9.2 per cent and that of the UK increased from 29.9 per cent to 32.8 per cent.[7] Ireland's stock position has not, however, deteriorated.[8] This probably reflects an absence of large-scale foreign disinvestment in the Irish case. Looking to the future, it is likely that Ireland's attractiveness regarding new investment inflows will be weakened by the accession of Spain and Portugal to the EEC, since both of these countries possess attractions comparable to Ireland for firms seeking secure access to EEC markets.

The second major problem for Irish industrial policy is the cost to the public finances of funding the industrialisation effort. As a result of the high rate of job loss which Ireland has experienced since 1973, the number of sustainable jobs created has fallen far short of the gross number of new jobs created. The average direct grant cost (excluding re-equipment grants) per job in new indigenous and foreign industry, based on calculations presented in the Telesis Report,[9] are set out in Table 3. It can be seen that while the grant cost per job created, in 1980 prices, in both indigenous and foreign industry was roughly equivalent to average annual earnings in manufacturing, the cost per job sustained was significantly higher. In foreign industry it was approximately twice average earnings and in indigenous industry three times average earnings.[10]

The high rate of job loss, which makes the cost of sustainable jobs so high, can be attributed to a number of factors, not all of which are under domestic control. However, one reason identified by the National Economic and Social Council (NESC)[11] is that, particularly in the case of indigenous industry, insufficient attention is paid to the structure necessary for a company to remain viable. A more general explanation, put forward by the OECD,[12] is that the incentive schemes offered in Ireland have not been as efficiently directed as they might have been. The OECD has referred in particular to the effects of incentives in reducing the cost of capital to

Table 3: Grant Cost Per Job in New Indigenous and Foreign Industry

£mm 1980 Prices	(000s)	1980 Prices
Indigenous Industry 1973-79		
		Approved grant cost
Grants approved	Jobs approved	per job
282.6	61.6	£4,587
Grants paid	Jobs created	Grant cost/job created
130.2	31.2	£4,173
	Jobs sustained	Grant cost/job sustained
	10.3	£12,640
Foreign Industry 1973-80		
		Approved grant cost
Grants approved	Jobs approved	per job
844.2	101.0	£8,358
Grants paid	Jobs created	Grant cost/job created
177.3	41.1	£4,211
	Jobs sustained	Grant cost/job sustained
	23.9	£7,413

Source: National Economic and Social Council, *Policies for Industrial Development: Conclusions and Recommendations,* (NESC Report No. 66) Dublin, 1982, Table 4.

firms. After allowing for inflation, it has been calculated that the cost of capital in 1983 was only about half of what it had been a decade earlier.[13] Over the same period, labour costs increased quite rapidly, partly as a direct result of government decisions to increase payroll taxes, with the result that the substitution of capital for labour has been encouraged. It is, therefore, not altogether surprising that increases in industrial employment have been so modest and the cost of sustainable jobs so high.

A RE-ASSESSMENT OF INDUSTRIAL POLICY

The difficulties and problems which became increasingly evident during the 1970s prompted a major re-examination of the aims and instruments of industrial policy. In 1979, the government requested the NESC to undertake a review of Irish industrial policy. The NESC produced five reports in all, but most attention has centred on Report No. 64, *A Review of Industrial Policy,* prepared by the Telesis Consultancy Group (The Telesis Report).[14] This formed the basis for the NESC's recommendations concerning the future direction of policy.[15]

The Telesis Report agreed with the broad thrust of Irish industrial policy and was complimentary about many aspects of implementation. Ireland, the report stated, has "a very sophisticated and extensive industrial policy, involving large numbers of people in a wide variety of activities to assist industrial development. The intentions expressed in the philosophy and goals of Irish industrial policy are intelligent and clear, the agencies are extremely inventive and energetic in devising programmes to carry out these goals, and substantial sums of money are being spent in support of these efforts." It was their view about how the money was being spent that was critical and controversial. This view focused on the balance between the promotion of foreign and of indigenous industry. Central to this was the argument that "no country has successfully achieved high incomes without a strong base of indigenously owned resource or manufacturing companies in traded businesses." In Telesis' view, Irish industrial policy devoted insufficient resources to developing indigenous businesses, and foreign investment could also be better utilised in the effort to do this. It also argued that Ireland was paying too much in grants and tax foregone for the number and type of sustainable jobs which foreign firms brought.

Telesis' recommendations regarding Irish policy towards foreign industrial investment were that:

— the average capital grants offered to foreign firms establishing factories in Ireland should be substantially reduced. Current levels of incentive should continue to be offered to particularly desirable projects, but the grants to most projects should be severely cut . . . .
— consideration should be given to further use of loan, loan guarantee, redeemable equity and participative loans, for providing incentives to foreign firms . . . .
— better advantage should be sought from foreign companies operating in Ireland to spur indigenous industry development.

Specific suggestions in regard to the development of indigenous industry were that:

— incentives directed towards new indigenous industry should be re-organised so as to emphasise the building of structurally strong Irish companies rather than strong agencies to assist weak companies;
— greater participation by large indigenous companies and by the indigenous financial community in traded and skilled sub-supply businesses in Ireland should be encouraged;
— grants to indigenous industry should be re-orientated so as to correct specific cost disadvantages and should be directed to the long-term removal of these disadvantages.

In addition, Telesis considered that government departments abdicated too much of their role in strategy formulation to state agencies and that they possessed neither the staff nor the information necessary to formulate strategy themselves or to oversee the development agencies on an ongoing basis. Consequently, it was recommended that government departments should pursue a more active policy role and that sufficient data be developed to facilitate this. An active review process was suggested as a means by which government could more clearly monitor and change the course of policy implementation.

TWO VIEWS ON THE ROLE OF GOVERNMENT

Parallel to the official review of industrial policy, a lively debate on the subject developed among economists in Ireland. Two polar views of the problems facing Irish industrial development and of the appropriate government action to solve these emerged from this debate. On the one hand, it is held that the economic environment in Ireland does not favour the development of industry, that existing government incentives are inadequate to compensate for this, and that government actions not primarily directed towards the industrial sector frequently have a harmful effect on industrial development. On the other hand, it is argued that Ireland, in common with a number of other late-industrialising countries, faces significant barriers to entry into international competition because of the advantages enjoyed by established competitors. These advantages relate mainly to economies of scale in production, marketing and finance, and to technological superiority and control. The limitations of an industrial policy which relies mainly on the attraction of multinational subsidiaries are acknowledged by holders of both views; the policy responses discussed below, therefore, relate mainly to the encouragement of domestic industry.

For those who hold the first view, the policy prescription is clear. The government should concentrate on developing an efficient and low-priced infrastructure, on restraining increases in labour and other input costs, and on restructuring tax and grant incentives so as to encourage more investment and entrepreneurial effort in industry, rather than in other sectors contributing less to national development. To date, it is suggested, the incentive structure in Ireland has favoured investment in property, residential housing and government securities over industrial investment.[16] The conclusion, therefore, is not that the private market is incapable of allocating funds efficiently to the industrial sector but rather that a poor economic environment and misguided government policies have not given market forces and private enterprise a fair chance.

Holders of the second view would concede that there are deficiencies in the economic environment and in the structure of government incentives. However, these deficiencies are not seen as major problems compared to the general difficulties facing firms in late industrialising countries. Consequently, correcting the deficiencies will not be expected in itself to lead to any significant improvement in industrial performance. Because of the disadvantages faced by new Irish firms in breaking into many industries which are dominated by strong established foreign firms, few if any private enterprises in Ireland could attempt to do so on their own initiative, even when local conditions and government incentives are favourable. This leads to the conclusion that government policy must assume a more active role. Rather than simply administering incentive schemes, development agencies must be prepared to take initiatives in developing new industries on a scale sufficient to overcome barriers faced by a late-industrialising country.[17] Holders of this view point to the success of industrial strategies in Japan, South Korea and Taiwan where outward-looking export-oriented policies have not relied on pure market forces but have taken the form of quite specific state initiatives to develop "targeted" industries characterised by barriers to entry. The process of selecting industries in these countries typically involved moving increasingly into large-scale, capital intensive and/or knowledge intensive activities, based on a technology policy of importing best-practice methods under licence for indigenous firms or, occasionally, through joint ventures with foreign firms.[18]

While it has been pointed out that these two views of what is required of government policy are not necessarily mutually exclusive,[19] their proponents in Ireland have tended to focus on the differences between them rather than on the potential compatibility of the suggested solutions. In this book, no attempt is made to evaluate the extent to which either view suggests the most appropriate policy prescriptions for Ireland. The authors of particular chapters, in discussing the policy implications of the empirical evidence which they present, do however, come down in favour of one or other approach. The short discussion on the policy debate provided here is intended to serve as a guide to the broader context within which these individual proposals should be assessed.

THE WHITE PAPER ON INDUSTRIAL POLICY

The government *White Paper on Industrial Policy,* published in July 1984, was the official outcome of the NESC-lead review of industrial policy of recent years.[20] The White Paper's main conclusions were also reiterated in the national economic plan, *Building on Reality 1985-1987,* published later in that year.[21] The White Paper begins by acknowledging that industrial policies which had clearly served Ireland well in the 1960 and 1970s are now having less success. This is largely attributed to changes in the external environment. Ireland now faces greater competition for a declining volume of mobile investment from both industrialised and developing countries, while the decline of our older labour intensive industries is considered to have been accelerated by the development of the same industries in low-wage Third World countries.

In view of the changed environment in which policy now operates, the White Paper seeks "to give a new impetus to industrial development."[22] To achieve this, official policy objectives are reformulated. These stated objectives are:
(i) to create and maintain the maximum number of sustainable jobs, as many as possible of them high-skilled, in manufacturing and international service industries;
(ii) to maximise value-added by these sectors and to capture the wealth thus created for further investment and employment creation in the Irish economy;
(iii) to develop a strong and internationally competitive indus-

trial sector in Ireland, made up of both Irish and foreign-owned industry;

(iv) to promote the more rapid development of our natural resource-based industries, particularly food and timber;

(v) to promote the integration of foreign industry into the Irish economy through greater linkage with Irish industry and educational institutions;

(vi) to improve the rate of return on the government's investment in the commercial State companies.[23]

The most notable change involved in the reformulation of objectives is the reduced emphasis on direct employment creation. For a quarter of a century, the success of Irish industrial policy was measured by the number of jobs "created" in both new foreign and domestic firms, with the number of job approvals secured by the IDA in each year being the main indicator of policy success. However, The Telesis Report had suggested that concentration on job numbers alone constituted too narrow a basis for industrial policy and called for a greater emphasis on domestic value-added as a target. This view was subsequently strongly endorsed by the IDA[24] and is now officially incorporated as a policy aim.

In addition to the broadening of policy objectives the White Paper also announced a number of new or improved incentives for:

(i) technology acquisition;

(ii) market research;

(iii) market entry development and distribution;

(iv) export finance and insurance;

(v) internationally-oriented service companies.

Existing incentives were retained, with the exception of re-equipment grants, but provision was made for greater selectivity in the case of these incentives. In exercising this selectivity, development agencies are to be guided by two main sets of criteria. The first relates to the products which firms produce. These must be primarily either for sale on overseas markets, for sub-supply to internationally-trading or other skilled firms in Ireland, or to supply niches of the Irish market now wholly or significantly supplied by imports. The second set of criteria relate to the proposed investment. Firms must be able to demonstrate that financial assistance is necessary for the investment to take place, that the investment is commercially viable, and that they have prepared a company development plan.

A further innovation announced in the White Paper is the "Company Development Approach". This approach involves the identification of promising firms, prepared to commit themselves to working closely with the appropriate State agencies. It is hoped that by taking an overall company development approach the aim of building up Irish-based companies capable of achieving a strong market position will be most effectively realised. Additional funds for the development of structurally-strong Irish firms are to be made available from the planned National Development Corporation, the proposed functions of which are also contained in the White Paper. This is to be a new State investment vehicle, taking equity stakes in new or expanding Irish business ventures.

Finally, to improve the monitoring of industrial performance and the effectiveness of agencies, a management committee comprising the Chief Executives of the main industrial development agencies has been established. Provision has also been made for a major review of industrial policies every three years in order to assess their effectiveness.

In general, the White Paper received a qualified welcome. Most commentators felt that there was little really new in it but, nevertheless, concede that any innovations and changes in emphasis which it contained represent improvements on the previous system.[25] Over the medium term some of the changes, such as the move towards problem-solving oriented incentives, the increased focus on marketing constraints and the increased emphasis on indigenous industry, may prove to be significant, although it is difficult at this stage to assess their impact. Perhaps even more so than at previous cross-roads in Irish industrial policy, changes this time will prove evolutionary rather than revolutionary.

Looked at in the context of the industrial policy debate that preceded it, however, the White Paper is likely to prove deficient both to those who favour an improved environment for industry and to those who see strong direct government intervention as necessary to assist Irish industry to enter international markets. In the first instance, the White Paper only deals with those policies which are the direct responsibility of the Department of Industry, Trade, Commerce and Tourism. As a result, policies which are not specific to the industrial sector but which nevertheless have an important impact on that sector, such as taxation and social insurance, labour legislation and energy pricing, were not addressed. This lack of comprehensiveness is an important failing for, as will be demonstrated later in this book, inconsistencies between government actions in different areas can have a serious negative impact on industrial development.

In the second instance, while interventionist, the model of industrial development proposed in the White Paper falls far short of the strongly interventionist action taken by many South-East Asian countries. There is also no questioning of the basis for government involvement in the industrial sector and no discussion of radical alternatives to existing policies. Thus, while some of the individual proposals, such as a greater emphasis on technology acquisition and greater selectivity in the distribution of incentives, are a step in the right direction they are likely to prove as insufficient to compensate for the disadvantages facing late-comers in international markets.

But perhaps the greatest weaknesses of the White Paper lie in its failure to specify policy instruments to achieve the objectives of building up indigenous firms and attracting overseas firms with key business functions and its omission of an industrial policy budget. Both of these short-comings have been pointed out by the National Economic and Social Council, who consider the absence of precision "in relation to the allocation of State resources" to be a major oversight.[26] In the Council's opinion, "this short-coming represents a failure on the part of government . . . . to convert the expression of broad strategic sentiments on industrial policy into an operational decision-making framework sufficient to the task of realising the strategic objectives."[27]

APPROACH OF THE BOOK

Despite the central role of industry in Ireland's economic development and the prominent role of government policy in the sector, economic and other researchers in Ireland have paid surprisingly little attention to industrial policy issues.[28] This subject has received relatively low priority by comparison with issues of, for example, macro-economic policy, and many of the important assumptions frequently made have not been subjected to much close empirical scrutiny. This has, however, been changing. In parallel with the official review of industrial policy of recent years, an increasing amount of academic and other research effort has been devoted to issues relating to Ireland's industrial experience. The purpose of the present book is to bring together the results of some of this empirical work and make it available to those for whom it might be a significant input to decision making now or in the future.

The approach of the book is to deal with a number of individual issues relevant to industrial policy in Ireland. Each chapter is written by a separate author (or authors) and deals with a separate topic. The book is not, therefore, an attempt to formulate a "grand plan" for Irish policy in the 1980s and 1990s. Rather, its approach is to deal with individual issues on which the authors of the chapters have undertaken research. The topics covered were, therefore, selected on the basis of availability of relevant empirical results. Consequently, coverage is not comprehensive and many important matters are not included. The methodology of the book and of the individual authors is essentially economic.[29] Therefore, matters are not examined from political, sociological or other viewpoints. The approach is also a national country-level one rather than one from an individual firm's perspective. The findings of this book are, therefore, seen as primarily for those involved or interested in national policy. This will clearly include government departments, state agencies, third-level education institutions and other parts of the public service.

This is not a book of interest only to the public sector, however. As outlined earlier, since the foundation of the state one aspect of government policy towards manufacturing industry in Ireland has remained consistent and is likely to remain so in the decade ahead. This is that the role of the state in deliberately influencing industrial development has been exercised primarily through a system of inducements to the private sector to take desired directions. The range of semi-state bodies offering grants, loans, technical assistance and other services to the private sector is evidence of this. Therefore, the business environment in which managers take their long-term or day-to-day corporate decisions is heavily influenced by government policy. The issues of concern to those who make this policy cannot, therefore, but be of interest to those who are affected by it, and this book is about those issues.

CONTENT OF THE BOOK

In its conclusion, the Telesis Report suggested that perhaps the greatest need for Ireland's industrial policy in the 1980s is to better manage the development of indigenous industry.[30] One area where important lessons for the improved management of indigenous industry may be learnt is from the past experience of such industry. In Chapter 1 of this book, entitled "The

Performance of Irish Indigenous Industry: Lessons for the 1980s", Eoin O'Malley reviews the performance of Irish-owned or indigenous industry since the foundation of the State. Developments during both the protectionist policy phase, which saw a rapid growth in indigenous import-substituting industry, and the later period of free trade and "outward-looking" policies are examined. Empirical data regarding the contribution of Irish-owned industry to overall growth of industrial employment, output and exports since the early 1960s are provided. Particular attention is paid to the issue of the effectiveness of free trade and export-promotion policies in developing internationally traded export industries in the indigenous sector. The empirical analysis presented in the chapter reveals that the performance of indigenous industry over the past two decades has been quite weak. This was masked by the rapid growth of new foreign industry, creating the overall impression of substantial industrial development in Ireland. There follows a discussion of alternative policies for the promotion of indigenous industry. In his concluding section O'Malley suggests a wide range of measures which could prove beneficial in this respect.

Chapter 2 of the book turns to an examination of a major component of indigenous Irish industry, namely small industry. In this chapter Kieran Kennedy and Tom Healy look at "Small-scale Industry in Ireland". The authors note that, like Irish industrial policy in general, economic analysts and policy makers in all countries have for long neglected the subject of small industry. This neglect arose from a general assumption that large sized firms were more efficient and that small firms accounted for only a small share of total manufacturing output and employment. However, increasing interest in small-scale industry has been evident in recent years. The chapter goes on to examine the quantitative significance of small industry in Ireland. In 1980, small firms defined as firms with less than 50 employees accounted for almost a quarter of manufacturing employment. The authors also examine the characteristics of small firms, the particular problems facing them, together with the experience of the IDA's Small Industry Programme. Kennedy and Healy conclude that there is a good case for continued specialised attention to small firms within the major development agency, the IDA, and also in some of the other development agencies. However, they say that the focus of this attention should not simply be on those with outstanding prospects but also on encouraging the formation of new small enterprise and increasing efficiency in those which survive but never grow large. The authors acknowledge that "there is a danger that great diversity in the experience of small firms, and in the problems facing them, could lead to a continuous accretion of services". Thus a service introduced to meet problems particular to one class of firms may be demanded even by those in less need of that service. Some safeguards in this regard are therefore necessary and are suggested by the authors.

Ireland's move in the late 1950s to a policy of export-led growth, based on participation in international trade, was followed by a progressive increase in the volume of both imports and exports during the 1960s and 1970s. While the contribution of export-oriented industry to industrial development has received considerable attention, the effects of the increased import volume on the industrial sector have been relatively neglected. In an attempt to redress this balance Chapter 3, entitled "Industrial Policy and the Import Dependence of the Irish Economy", is devoted to an examination of the import dependence of the Irish economy and the implications of this for industrial policy. In the early part of this chapter the authors, Alan Gray and John Kelly, are concerned with an empirical examination of imports at a twenty-sector level of disaggregation. This permits trends in the growth of imports in each of these industrial sectors to be identified. The reasons behind the level of and movements in import penetration are analysed by comparing industries with high import penetration to industries with low import penetration. The policy implications of the earlier findings are then discussed and a number of specific proposals are put forward. These relate in particular to the development of intra-industry trade, the enhancement of the competitiveness of Irish industry, and the exploitation of the sub-supply market in Ireland.

In Chapter 4, Jim Fitzpatrick examines a more specific aspect of import competition facing Irish manufacturing industry, namely competition from less developed countries. The chapter, entitled "Competition from the Less Developed Countries and Irish Manufacturing Industry", notes that one of the major international economic changes of the 1960s and 1970s was the emergence of a number of newly industrialising developing countries (NICs) as prominent exporters of low-cost manufactured goods. The chapter describes this emergence and discusses its implications for Irish industry and Irish industrial policy. The chapter has four parts. The author begins by clarifying to which countries the term "NICs" is applied. The chapter then looks at the role which this group of countries play in world trade and in Ireland's foreign trade. The nature and extent of import competition from them is then examined. Finally, the chapter reviews the policy response of the industrialised western countries to such competition and it discusses the forms of response which Ireland's industrial policy-makers might consider. The author argues for a "positive adjustment" approach by Ireland involving decisions in two areas, namely foreign trade policy and domestic industrial policy. In the field of industrial policy the need is not for new policy instruments but for an appropriate orientation and co-ordination of the wide range of instruments which already exist in the areas of grant assistance, manpower, technology and other industrial aids and services. The author's view is that the evidence of the chapter points to the feasibility of adopting such a positive approach to low-cost competition from developing countries. Such competition, the author states, "while significant and growing, is not as sweeping or as dramatic as may sometimes be supposed".

Financial behaviour of multinational companies (MNCs) operating in Ireland are the subject of Chapter 5, "Aspects of the Financial Behaviour of Multinational Companies in Ireland". Statistics relating to financial behaviour are typically difficult to obtain. In this chapter James Stewart uses a unique data set built up over a number of years to provide some insights into the financial behaviour of MNCs. Three areas in particular are examined; "crowding-out", "transfer pricing", and the balance of payments effects of direct foreign investment. Crowding out is often perceived as an issue in LDCs. It means that foreign investment tends to absorb most of the available savings/credit in an economy to the detriment of the domestic corporate sector. Data on bank lending to a sample of 20 multinational company subsidiaries over the period 1972 to 1980 are used here to assess the seriousness of this effect in Ireland. Transfer pricing is generally used to switch profits from one country to another and for that reason, in this chapter, is referred to as 'profit switching transfer pricing'. Where foreign investment generates profits from exports and hence is tax free, transfer pricing may not have much effect on tax revenues. However, in the case where profits are generated domestically, 'profit switching transfer pricing' can result in a loss in tax-revenue to the Exchequer. Transfer pricing may also distort trade statistics and data on company profitability, and act as a mechanism by means of which funds may be transferred within the MNC. Data relating the profits of Irish subsidiaries to total company profit are presented as a measure of the existence of transfer pricing and trends in value-added by "new industry" in Ireland are examined. In looking at the balance of payments effects of MNCs, financial flows which indicate the degree to which MNCs are reinvesting within the Irish economy, their reliance on the parent company for finance, and the extent to which they tend to take 'positions' on the currency are examined.

Another important aspect of the role of multinational manufacturing companies in industrial development is their potential for helping to build a high technology industrial base in host countries. In Chapter 6, "Technology and Industrial Development: Irish Electronics in an International Context", Ronan O'Brien examines the issue of technology and industrial development in Ireland with reference to the electronics industry. The central issue which the chapter addresses is how a country such as Ireland which is industrialising relatively late can build up a capability in a group of growing industries which in turn can provide the base for further expansion over the long run. Within this general issue, the focus is on the role of technology in the process. As a background the first section examines the role of technology in industrial competition. The second section examines the effect of location on national technological capability. The third section of the chapter draws some important lessons for Ireland from the approaches of other successful late industrialising countries competing in the electronics industry. The experience of the electronics industry in Ireland is examined in the fourth section. The chapter considers three possible approaches by which an electronics industry base, capable of self-sustained growth, can be built up in the particular conditions existing in Ireland. The first approach, which relies on attracting multinational firms, is found to be inadequate for building this type of base despite its contribution to employment. The second approach, the "Silicon Valley" process whereby many high technology firms start up, enter new industry segments, and grow rapidly, is found not to be a feasible proposition in Irish circumstances. In considering the third approach, namely the build-up of large indigenous companies, the author argues that measures which lie outside the standard prescriptions are necessary in Ireland's specific circumstances and that much can be learned from the measures adopted in other countries facing comparable obstacles. In rapidly changing industries such as electronics, O'Brien states, "it appears that to provide the necessary environment for building individual and organisational capabilities requires intervention by the State in the structure of the domestic industry".

xl

NOTES AND REFERENCES

1. See, for example, J.W. O'Hagan and K.P. McStay, *The Evolution of Manufacturing Industry in Ireland*, (Dublin: Helicon, 1981).
2. *IDA Annual Report*, 1982.
3. Data from Chapter 6, Table 6.5.
4. D. McAleese, *A Profile of Grant-Aided Industry in Ireland* (Dublin, IDA, 1977).
5. *Revisions to the Balance of International Payments and the National Accounts*, (Dublin, CSO, May 1984).
6. This point is discussed at greater length in Chapter 3. For the most recent comprehensive measure of linkages see P.N. O'Farrell and B. O'Loughlin, *An Analysis of New Industry Linkages in Ireland* (Dublin: IDA, 1980).
7. OECD Economic Survey, *Ireland*, (December 1983), footnote 33.
8. See J. Fitzpatrick, *Republic of Ireland: Economic Prospects 1984-88*, (London, The Economist Intelligence Unit, 1984), Table 27.
9. Telesis Consultancy Group, *A Review of Industrial Policy* (Dublin: National Economic and Social Council (Report No. 64) 1982).
10. *Policies for Industrial Development: Conclusions and Recommendations* (Dublin, National Economic and Social Council (Report No. 66) 1982).
11. ibid.
12. OECD Economic Survey, *Ireland*, op. cit.
13. J. Flynn and P. Honohan, "Notes on the Cost of Capital in Ireland", *Journal of Irish Business and Administrative Research*, Vol. 6, No. 1, (April 1984).
14. Telesis Consultancy Group, op. cit.
15. NESC Report No. 66, op. cit.
16. See, for instance, F.P. Ruane, "Government Financial and Tax Incentives and Industrial Employment", *The Irish Banking Review*, (June 1983).
17. See, for instance, E. O'Malley, "Late Industrialisation under Outward-Looking Policies in the Republic of Ireland", paper read to the Development Studies Association Annual Conference (September 1982), and Chapter 1 of this book.
18. Ira C. Magaziner and Thomas M. Hout, *Japanese Industrial Policy* (London: Policy Studies Institute, Paper No. 585, 1980); N. Rosser "Latecomer Advantage in the Eighties and the Lessons of Postwar Japanese Industrial Policy", M.A. Thesis, University of Sussex, 1980.
19. D. McAleese, "Ireland in the European Community: An Economic Evaluation", *Export Review*, Vol. 2 No. 1, April 1983.
20. *White Paper on Industrial Policy* (Dublin: The Stationery Office, 1984).
21. *Building on Reality 1985-1987*, (Dublin: The Stationery Office, 1984).
22. ibid. p. 3.
23. ibid. pp. 5-6.
24. P.A. White, "A Concept of Industrial Development in the 1980s", paper read to the Statistical and Social Inquiry Society of Ireland, 2nd December 1982.
25. F.P. Ruane, "The White Paper on Industrial Policy" *The Irish Banking Review*, (September 1984).
26. *Economic and Social Policy Assessment* (Dublin: National Economic and Social Council (Report No. 79) 1985) pp. 37-38.

27. ibid., p. 39.

28. For a literature review see E. O'Malley, *Industrial Policy and Development: A Survey of Literature from the Early 1960s to the Present,* (Dublin: National Economic and Social Council (Report No. 56) 1981).

29. For alternative approaches see C. Carroll, *Building Ireland's Business Perspectives from PIMS,* (Dublin: Irish Management Institute, 1985), and S.A. Brophy, *The Strategic Management of Irish Enterprise 1934-1984, Case Studies from Leading Irish Companies,* (Dublin: Smurfit Publications, 1985).

30. Telesis Consultancy Group, op. cit.

1

The Performance of Irish Indigenous Industry: Lessons for the 1980s

Eoin O'Malley

It was pointed out in the Introduction that the outward-looking free market industrial policies introduced in the late 1950s semed notably successful by the standard criteria until quite recently. The rate of growth of industrial output, for instance, was several times greater in the 1960s and 1970s than it had been in the 1950s. It has, however, now been widely recognised that this overall improvement in industrial performance was due largely to the establishment of many new foreign-owned firms in Ireland, while indigenous or native Irish industry showed rather less improvement. The present chapter examines the performance of Irish indigenous industry and considers the implications for industrial policy.

In order to understand and explain the weak performance of Irish native industry, the theoretical interpretation in this chapter will start by recognising that the relatively long-established industries of advanced economies have generally built up substantial competitive advantages over aspiring newcomers to industrialisation. Thus the existing competitive strength of established industries creates *barriers to entry* for newcomers in many sectors. This problem would affect the *indigenous* industries of a relatively late-industrialising country such as Ireland, but not the subsidiaries of advanced foreign firms which have come to Ireland. Thus it can account for the fact that there has been a substantial difference in the

1

performance of native and foreign industries in Ireland, despite the fact that both groups operate in much the same environment.

According to this interpretation, therefore, the behaviour of foreign firms in Ireland would have to be considered primarily in the light of factors which influence the plant location decisions of *strong established* industrial firms. But because Irish indigenous industry was clearly very weak by international competitive standards up to the 1950s, an analysis of its performance since then would have to take account of the pervasive influence of barriers to entry constraining the development of relatively new and weak industries.

This theoretical interpretation differs from the view of industrial development based on neo-classical economics, which would regard barriers to entry as rather exceptional 'imperfections' in a generally efficient world market economy. Thus according to the neo-classical view the way should generally be open for latecomers to industrialise if they create an attractive environment and the right incentives for industrial investment. There would be a considerable problem for the neo-classical interpretation as applied to Ireland, however, in trying to explain why foreign firms have found Ireland an attractive environment (and why *some* native Irish industries have grown rapidly, as will be shown below), while many Irish indigenous industries have tended to decline. The theoretical interpretation adopted in this chapter, however, aims to show why these trends have occurred and to provide a basis for different policy conclusions than those put forward by pure neo-classical economists.

Although this chapter is concerned only with the experience of Ireland, it is worth pointing out that the effect of the same constraints arising from barriers to entry can be observed in the less-developed and newly industrialising countries in general. The industries of most of these countries produce mainly for artificially protected domestic markets and show little ability to compete with established industrial economies in export markets. Some exceptions to this rule are a narrow range of industries which are easily penetrated due to low barriers to entry (textiles, clothing, toys, etc.), as well as exports from subsidiaries of foreign companies, as in Ireland. But the opportunities presented by these exceptions are very limited, especially in relation to the size of the less-developed world.

There are, however, a few examples of relatively late-industrialising countries which have succeeded in developing competitive indigenous industries in a wider range of sectors. These examples — notably South Korea and Taiwan recently, and Japan some decades ago — used strong protection and active government policies to overcome barriers to entry. They did not rely only on free market forces and passive incentives to private enterprise as the neo-classical analysis recommends. Accordingly, the policy conclusions of this chapter recommend a far more *active* governmental strategy for the development of Irish indigenous industries capable of overcoming barriers to entry.

BARRIERS TO ENTRY FOR LATECOMERS

Unlike the neo-classical theory, a number of other strands of the literature on industrial development share a recognition of the fact that long-established industries, which are mainly based in the most advanced industrial countries, have built up competitive advantages over aspiring newcomers. These advantages are so strong as to create serious barriers to entry in many sectors. Barriers to entry arise for various reasons, and both their nature and the degree of difficulty they present for newcomers vary from one activity to the next. Some types of barriers to entry apply to individual firms and others apply at a broader, industry-wide level.

One source of entry barriers for indigenous firms in relatively late-developing countries such as Ireland is the existence of *economies of scale* in production in many activities which means that costs per unit of production decline as the scale of output increases.[1] This creates entry barriers because the development of production to the large scale required to be competitive can be not only very demanding on capital for investment, but also difficult or impossible for new firms to achieve without substantial initial losses when competing with existing large producers. To take just one example of an industry with significant economies of scale, one Swedish producer of ethylene oxide had to build a plant in the 1960s which was large enough to supply the whole Scandinavian market of over 20 million people in order to attain a competitive scale. Since then the minimum efficient scale has increased tenfold. Similar stories are true of dozens of important sectors, such as the older technically mature branches of the chemicals, metals, pulp, paper and machinery industries.[2] Increases in economies of scale over time have squeezed out smaller established firms in many maturing industries and simultaneously created rising barriers to entry for latecomers.

The *technological strength* of established firms in the most advanced countries can also impede latecomers from competing effectively in technically demanding industries. In some industries the problem arises because the necessary overhead expenditures on Research and Development (R&D) may be too large for initially small newcoming firms. The advantages of conducting industrial R & D on a large scale mean that a large proportion of it is carried out by very large firms. More than half of industrial R & D in all the OECD countries is accounted for by only 40 firms, each of which has an R & D budget substantially greater than the whole of Irish industry. Most small to medium size firms, on the other hand, do not attempt to engage in heavily R & D intensive activities as shown by the fact that only about 10 per cent of OECD industrial firms employing under 500 people have any R & D capability.[3] Not many Irish indigenous industrial firms employ more than 500 people.

Significant technological barriers to entry for indigenous firms in late-developing countries also arise for a number of other reasons. First, the quality of products and efficiency of production by established firms have already had time to benefit from the learning effects which commonly occur in technically advanced industries. Second, the proprietary technology already developed and controlled by many established firms confers exclusive competitive advantages. And third, established firms have most experience in tapping the supply of technical information, ideas, and licensing opportunities which may be available from sources outside the firm.

Sales promotion or marketing (including acquisition of market knowledge, aspects of design, establishment of distribution and after-sales service networks, and advertising) also creates entry barriers for newcomers because it can involve heavy expenditures and takes time to develop effectively. And firms newly entering the market may need to achieve large sales quickly to earn a return on capital, to develop a sufficiently large scale of production and to cover overheads like R & D. There is evidence that senior managers of large USA companies regard sales promotion as more important for sales success than pricing in many industries, indicating that this area is important and its skills are highly developed.[4]

Capital requirements have been a source of continuously growing barriers to entry for latecomers. This is partly due to the continually increasing scale and capital-intensity required for competitive production in many industries. But financial entry barriers can also be significant if capital is required for risky or unrecoverable investments such as advertising or R & D, rather than physical assets or stocks which at least have some sales value in the case of failure. Substantial investments of working capital may also be necessary for customer credit or covering start-up losses.[5]

As Hobsbawm observes, from the long-term perspective of an economic historian, the techniques used early in Great Britain's pioneering industrial revolution required little initial investment and their expansion could be financed out of accumulated profits. Industrial development was within the capacities of a multiplicity of small entrepreneurs and skilled traditional artisans. No twentieth century country setting about industrialisation has, or can have, anything like these advantages.[6] The point here is not simply that the total amount of capital available in a latecomer *country* may be inadequate (which is often not the immediate problem) but also that even where there is no general capital constraint, few business people can accumulate sufficiently large amounts of capital themselves. And private financial institutions would often be taking substantial and (from the private point of view) unwarranted risks if they were to finance major new, unproven manufacturing ventures faced with established competitors. This point is all the more significant when other more secure and attractive investment opportuntities are available in services, property, government securities, shares in existing firms and investment abroad.

Finally, further barriers to entry for the development of whole groups of industries in late-developing countries arise from *external economies,* or the advantages of industrial centralisation which are enjoyed in many activities in large established industrial centres. These advantages consist mainly of the benefits of close contact between related firms and specialist suppliers and services, the advantages of having large pools of skilled labour and specialised knowledge, and the advantage of a large local market. Although the advantages of external economies appear to have weakened for some industries since the 1960s, they still seem to be particularly important for industries in the early stages of their development based on newly emerging and rapidly developing technologies. Thus, even though many new, initially small firms can appear in these industries, such as electronics since the 1960s, this tends to occur mainly in concentrated industrial centres in the most advanced countries and could not readily arise in late-industrialising countries. Hence such geographically concentrated developments as 'Silicon Valley', California.

The combined influence of a number of the factors discussed above tends, in many industries, to generate increasing concentration of production in a small number of successful firms, which squeeze out smaller competitors. Inevitably, barriers to entry into such increasingly oligopolistic industries are continuously raised by the same process. A broad indication of increasing concentration is the fact that in the USA the 500 largest firms accounted for 40 per cent of manufacturing and mining assets in 1955, rising to 70 per cent by 1970; by 1970 the top nine firms alone accounted for 15 per cent of assets and sales.[7] Similarly, in the UK, the top 100 firms accounted for 21 per cent of manufacturing net output in 1948, rising to 41 per cent by 1972; 85 industrial firms, employing over 10,000 people each, accounted for 35 per cent of UK manufacturing employment in 1972.[8] By comparison, no Irish indigenous manufacturing company employs over 10,000 people in Ireland.

But although it is perhaps most clearly the case that oligopolistic industries dominated by very large firms are characterised by high barriers to entry for indigenous firms in late-industrialising countries, it should also be recognised that other types of industry too can be difficult for late-developing countries to enter. This can arise for reasons of technology, marketing or external economies, as outlined above.

BARRIERS TO ENTRY AND IRISH INDIGENOUS INDUSTRY

If barriers to entry for newcomers are prevalent in many manufacturing industries this has significant implications for Irish indigenous industry, since Ireland in the twentieth century could be described as a relatively late-industrialising country. With the exception of a few large long-established firms, Ireland has had a relatively weak indigenous industry that was scarcely capable of competing internationally in the

1950s. Most Irish firms were largely confined to producing for the highly protected domestic market at that time. Following the introduction of outward-looking, free trade policies in the 1960s, one might expect that most Irish indigenous firms would be deterred from even trying to enter any internationally traded industry where barriers to entry are significant. And many of those which had previously invested in such industries, producing for the small domestic market behind protectionist import barriers, might be expected to succumb to stronger foreign competition under free trade.

Thus Irish indigenous firms would tend to be confined to investing in a limited range of industries. These would include virtually 'non-traded' industries which produce goods that are rarely traded internationally, the narrow range of internationally traded industries which only have low or negligible barriers to entry, and limited or low value-added processing of local primary products. Confinement to such a narrow range of industries might well be inadequate to allow employment or output to expand in accordance with the goals of economic policy.

The rest of this chapter examines the performance of Irish indigenous industry, assessing whether these suggested adverse effects of the prevalence of barriers to entry have, in fact, been in evidence. Before focussing on the period since the 1950s, however, the history of Irish industry before that time is briefly considered.

IRISH INDUSTRY BEFORE THE 1950s

The history of Irish industry before the adoption of an outward-looking, free-market strategy in the 1950s is of some relevance to the issues discussed above. Throughout the nineteenth century and until the early 1930s Ireland was in a position somewhat analogous to that of present-day latecomers adopting outward-looking policies and relying on market forces. For most of that time, Ireland was in a relationship of free trade with Great Britain (then the most advanced industrial country in the world) under classic 'laissez-faire', free market conditions as part of the United Kingdom. For the first ten years after the establishment of the Irish Free State in 1922 only minor modifications were made to this economic position. The consequences for most of Irish industry, except in the Belfast region in the north-east, were quite destructive.

Industry had, in fact, developed to quite substantial proportions in Ireland by the early nineteenth century. For example, the census of 1841 showed that about 700,000 people, or about one-fifth of the labour force, were occupied in the textile industry alone. Although many of these people would in fact have had little work by 1841, since employment in textiles had begun to decline about a decade earlier, the fact that they reported their principal occupations as they did nevertheless indicates the existence of a major textile industry at some stage in the early nineteenth century. There were, in addition, a number of other less important industries such as brewing, grain-milling, sugar-refining, shipbuilding and the manufacture of luxury consumer items. Industry was to some extent concentrated in Ulster but industrial activity was by no means confined to Ulster. The 1821 census, for instance, reported that 6 out of 23 counties outside Ulster had a greater number of people working in industry, handicraft or trade than in agriculture. But although Ireland was not very backward industrially early in the last century compared with most countries at that time, it was nevertheless some way behind Great Britain which led the world in industrial development.

The decline of industry which followed in most of Ireland indicates that reliance on market forces is not sufficient to generate sustained industrialisation in a country making a relatively late start on a relatively small scale in developing mechanised industry (i.e. relative to Great Britain's pioneering industrial revolution). As the development of mechanised industry proceeded, the growing advantages of having a relatively large scale of production, relatively large advanced industrial centres and strong technological capabilities created ever stronger concentrated industrial centres in those areas of the UK which began the process of mechanised development on a large scale first. Those starting relatively late and/or on a smaller scale were gradually eliminated by competition. This process generally worked in favour of the earlier-starting British industries and against Irish ones, except in the Belfast area where a large mechanised textile centre developed quite early. The same process would have involved the simultaneous creation of ever higher barriers to entry for newcomers.[9] By the 1920s manufacturing industry was very weak in the new independent Irish State, employing 60,000 people, or little more than 4 per cent of the labour force.[10]

When strong protectionist policies were introduced by the Irish Free State in the early 1930s to restrict imports and encourage new native 'infant industry' development, rapid industrial growth followed for a period of two decades, apart from the interruption caused by the difficulty of importing fuel and materials during the Second World War.[11] This industrial growth was heavily concentrated on the protected domestic market, however, and few of the 'infant industries' developed a mature capability to compete in export markets. The proportion of manufactured output exported in 1951 was 16 per cent, but the proportion was only 6 per cent in sectors other than food, drink and tobacco, which consisted largely of basic processing of local agricultural output. Since economic growth depended on growing imports of the many capital goods, components, materials and fuel still not available domestically, while export growth was weak, a chronic balance of payments crisis developed by the 1950s. The deflationary measures taken to cut demand for imports resulted in prolonged recession, rapid decline in employment and high emigration.[12]

The prevailing view regarded the experience of the 1950s as evidence that protection created inefficiency and stagnation and it was concluded that outward-looking, free market policies would stimulate growth. But seen in the long-term perspective of experience since the early nineteenth century, it is evident that protection was not the *original cause* of these problems. What were effectively outward-looking policies and reliance on market forces for more than 100 years before the 1930s had already produced very poor results long before protection proved to be of considerable value for a time. But protection was ultimately *inadequate* to overcome the constraints on latecomers, in view of the level to which barriers to entry into international competition had been raised by the mid-twentieth century.

Nevertheless, the prevailing view favoured a return to the outward-looking free market approach rather than, say, the use of stronger systematic and selective State initiatives to supplement protection as a means of overcoming barriers to entry. General incentives such as grants and tax concessions to promote export industries and to attract foreign investment were introduced in the 1950s. The removal of protection followed, beginning in the mid-1960s with the introduction of a free trade agreement with the UK, followed by Ireland's decision to join the EEC in 1973.[13]

THE GROWTH OF IRISH INDIGENOUS INDUSTRY

Roughly coinciding with the change of policies, economic recovery began in the late 1950s, and industrial output in the 1960s and 1970s grew at over three times the rate of the 1950s. Manufactured exports grew particularly rapidly as Irish exports' share of foreign markets increased continuously. Considerable diversification occurred into a wider range of products including technically advanced products such as computers, machinery and fine chemicals/ pharmaceuticals, and Irish industrial wages rose to close to UK levels by 1979. Perhaps not surprisingly, the experience of industrial growth since the 1950s has been widely regarded as a fundamental breakthrough, and Ireland has for some time conventionally been classified as an advanced industrial country.

It is widely recognised, of course, that these developments were at least partially attributable to Ireland's success in attracting a good deal of mobile foreign industry. The questions to be answered in this chapter are, first, to what extent has indigenous Irish industry contributed to industrial growth? And, second, has the development of indigenous industry been constrained significantly by the problems of overcoming barriers to entry? This section reviews the overall growth of Irish indigenous industry, and subsequent sections examine the record in greater detail.

A number of issues of definition and data availability arise in seeking to distinguish 'indigenous' from 'foreign' industry. There is no single correct definition of these categories, since the appropriate definition depends on the purpose of any particular analysis, and feasible definition for empirical study will generally be constrained by the data. In principle, the most appropriate definition of indigenous industry, which would be relevant to the discussion above concerning barriers to entry for newcomers in a late-industrialising country, would be firms which *first* arose in the country concerned as opposed to those established there as subsidiaries of companies already in existence elsewhere. By this definition 'indigenous' industry might differ somewhat from majority native-owned industrial firms, since firms can pass into majority foreign ownership after originating quite independently in the native economy.

In the case of Ireland, however, there are special grounds for regarding as genuinely 'foreign' most of the firms which passed into foreign ownership after being originally Irish-owned. This is because the many industrial firms established between the early 1930s and the early 1960s were subject to the Control of Manufactures Acts. These Acts required that majority owner-ship of new manufacturing firms had to be in the hands of Irish citizens or residents. As a result, many of the firms set up before the 1960s which were *apparently* independently set up and owned by Irish people, and not as subsidiaries of foreign companies, were in fact initiated and controlled by foreign companies in all but name. It was possible for foreign firms to take initiatives in forming new manufacturing companies in Ireland, with majority Irish ownership, and then virtually to direct the operations of such companies by various means. For example, the foreign firms could own *sales* companies to which the Irish-owned manufacturing companies were tightly bound by sales contracts or various types of licensing agreements.[14] In such cases it would seem more realistic to treat the firms concerned as foreign.

After the Control of Manufactures Acts were repealed in the early 1960s, it was possible for the firms set up since the 1930s with heavy foreign involvement to be openly taken over by the foreign firms which had initiated and virtually controlled them all along. Thus, in general, it would probably be more accurate to regard *currently* foreign-owned firms as genuinely and originally foreign — even if they originally had Irish owners when established in the period from the 1930s to the 1960s. In contrast, firms established in that period which have remained Irish-owned up to the present could more legitimately be regarded as original 'indigenous' firms. Thus, data on *present* nationality of ownership of firms set up in the period 1930s to 1960s can serve as a rough guide to indicate which companies established at that time should be defined as indigenous and which as foreign. But in the case of firms established before the 1930s or since the early 1960s, when the Control of Manufactures Acts were not in force, the *original* nationality of ownership would best fit our desired definition if the nationality of majority ownership has changed. For this reason, although the available data categorised by present nationality of ownership can usually be accepted as fitting our desired definition fairly well, a number of large firms established in these periods, whose nationality of ownership has changed, are categorised according to their original nationality for the purpose of this chapter.

A further complication which might be raised is the fact that indigenous firms could still be effectively constrained or controlled in some important respects by foreign firms. This could happen if, say, they have signed restrictive agreements for the use of foreign firms' patented processes, products or trade marks under licence, if they sell their output to one dominant foreign buyer, or if foreigners have acquired substantial minority shareholdings. For our purpose, however, considerations of this type need not mean that such dominated Irish firms should be excluded from 'indigenous' industry. Since the major focus of interest here is the constraints on, and opportunities for, the development of industry originating in Ireland, this type of influence or control from abroad may be regarded as *one form* of constraint on, or opportunity for, indigenous development. Presumably the indigenous firm enters into a foreign licensing or trading agreement, or sells shares to foreign firms, because it judges that this will enable it to operate more effectively than otherwise — to overcome to some extent, in fact, technological, marketing or financial barriers to entry. The constraints which also go with such agreements, then, are one form in which barriers to entry into wider markets or other activities are experienced. For our purposes, therefore, such a licensee or sub-contractor firm may be included as indigenous and indeed to exclude it would be effectively to prejudge as invalid one possible way around barriers to entry.

To sum up, the distinction between Irish indigenous and foreign industry is generally defined here by current nationality of majority ownership. But some exceptions are made so as to define according to their *original* status firms which were set up either before the 1930s or during the past two decades, and subsequently changed their nationality of ownership. The main example of such an exception is Guinness (originally indigenous, although later foreign-owned).

Besides the distinction between Irish indigenous and foreign industry, some of the discussion below also refers to a distinction between 'New' or 'New and Small' industry on the one hand, and 'Old' or the 'rest of' industry on the other. New and Small industries are those which have received the IDA grants payable since the 1950s for the establishment of new projects. The vast majority of foreign projects established since that time (with over 90 per cent of their employment) have received these grants, so foreign New and Small Industry is virtually synonymous with foreign industries set up since the 1950s. It is necessary to use these categories in some cases because much of the data are available only for foreign and Irish New and Small industries, and for all industry. This means that in many cases the closest available approximation to data on Irish indigenous industry is to subtract the figures for foreign 'New and Small' from the total for all industry, leaving figures for Irish indigenous *plus* 'old' foreign industry. While this is not fully satisfactory, the relatively small size of 'old' foreign industry means that these data are still useful as indicators of the performance of indigenous industry.

Table 1.1 shows that employment in industry other than new foreign industry increased by almost 20,000 between 1960 and 1966 while protection still remained in force, but has declined slightly under freer trade since the mid-1960s. The data on indigenous or Irish-owned industry, which are available only since 1973, show a similar slight decline between 1973 and 1980.

Output in industries other than new foreign industry has grown since the mid-1960s but, as the decline in employment indicates, the rate of growth has been too low to keep up with the growth of labour productivity (output per worker). The output of these industries, in fact, has grown more slowly than demand which has resulted in declining market share — a trend that may be described as one of relative decline. Relative decline in the domestic market is evident from the growth of competing imports, which had gained only an extra 0.2 per

15

Table 1.1: Manufacturing Employment by Nationality of Industry, 1960-80 (thousands)

	1960	1966	1973	1980
New and Small Foreign Industry	3	10	36	61
Industry other than New Foreign	169	188	186	182
Irish Indigenous Industry	n.a.	n.a.	166	161
All Industry	172	198	222	243

Sources: Trend in Employment and Unemployment for all industry; *IDA Employment Survey* for New and Small Foreign in 1973 and 1980; New Foreign in 1960 and 1966 estimated from *Survey of Grant-Aided Industry* (1967); Industry other than New Foreign obtained by subtracting New and Small Foreign from All Industry. Irish Indigenous Industry from *IDA Employment Survey*, which only began in 1973.
Note: Indigenous Industry is a somewhat narrower definition than 'Industry Other than New Foreign', which also includes some older foreign-owned firms that have not received New or Small Industry grants.

cent of the Irish market per annum between 1960 and 1967, but then gained an extra 1.5 per cent p.a. between 1967 and 1973, and 1.1 per cent p.a. between in 1973 and 1979.[15] Since new foreign firms have always been very highly export-orientated they have never accounted for more than 5 per cent of sales on the domestic market, so the rise in import penetration has taken market shares almost exclusively from indigenous and older foreign firms.

It might be thought, of course, that a rise in import penetration was only to be expected under freer trade and that the accompanying development of exports would compensate (or more than compensate) for the decline at home. The proportion of output going for export from industries other than new foreign industry has in fact increased, especially in the period 1966 to 1973. About 18 per cent of the output of these industries was exported in 1960, rising to 19 per cent in 1966, 26 per cent in 1973 and 27 per cent in 1976. No more recent figure is available for all industries other than new foreign industry, but 29.5 per cent of output of indigenous (Irish-owned) industry alone was exported in 1979.[16] This increase in export-orientation, however, has been due primarily to slow growth of domestic sales rather than a strong export performance. The exports of industries other than new foreign industry increased more slowly than OECD manufactured imports in 1966-73, so that their share of OECD imports declined.[17] However, comparison with UK imports, which grew more slowly than in the rest of the OECD, may be more appropriate. Assuming that in 1966 as much as 70 per cent of the exports of industries other than new foreign industry went to the UK and 30 per cent to the rest of the OECD, the maintenance of constant shares in both these export markets would have raised their export-gross output ratio to 24 per cent by 1973 (due to slow growth of domestic sales) compared with the actual figure of 26 per cent referred to above. So by this estimate, a small part of the increase in the export/gross output ratio would have been due to a slight increase in export market shares.

It may be concluded from this examination of trends at an aggregate level that rather little progress appears to have been made in Irish industrial development under outward-looking free market policies, apart from the development of the country as a site for mobile foreign industries. The more detailed analysis which follows tends to support the view that the basic problem is the existence of barriers to entry which impede latecomers from competing in many internationally traded industries and confine them to a limited range of virtually non-traded activities, basic processing, and 'easily-entered' traded industries.

SECTORAL ANALYSIS OF IRISH INDIGENOUS INDUSTRY

Some types of Irish indigenous industry have fared quite well over the past two decades while others have tended to decline rapidly. Using the standard classification of manufacturing industry into ten major sectors, one can identify four relatively strong sectors, three particularly weak sectors and three with a more mixed record. Table 1.2 shows a number of performance indicators for each sector of indigenous industry, divided into these three broad groups.

As the table shows, four sectors — Clay, Glass & Cement, Drink & Tobacco, Food and Paper & Printing — seem quite strong by a number of indicators. They have resisted import penetration relatively well, they have had considerably lower than average rates of job loss, and they have suffered little or no loss of employment in established firms which were already in operation by the early 1970s.[18] In addition, all four recorded a net expansion of employment in 1973 to 1980, taking into account new firms starting up as well as previously existing firms. In contrast, Chemicals, Textiles and Clothing & Footwear have the weakest record on all these indicators and show signs of significant decline. The performance of the remaining three sectors — Metals & Engineering, Wood & Furniture and 'Other' Manufacturing — is in the intermediate range between the strong and the weak sectors on the first three indicators. Their net employment growth, however, is generally relatively strong. Metals & Engineering, in particular, has had much the highest rate of growth in net employment, despite a marked decline in employment in the longer established firms. These patterns of change by sector and their underlying causes will now be considered in more detail.

The relatively strong performance of Clay, Glass & Cement, Drink & Tobacco, Food and Paper & Printing may be explained by the fact that these sectors consist largely of activities which are not subject to the constraints imposed on latecomers by barriers to entry. There are three main reasons for this. First, some of the activities in these sectors enjoy a significant degree of natural protection against foreign competition in the domestic market due to transport or logistical costs for more distant competitors. Such industries

Table 1.2: Performance Indicators for Indigenous Industry, by Sector

	Increase in competing imports' Irish market share 1967-79 (% p.a.)	Rate of job loss 1973-80 (% p.a.)	Employment change (%) 1973-80 in firms set up before 1973	Net Employment change (%) 1973-80
Clay, Glass & Cement	0.2	2.7	6.5	16.4
Drink & Tobacco	0.3	2.0	1.1	1.6
Food	0.5	3.8	− 2.1	4.9
Paper & Printing	1.4	3.3	− 2.0	16.0
'Other' Manufacturing	1.4	5.1	− 14.2	5.2
Wood & Furniture	2.0	6.0	− 16.0	6.8
Metals & Engineering	2.3	5.5	− 8.7	23.9
Chemicals	2.3	6.7	− 27.1	− 9.1
Textiles	2.8	8.7	− 39.9	− 33.4
Clothing & Footwear	4.6	8.2	− 36.3	− 24.6
All Sectors	1.2	5.1	− 12.8	1.1

Sources: Competing imports data as explained in endnote 15. Job losses data from John Blackwell, Gerard Danaher and Eoin O'Malley, *An Analysis of Job Losses in Irish Manufacturing Industry,* (Dublin, National Economic and Social Council Report No. 67, 1983), Table 6.4. Employment data from IDA Employment Survey.

Note: The slight net employment increase shown in the total for column four differs from the slight decline shown in Table 2.1 because data are not available by sector for some small firms in 1973; these employed about 7500 people in 1973.

are often loosely described as 'non-traded' since little international trade occurs in the products concerned. *Some* trade generally occurs in these products, however, since completely effective natural protection is rare. Thus so-called non-traded industries would generally be characterised by a substantially *lower* level of imports and exports than other industries, rather than no international trade whatsoever. A low level of imports alone could indicate that a sector is competitively strong, and a low level of exports alone could indicate that it is weak. But an exceptionally low level of *both* imports *and* exports defines a virtually non-traded sector.

Second, some of the activities in the four sectors mentioned above involve exceptionally low value-added processing of local resources. This type of industry is also not subject to the constraints imposed on late-comers by barriers to entry, because there is often a significant advantage in conducting low value-added basic processing close to the source of supply of the material inputs concerned. And third, the indigenous Drink & Tobacco sector does produce some internationally traded, high value-added products but these have been little subject to the constraints of barriers to entry for a different reason. This is because most of the sector's output comes from a few large firms which are exceptionally long-established so that, unlike most of Irish industry, they have not had to overcome barriers to entry as newcomers.

Clay, Glass & Cement quite largely consists of virtually non-traded activities, which are naturally protected against foreign competition in the domestic market because transport costs are high for products with a low value in relation to their weight. Examples of such products include cement, concrete, other building materials and glass bottles. This sector does include some internationally traded industries, such as glassware, china and pottery. But its predominantly non-traded nature is shown by the fact that it has resisted import penetration quite successfully *at the same time* as showing little ability to develop exports. The rate of increase in competing import penetration in Clay, Glass & Cement has been the lowest of all sectors (Table 1.2), while the percentage of output exported by firms other than new foreign firms in this sector was only 15 per cent in 1973 — a slight decline from the percentage in 1960 and well below the 1973 average of 26 per cent for all industries other than new foreign industry.[19]

The indigenous Drink & Tobacco sector also includes a virtually non-traded sub-division, namely soft drinks. But probably the main explanation for its relatively strong performance, despite the prevailing constraints on latecomers, is that the bulk of the sector's output in Ireland is produced by a number of large old firms which survived the general decline of the nineteenth century. The long-established position of these firms — notably Guinness, Carroll Industries and Irish Distillers — is quite exceptional in Ireland and it means that they have not had to overcome, as newcomers, the marketing, economies of scale and financial barriers to entry which would now be quite substantial in their main activities.

The indigenous Food industry also includes some products, such as bread, which are virtually non-traded. But its relatively successful performance has probably been due to the fact that it consists mostly of low value-added, basic processing of commodity type products. These activities are naturally located close to the source of supply of material inputs and they do not face the marketing barriers to entry which prevail in higher value-added, branded food products. Thus in 1973, 80 per cent of Food gross output (including the relatively small number of foreign firms in this sector) was accounted for by dairy products, bacon, other meat and milling. These subdivisions all had low levels of value-added to materials ranging from 13 to 21 per cent of gross output, as compared with 44 per cent in non-Food manufacturing. The same four divisions of the Food sector together accounted for 90 per cent of food exports in 1973, and food exports in turn accounted for just over half of the exports from industries other than new foreign industry in 1960 and 1973. Thus low value-added food products, which are not subject to the constraints on late-comers, have been the source of roughly half the exports of indigenous industry. It is very likely that the relative importance of low value-added Food products in indigenous industrial exports has remained at least as great since 1973, particularly because this type of industry has benefitted from EEC policies since Ireland became a member in 1973. But unfortunately the detailed export data are not available to show this for recent years. In industries other than new foreign industry, the percentage of food output going for export rose from 28 per cent in 1960 to 35 per cent in 1973 — the highest percentage among the ten sectors and well above the average in both years.

In the case of Paper & Printing, the relatively strong performance appears to be due to the fact that much of the sector is involved in virtually non-traded industries. For many products of this sector — such as newspapers, magazines, packaging and general printing — there is a substantial, although not complete degree of natural protection against foreign competition in the domestic market because of the advantages of local knowledge and contacts, and flexibility and speed of response to local demand. Quite a large minority of this sector's output, however, is internationally traded, such as paper itself and various paper products.

As in Clay, Glass & Cement, the predominantly non-traded nature of Paper & Printing is indicated by a relatively low rate of increase in import penetration (though the rate has been somewhat higher than in Clay, Glass & Cement — Table 1.2) combined with a low level of exports. Only 13 per cent of the output of firms other than new foreign firms in Paper & Printing was exported in 1973 — a decline from the percentage in 1960 and only half the 1973 average of 26 per cent for all industries other than new foreign industry. Import penetration and employment decline, however, has been substantial in paper manufacture, which is an internationally traded sub-division of this sector dominated by relatively large firms abroad which benefit from superior economies of scale.

In contrast with the four relatively strong sectors discussed above, Chemicals, Textiles and Clothing & Footwear seem to be the weakest sectors of Irish indigenous industry to judge from the indicators in Table 1.2. The particularly marked decline of these sectors may be explained, first, by the fact that — unlike the other sectors — they include few naturally pro-tected activities and were therefore wide open to international competition following the removal of protection. The decline of many firms in the Irish Chemicals industry would then be understandable in view of the fact that they were relatively small, whereas the Chemicals industry internationally is dominated by large strong European and American firms so that the industry is highly concentrated and characterised by high barriers to entry. In fact the decline of Irish indigenous employment in Chemicals has been even greater than in Clothing & Footwear if the State enterprise, NET, is excluded on the grounds that it has had to be heavily subsidised to survive.

Textiles and Clothing & Footwear, however, evidently include many activities with relatively low barriers to entry, as shown by the rise of these industries in many newly indus-trialising countries (NICs), so that it might be expected that Ireland, as a latecomer, should have some success in competing internationally in these industries. There have in fact been some successes in developing exports, with all of the eight largest Irish Textiles and Clothing firms exporting excep-tionally large proportions of output — ranging from 31 per cent to over 90 per cent in 1978.[20] Evidently, however, many Irish firms did not succeed in developing the scale, degree of specialisation and marketing sophistication required for international competition (although such requirements would be less in these industries than in most others, making them *relatively* easily-entered by latecomers). A further problem for some sub-divisions of these sectors has been competition from low-wage NICs which can also easily enter the same activities, though this appears to have had a limited overall impact, as yet.[21]

The remaining three sectors — Metals & Engineering, Wood & Furniture, and 'Other' Manufacturing — would also contain many unsheltered, internationally traded activities. But they each include, in addition, a considerable proportion of, mainly small-scale, non-traded activities — such as carpentry workshops, simple metal fabrication, welding and pressing, structural steel, mechanical repairs and maintenance, plastic moulding and tyre remoulds. These would be naturally protected by transport costs and/or the advantages of proximity to the market for activities in which frequent local contact and flexibility of response is important. Due to the combination of internationally traded and non-traded activities, the rate of import penetration and job loss in these three sectors has been less than in the three weakest sectors but greater than in the four strongest sectors.

As a result of rising import penetration and job losses, employment has declined quite markedly in firms set up before 1973 in Metals & Engineering, Wood & Furniture and 'Other' Manufacturing, though the rate of decline has been less than in the very weakest sectors (Table 1.2). Yet net employment growth in these three sectors has been relatively strong, especially in Metals & Engineering, indicating that a good deal of employment has been generated in *new* firms set up since the early 1970s. These trends are due mainly to the rapid decline of a number of relatively large firms in internationally tradeable activities, which had been previously established behind protectionist barriers, combined with rapid growth of the *small-scale* non-traded activities (including the establishment of many new small firms) within these sectors, in response to growing domestic demand for their products.[22]

Generally, the larger firms would have been involved in activities with significant economies of scale, as indicated by their own relatively large size by Irish standards, but they would probably have been too small and/or too weak in marketing and technology to break into and survive in open international competition following the introduction of freer trade. Table 1.3 shows that employment decline among firms already set up before 1973 has been most marked in the larger size categories, while growth occurred only in the smallest (mainly non-traded) category. Similarly, the establishment of new firms since 1973 in these sectors has been concentrated in the relatively small-sized categories; of the 11,100 jobs existing in 1980 in such new firms, none were in plants employing over 500 people, and less then 10 per cent were in plants employing over 200.

Table 1.3: Employment, by Plant Size, in Irish Indigenous Metals & Engineering, Wood & Furniture and 'Other' Manufacturing

Employment size	Plants established before 1973		
	1973	1980	% change
Over 500	2263	923	− 59.2
201 − 500	7352	4772	− 35.1
101 − 200	8226	7615	− 7.4
51 − 100	5584	5102	− 8.6
Under 50	17155	17451	+ 1.7
	40579	35863	− 11.6

Source: IDA Employment Survey.

To conclude this section, growth has occurred in industries which would not generally be subject to the constraints on late-developers discussed at the start of this chapter, mainly because they are non-traded, basic processing or very long-established activities. Such activities are found mainly in Clay, Glass & Cement, Paper & Printing, Food and Drink & Tobacco, in which employment in indigenous firms increased by 11 per cent in 1973 to 1980, and also in the relatively small-scale plants in Metals & Engineering, Wood & Furniture and

'Other' Manufacturing, in which employment in indigenous firms with under 200 workers increased by 32 per cent in 1973 to 1980. But employment in other, internationally traded, indigenous industries has declined rapidly — by 26 per cent in the period 1973 to 1980 in Chemicals, Textiles and Clothing & Footwear, and by 30 per cent in the larger-scale plants with over 200 workers in Metals & Engineering, Wood & Furniture and 'Other' Manufacturing.

Generally, then, it appears that Irish indigenous industry has prospered relatively well in the limited range of activities which are not subject to the constraints imposed on latecomers by barriers to entry, but has declined markedly in internationally traded activities subject to these constraints. Some further confirmation of this trend is found in data on Research and Development (R & D) expenditures. R & D intensity (which has consistently been low by OECD standards) declined between 1971 and 1979, since real R & D expenditures by industry increased by 3.7 per cent per annum which was lower than the rate of growth of industrial output at 5.5 per cent per annum. This indicates that Irish industry has made little or no progress in developing technically demanding industries, which is one of the major categories of industry subject to barriers to entry.

THE LARGEST IRISH INDIGENOUS FIRMS

In order to investigate further whether the development of Irish indigenous industry has been constrained by the problems of overcoming barriers to entry for latecomers, it is useful to examine the activities of the largest indigenous manfacturing firms.

As was pointed out earlier, barriers to entry for latecomers often arise from much the same causes that have given rise to the development of increasingly large firms in the advanced industrial countries and growing concentration of industrial production. Factors such as economies of scale in production, and advantages of large firm size with regard to finance, marketing or research and development, have encouraged this prevalence of large firms and increasingly concentrated industrial structures, at the same time as creating barriers to entry for latecomers into the industries where they are important. If this is so, it follows that it is primarily among the largest firms in Ireland too that one should look to find examples of companies which have succeeded in developing industries where barriers to entry prevail. The largest Irish firms would be the ones with the greatest capacity to enter industries where there are special competitive advantages generally associated with large size. Thus inspection of the activities of the *largest* Irish indigenous firms should be quite a good test of whether indigenous firms have successfully engaged to *any* significant extent in activities with substantial entry barriers.

For this purpose, a list was compiled of the 100 largest Irish indigenous, private-sector, manufacturing firms in 1981/82. This list was drawn up by selecting from the largest such firms, ranked in terms of sales, in *Irish Business,* January, 1983, the first 100 which employed at least 145 people.[23] The list is probably quite comprehensive, although there may be a few relatively insignificant omissions of small companies that ought to be included towards the bottom end of the list. The full list of 100 companies, with details of their sales, employment and main activities, is too lengthy to present here. Table 1.4 summarises the sectoral distribution of all 100 firms, and Table 1.5 lists the top 20 companies individually. For various reasons the data in these tables may not be completely accurate, but they do illustrate the main features.

In Table 1.4, the Food sector emerges as by far the most important sector of activity of the largest Irish manufacturing firms in terms of its share of the top 100 companies and their sales. It is also, by a lesser but still substantial margin, the largest sector in terms of its share of employment in the top 100, with the difference arising from the sector's basic processing nature which results in low value-added to material inputs and high sales per worker. Metals & Engineering is second largest in terms of the number of companies included in the top 100, but ranks only fifth in terms of its share of sales and employment in the top 100. This is due to the relatively small size of the companies concerned, since 9 of the 12 included rank below no. 60 on the list of 100. Drink & Tobacco, Paper & Printing and Clay, Glass & Cement are all considerably larger than Metals & Engineering in terms of sales and employment. These three, together with Food, are the only sectors which account for a greater share of employment in the largest firms than in all Irish indigenous industry. Between them, these four sectors account for 85 per cent of sales and 77 per cent of employment in the group of 100 largest firms, compared with 51 per cent of employment in all indigenous industry in 1980.

These four sectors, which account for a disproportionately large share of the activity of the biggest Irish firms, are the same ones which emerged above as being largely composed of non-traded or limited processing activities. They also include some long-established firms which are engaged in less sheltered activities with significant entry barriers, but have not had to overcome these barriers as newcomers due to their long-established position.

To look at the very largest firms in more detail, Table 1.5 lists the top 20 Irish indigenous, private sector, manufacturing companies. One of the most striking features of this list is the virtual absence of firms engaged in Metals & Engineering, Chemicals or 'Other' Manufacturing . These are the sectors which tend to be most dominant among the activities of the biggest firms in advanced industrial countries — in branches such as metals, transport equipment, machinery, aerospace, electronics, armaments, consumer durables, industrial chemicals, pharmaceuticals, petroleum products, rubber products and technical instruments. These types of industry are generally characterised by barriers to entry for latecomers, and their absence from the list of the top 20 Irish companies indicates that Irish indigenous firms

Table 1.4: Sectoral Distribution of the 100 Largest Irish Indigenous Manufacturing Firms, 1981/82

Sector	Companies	Sales (%)	Employment (%)
Food	44	40.3	26.8
Drink & Tobacco	10	19.3	13.8
Textiles	5	2.5	6.1
Clothing & Footwear	5	1.3	3.1
Wood & Furniture	2	0.9	0.6
Paper & Printing	7	13.1	18.5
Chemicals	2	1.4	0.6
Clay, Glass & Cement	5	12.1	18.1
Metals & Engineering	12	5.6	8.8
Other Manufacturing	3	1.2	1.5
Multi-Sectoral*	5	2.3	2.2
	100	100	100

Source: Calculated from data on the indigenous, private-sector, manufacturing companies included in Sweeney, Marie Claire, 'Ireland's Largest 500 Companies', *Irish Business*, January, 1983.

Note: Companies involved in more than one sector are allocated to a sector according to their major manufacturing activity. Only the few which are not *predominatly* engaged in one manufacturing sector are categorised here as 'multi-sectoral'. Some companies are also engaged in non-manyfacturing activities, and they are included here only if their scale of manufacturing is believed to exceed the minimum level mentioned in the text; in these cases, however, sales and employment data used here are for the whole company.

have had little notable success in overcoming such barriers.

In contrast with the Irish situation, even the smallest advanced European countries have numerous relatively large firms in these sectors. For example in 1979, Belgium and Denmark each had 17 indigenous engineering firms employing over 1000 people, half of these employing over 2000 people, and one-quarter employing 5000 or more.[24] In Ireland the only engineering firm in the 1981/82 top 20 (O'Flaherty Holdings, no. 14) employed under 1000 people, was more involved in distribution than manufacturing, and benefited from a form of legal protection for the car assembly industry. Looking beyond the list of top 20 Irish firms, only 1 out of 23 indigenous private manufacturing companies employing over 1000 people in 1981/82 was engaged in Metals & Engineering, Chemicals or 'Other' Manufacturing. This company, however, is really more involved in construction and services, with only relatively small-scale manufacturing subsidiaries.

Table 1.5: The Largest Irish Indigenous Private Sector Manufacturing Companies, 1981/82

Company	Sales	Employ-ment	Main Activity	Main Manufac-turing Sector
1 Smurfit Group	£491.7m	11,207	Print and packaging	Paper and Printing
2 Cement Roadstone	£354.5m	7493	Building materials, construction	Clay, Glass and Cement
3 Guinness* (Ireland)	£352.6m	6000	Brewing	Drink and Tobacco
4 Carroll Industries	£219m	1451	Tobacco Manufacture	Drink and Tobacco
5 Waterford Glass	£190.3m	7009	Glassware	Clay, Glass and Cement
6 Cork Co-op	£154m	960	Agricultural co-operative	Food
7 Mitchelstown Co-op	£149.5m	2100	Agricultural co-operative	Food
8 Avonmore Creameries	£143.6m	1300	Agricultural co-operative	Food
9 Irish Distillers	£132.1m	1050	Distilling	Drink and Tobacco
10 Waterford Co-op	£127.9m	1200	Agricultural co-operative	Food

Company	Sales	Employ-ment	Main Activity	Main Manufac-turing Sector
11 Golden Vale Co-op	£110.1m	1219	Agricultural co-operative	Food
12 Ballyclough Co-op	£105.5m	1020	Agricultural co-operative	Food
13 Anglo Irish Meat	£102m	700	Meat processors	Food
14 O'Flaherty Holdings	£ 92m	722	Car assembly, distribution	Metals and Engineering
15 Kerry Co-op	£ 87.7m	1000	Agricultural co-operative	Food
16 Cantrell and Cochrane	£ 73m	1540	Soft Drinks	Drink and Tobacco
17 North Connaught Co-op	£ 68.8m	260	Agricultural co-operative	Food
18 Clover Meats	£ 67.4m	950	Meat processors	Food
19 Premier Hughes	£ 65m	1950	Dairy products	Food
20 Youghal Carpets	£ 63.6m	2662	Carpet manufacture	Textiles

Source: Irish Business, January 1983.
Note: Figures and ranking refer to Guinness *(Ireland)* only.

Looking at the activities of the firms which *are* in the Irish top 20, again one is struck by the dominance of the Food, Drink & Tobacco, Clay, Glass & Cement and Paper & Printing sectors, which account for 18 of the top 20 firms. The 11 Food companies are predominantly engaged in only low value-added basic processing of Irish primary produce, and as such have a

31

natural advantage which means they have not had to overcome difficult entry barriers for latecomers.

The Smurfit Group (no. 1), Cement Roadstone (no. 2) and Cantrell & Cochrane (no. 16) are mainly engaged in industries which are virtually non-traded internationally; this is indicated by home market success combined with a low export-orientation. (Smurfit and Cement Roadstone both exported only 4 per cent of output in 1978/79.)[25] Guinness (no. 3), Carroll's (no. 4) and Irish Distillers (no. 9) *are* engaged in internationally tradeable activities with considerable barriers to entry, but all three are exceptional in Ireland in having very long-established roots. Carroll's, the newest of these three, was set up in 1824. Consequently, they have not had to overcome entry barriers *as newcomers.*

Waterford Glass (no. 5) is something of a special case since its main business, the manufacture of high quality glassware, or crystal, is an internationally tradeable activity in which marketing and skill development on the job must be significant barriers to entry for newcomers. Yet the present Waterford Glass firm was set up only in 1951. This industry, however, is based in a tradition dating back to the eighteenth century, and before the advent of cheap mass-produced glass destroyed the market for the hand-made Waterford product in the mid-nineteenth century, forcing the closure of the industry in 1851, Waterford Glass had developed a high reputation. This tradition and the established name lingered on until the twentieth century, as seen in the considerable antique value of old Waterford Glass. Presumably this was a major asset when the appearance of high-income mass markets (especially in the USA) reopened the opportunities for large-scale manufacture of expensive hand-made glassware. Marketing is probably the main factor influencing competitive success in this business, together with design and labour skills. Thus the new Waterford firm would have had quite an advantage in marketing due to the established reputation when it started out — relatively early, in fact, in terms of the timing of the new phase of regeneration of the industry. In addition, the skill development barrier could be overcome at that particular time by hiring skilled glass-workers from central Europe, who were displaced as a result of the Second World War and were willing to work in Ireland and train local workers.

Of the other two companies in the top 20, O'Flaherty Holdings (no. 14) was exceptional in continuing to benefit from a form of legal protection, while Youghal Carpets (no. 20) is in a traded but relatively easily entered sector without major barriers to entry.

One could conclude, therefore, that the activities of the largest Irish indigenous firms show little sign of a capacity to initiate and develop internationally traded industries characterised by significant entry barriers. This conclusion tends to be confirmed by the patterns of expansion and diversification of the largest firms, which for the most part have only expanded beyond their base business successfully in services, non-traded industries in Ireland, and the acquisition or establishment of subsidiaries abroad. The Smurfit Group has become involved in distribution, finance and property, and has acquired many subsidiaries abroad — in the USA, UK, Nigeria, Australia, Channel Islands and the Netherlands, which account for more than four-fifths of the Group's sales. Guinness set up its first brewery outside Ireland in 1936 (in London) and Guinness is now brewed in more than a dozen countries on five continents. Guinness has also taken over some other breweries and diversified into numerous service sector activities in Ireland and elsewhere. The whole international Guinness group has long ago moved its head office to the UK and now employs at least three times as many people outside Ireland as it does in Ireland.

Cement Roadstone, too, has acquired numerous subsidiaries abroad, in the UK, USA, Netherlands, Belgium and Cyprus. Its joint venture with a British partner in a large magnesia plant, Premier Periclase, is in an internationally traded industry in Ireland, but this enterprise has consistently made losses since its establishment and could therefore scarcely be called a success. Carroll Industries has successfully diversified from tobacco manufacture into (largely non-traded) printing and packaging, and into pharmaceutical distribution. Its main new venture into internationally traded manufacturing, however, as a partner in the Fieldcrest plant, has collapsed. Waterford Glass has taken over retail outlets (60 per cent of the Switzer Group), sheltered non-traded manufacturing operations (the Smith Group's protected car assembling, and a printing firm), and a subsidiary in the UK. Similarly, further down the list, Youghal Carpets, Clondalkin Mills (no. 23), Independent Newspapers (no. 24), James Crean (no. 27), Doreen Holdings (no. 47) and others have expanded significantly overseas and/or into services.

These patterns of expansion presumably reflect the generally poor prospects of making secure and attractive profits in attempting to overcome barriers to entry for newcomers by developing internationally traded industries.

POLICY CONCLUSIONS

It may be concluded that over the past two decades Irish indigenous industry has contributed relatively little to industrial development. The growth of industrial employment and exports and diversification into a wider range of more advanced products have resulted very largely from the establishment of many new foreign firms in Ireland.

The major weakness of Irish indigenous industry is its poor ability to compete in internationally traded, high value-added industries. This is seen in the marked (and increasing) degree of concentration of indigenous firms in non-traded industries, low value-addded basic processing industries, and a limited range of traded activities with low barriers to entry which will probably become increasingly liable to low-wage competition from newly industrialising countries. This confinement to such a limited range of activities has constrained the development of indigenous industry quite severely, resulting is no net contribution to employment creation and little contribution to export development.

It must be considered vitally important for industrial policy to aim to develop *indigenous industries* in *internationally traded, high value-added* activities. Greater efforts to develop *indigenous* industry are necessary because foreign industries alone, despite their quite rapid expansion, have not proved sufficient to meet Ireland's development and employment aspirations, and increasing difficulty has been encountered in attracting new foreign investment since 1979. Having established a most attractive set of grant and tax incentives and a strong institutional structure to encourage foreign investment, there seems to be little more that can be done by such methods to increase it significantly. There is, however, much ground to be made up in developing indigenous industry. Furthermore, if the range of skills and sub-supplier firms in indigenous industry could be improved, this could ultimately serve to improve the attractions of Ireland as a site for a wider range of more sophisticated foreign firms.

The importance of focusing on developing indigenous industries which are internationally *traded* arises for several reasons. To develop a number of such industries successfully would open up currently untapped opportunities for generating employment and incomes directly. Such industries would also earn foreign exchange to facilitate the expansion of other sectors such as the many non-traded, domestically-orientated industries and services. Since a high proportion of fuel, materials and machinery inputs for all sectors must inevitably be imported in such a small country as Ireland, and since a good deal of consumer spending resulting from income increases is also spent on imports, rising imports are both a prerequisite for economic growth and rising employment, and a result of such growth. Thus Ireland's ability to sustain growth and to increase employment ultimately depends on the country's ability to obtain foreign exhange to pay for imports. This in turn means that the development of internationally traded industries, capable of earning foreign exchange, should be the main priority for industrial policy. Finally, the development of internationally traded indigenous industries would raise the level of skills and provide a greater market for skilled sub-supply industries, which would also serve to make Ireland more attractive for foreign firms.

In aiming to develop traded indigenous industries, it would also be important to focus on *higher value-added* traded industries. These are industries which require factors such as a high level of skills, technological capability or strong marketing. They can sustain relatively high wage levels and are least vulnerable to overwhelming competition from low-wage, low-skill, newly industrialising countries.

It was indicated above that a major problem constraining the development of such indigenous traded industries has proved to be the difficulty of overcoming barriers to entry for latecomers due to strong established foreign competitors. This fundamental problem has, for the most part, been overlooked in Ireland, while other issues that in fact are probably less serious impediments to development have often been regarded as the main or only problems. The fact that barriers to entry for latecomers, posed by strong external competition, have presented a major constraint on the development of Irish indigenous industry is indicated by the detailed trends in Irish industry discussed above. To support this idea it is worth referring to certain indications that Irish 'supply-side' conditions (although perhaps deficient in some respects) can scarcely be solely responsible for the poor performance of indigenous industry.

Thus the rapid expansion of foreign industry in Ireland in the 1960s and 1970s indicates the existence of reasonably favourable general conditions in the physical infrastructure, the political and bureaucratic environment, financial and professional services, and the attitudes and commitment of the labour force. Although there may well be room for improvement in these matters, they could scarcely account adequately for the the weakness of Irish indigenous industry since foreign industry expanded quickly in the same environment. Nor does a lack of a spirit of enterprise in Ireland seem to be an adequate explanation for the problems of Irish industry. Irish entrepreneurial activity has been booming, in fact, although it has become clear that this need not lead to satisfactory industrial development involving the growth of internationally traded industries. Thus almost 1500 new indigenous manufacturing firms were established between 1973 and 1980, and these accounted for as much as 37 per cent of Irish manufacturing firms by 1980. Many more new firms were also established in services and building. But the new manufacturing firms are mostly small and (like building and services) largely naturally protected against foreign competition. So the decline in older larger firms has meant a net decline in indigenous manufacturing employment while there was also little export development — despite the emergence of many active entrepreneurs. The fact that many firms originating in Ireland, including non-traded businesses, have established or acquired operations abroad since the early 1970s also indicates an entrepreneurial willingness to compete internationally, although in a manner which contributes little to Irish industrial development.

Thus the fact that Irish firms have not developed many internationally traded industries in sectors with substantial entry barriers could not be put down merely to a general lack of entrepreneurial initiative. There may well be room for improvement in specialised entrepreneurial skills and competence. However, the general reluctance to invest in such new traded industries could quite reasonably be interpreted as rational and realistic behaviour, which even the best of profit-seeking private businessmen would adopt in similar circumstances, since there are other more certain ways for latecomers to make profits.

It may be concluded, therefore, that while there may be some merit in policies and exhortations which aim to improve the general business environment, to secure greater co-operation and effort from the labour force, or to stimulate entrepreneurship, such efforts fail to confront the major problem of overcoming barriers to entry.

Similarly, the frequently repeated calls for wage 'restraint' as the key to competitive success tend to overemphasise the importance of labour costs. As indicated above, the central aim with regard to traded industries should be to try to develop the higher value-added traded industries, rather than only low value-added activities with low barriers to entry in which labour costs *are* important for competitive success but which are correspondingly subject to irresistible competition from very low-wage newly industrialising countries. So if a sustainable strategy requires shifting out of such low-wage industries and into higher value-added industries with significant entry barriers, then wage 'restraint' is no longer the key to success (though it might help sustain certain of the existing low-wage industries a little longer). Rather, the development of sufficiently large-scale firms which would be strong in technology and marketing, and the development of advanced high-level skills, would be the key to success in overcoming barriers to entry into high value-added industries which can readily sustain quite high wage levels.

Because labour costs are only one of many factors influencing competitiveness (and not the most important factor in relatively high value-added industries), Japan, for example, was able to sustain greater increases than her competitors in labour costs per unit of output during the 1960s and 1970s, at the same time as continuously making gains in shares of export markets. This was a reflection of Japan's industrial transformation, involving a continuing shift into higher value-added industries in which labour costs have relatively little influence on competitive success in comparison with factors such as scale, technology, marketing or skills.

It is not sufficient, therefore, to concentrate only on labour costs, infrastructure, the stimulation of enterprise and other such factors, which have habitually received a good deal of attention from policy-makers and commentators. The effective development of Irish indigenous industry calls for a change of emphasis in the formulation of policies, with greater efforts being focused on overcoming barriers to entry into higher value-added traded industries. Or to put it another way, it is not sufficient to aim to create an attractive business environment and to stimulate business enterprise. It is also necessary for government policy to *take initiatives* in building up selected traded industries in which private business would not be motivated to invest because a viable competitive stature could only be attained by newcomers over a period of some years, during which initial losses may have to be sustained.

The suggestions which follow concerning a new direction for industrial policy are broadly in line with the proposals of the Telesis Report to the NESC. The implementation of a more selective and directed industrial policy would involve (1) the development of a *strategic planning* capability to select target industries and assess their requirements for competitive success; (2) a commitment by the State to take the *initiative,* where necessary, in developing the target industries, rather than awaiting private initiatives which may not be forthcoming; (3) *redeployment of development aids and incentives* to focus more on assisting indigenous traded industries — especially to help new selected projects through the 'infant industry' stage to a viable competitive stature.

The primary function of *strategic planning* would be to select suitable new high value-added traded industries for development — making selections at quite a detailed level of the sub-sector or product group rather than the broad industrial sector, though the final precise choice of products is a matter for enterprises themselves. This selection would have to be based on exhaustive analysis of the requirements for international competitive success in specific industries, as compared with the competitive capabilities that could be developed most readily in Ireland. It must be recognised that such strategic planning expertise is in short supply in Ireland at present largely because there has been little attempt to operate a selective directed industrial policy to date. Thus it would be necessary to tap foreign sources for advice initially, while considerable effort should be devoted to education and training to develop the necessary expertise, in corporate strategy and the analysis of the international competitive process in industry, in public agencies concerned with planning and development. At present, a number of bodies have some role in industrial planning, including the Industrial Development Authority, the Department of Industry, Trade, Commerce and Tourism, the Sectoral Development Committee and the Shannon Free Airport Development Company. If effective strategic planning is to be carried out, to co-ordinate policy measures to achieve specific goals rather than being merely a mild and general form of 'indicative planning', this will have to be organised by a strong institution directly responsible to government.

Selection of suitable target industries is a complex matter but a few general considerations of relevance may be suggested.[26] For example, industries which have chronic excess capacity internationally should generally be ruled out (e.g. steel or shipbuilding). Very large-scale industries should also be avoided in view of Ireland's small size and limited resources (e.g. cars, industrial chemicals). Similarly industries based on an advantage in direct development of new basic technologies (e.g. laser technology, fibreoptics) would have to be ruled out since the largest advanced countries dominate such industries, often backed by massive military or space research pro-grammes. A more suitable type of industry for Ireland would be specialised 'niche' industries — aiming at relatively narrow markets which may be specialised by product, by customer, by geographical area or by a combination of these. Selection of such 'niches' would mean identifying product groups and target markets at quite a detailed level, rather than broad industrial sectors. Emphasis on 'niche' industries would often imply importing new basic technologies and developing further specialised applications for such technologies — thus avoiding direct competition with the major technological leaders and the very large high-volume producers.

Perhaps a suitable goal for Ireland would be to develop, say, 50 sizeable indigenous firms in new traded industries, each of them relatively large by present Irish standards but small enough and sufficiently specialised in 'niches' to avoid competing directly with the very largest firms abroad. These 50 or so firms would each be employing about 500-5000 people, many of them in specialised product areas within mechanical engineering or electronics for example.

Initiatives by the State to develop such industries could take several forms. One way would be direct State investment in new enterprises, for example through the proposed National Development Corporation. Another possible way would be to build on selected existing private firms by drawing up specific company development plans in consultation with the businesses concerned. Payments of loans, grants and other incentives could then be linked to progress in the planned development of new traded activities. A third possible method, as suggested in the Telesis Report (pp. 232-4), would be to establish an entirely new 'corporate shell' to undertake a selected project, by assembling a consortium of diverse interests (State or private, with or without some foreign participation) with the required capital and managerial skills. Or, finally, new 'development companies' could be established; these would be new organisations that would acquire the technical, marketing and managerial capabilities needed for high value-added traded businesses, but would sub-contract component manufacturing and sub-assembly to existing small manufacturing firms.

Each of the options just mentioned would involve quite substantial new departures in industrial policy, requiring planning skills and expertise of a type that has not previously been greatly developed in Ireland. Consequently, it may be prudent to proceed initially with a relatively small number of such major initiatives (each of which would need to be undertaken on a substantial scale, by Irish standards) followed by a phased introduction of an increasing number of new projects as improved skills and techniques are acquired with experience.

Having chosen and initiated such projects, a battery of co-ordinated *development aids and incentives* would be required to ensure the best possible prospects for them to attain an internationally competitive stature. Strong general protection against imports to shelter such 'infant industries' would presumably not be readily acceptable in the context of EEC membership. But substitutes for protection could be found in planned public procurement, specific grants to encourage other firms to purchase the new products, and investments in the new industries by State enterprise which would be willing to absorb initial losses. To maintain the incentive to become competitive, schedules could be drawn up for phasing out such special supports.

Grants to industry would need to be made more selective, focusing primarily on target traded industries. They would need to be more selective too in the sense of focusing on overcoming specific entry barriers, such as marketing or skill-training, rather than being very largely capital grants as at present. As further aids to overcoming marketing barriers to entry, one or more large State trading companies could be established, with the aim of improving access to distribution channels in Ireland and abroad.

Technological entry barriers could be tackled by assisting firms with the costs of seeking out and importing best-practice technology, whether under licence or embodied in capital goods or materials. Aids for technology import could also be linked to commitments by the firms to avail of grants for further R & D work to improve on or develop new applications for the imported technology. In addition, technology could be acquired by employing foreign engineers, by arranging joint ventures with foreign firms, and by gaining control of (necessarily relatively small) technically advanced foreign firms with a view to training Irish staff, making licensing arrangements or even diverting much of the firms' future expansion to Ireland.

Finally, new investment initiatives and development incentives would need to be carefully co-ordinated in the case of target industries which are related in skills, technology or linkages, in order to develop the advantages of 'external economies'. For example, an engineering skill-training programme in a selected area, coupled with initiatives to establish a number of inter-related engineering projects located in the same area, could serve to provide additional support for each individual project. It would also help to provide the basis for a process of further autonomous development, through the creation of a structure of specialist sub-suppliers and services to support and sustain new projects.

As mentioned above, these suggestions for a more active and selective industrial policy are broadly in line with the proposals of the Telesis Report and the NESC's conclusions on industrial policy. The Government's White Paper on this subject, published in July 1984,[27] appears to endorse some recommendations of the type outlined above, particularly those concerning more grants for purposes such as marketing and technology acquisition, rather than concentrating grants heavily on capital assets alone. However, the White Paper's commitment to a generally more active approach, with State initiatives to develop large indigenous enterprises, seems a good deal less than wholehearted. Although the White Paper does contain proposals for company development plans for selected firms and for a new National Development Corporation, both these sets of proposals are rather circumscribed and do not clearly indicate a significant shift in the thrust of industrial policy. As a result, there is, unfortunately, a danger that rather little will come of these proposals in practice.

NOTES AND REFERENCES

1. Economies of scale is mentioned as an entry barrier for late-developers by, for example, Furtado, Celso, *Development and Underdevelopment* (Berkley, University of California Press, 1971); Thomas, Clive, *Dependence and Transformation*, (New York and London: Monthly Review Press, 1974).
2. Magaziner, Ira, 'The Rationale and the Competitive Economics of Public Policy for New Industries', paper read to OECD Conference on Industrial Policy, Madrid, 1980.
3. OECD Committee for Scientific and Technological Policy *Innovation in Small and Medium Firms* (Paris: OECD, 1982).
4. Lee, N., 'Pricing and Advertising' in P.J. Devine *et al.* (eds), *An Introduction to Industrial Economics* (3rd ed., London: George Allen and Unwin, 1979).
5. See Porter, Michael E. *Competitive Strategy — Techniques for Analysing Industries and Competitors* (New York: Free Press, 1980), pp. 9, 10.
6. Hobsbawm, E.J., *Industry and Empire* (Pelican Economic History of Britain, Vol. 3, London: Pelican, 1976), p. 25.
7. Aaronovitch, Sam, 'The Firm and Concentration' in Francis Green and Petter Nore (eds), *Economics — An Anti-Text* (London: Macmillan, 1977).
8. Devine, P.J. 'The Firm', in P.J. Devine et al. (eds), *op. cit.*
9. The causes of the nineteenth century decline of most Irish industry, in contrast to the Belfast area, are discussed in more detail in O'Malley, Eoin, 'The Decline of Irish Industry in the Nineteenth Century', *Economic and Social Review*, Vol. 13, No. 1 (October 1981).
10. Census of Industrial Production data.
11. Manufacturing employment grew from 62,000 in 1931 to 101,000 in 1938 and 140,000 in 1951 (Census of Industrial Production).
12. The rate of emigration in the 1950s was the highest since the 1880s and was equivalent to over 70 per cent of the numbers reaching the age of 15.
13. Details of the steps by which these policies were introduced are contained in O'Malley, Eoin, *Industrial Policy and Development: A Survey of Literature from the Early 1960s to the Present*, National Economic and Social Council paper No. 56 (Dublin: Stationery Office, 1980).
14. See Stewart, J.C., 'A Study of the Financing of Multinational Companies in Ireland 1964-1980' *Journal of Irish Business and Administrative Research*, Vol. 4, No. 2 (October 1982).
15. Competing imports are imports of manufactured goods which compete with existing producers of similar goods in Ireland. Data on competing imports for 1960-73 are from the *Review of 1973 and Outlook for 1974;*

1973-77 data are derived from Trade Statistics of Ireland by summing up import items classified as 'competing' according to a list provided by Alan Matthews of Trinity College, Dublin; 1977-79 data were provided by the Department of Industry, Commerce and Tourism.

16. The figures quoted for industries other than new foreign industry are calculated by subtracting export and gross output data for new foreign industry from national totals. The data on new foreign industry are derived from the *Survey of Grant-Aided Industry*, a survey team's report to the IDA, (Dublin, Stationery Office, 1967); McAleese, Dermot, *A Profile of Grant-Aided Industry in Ireland* (Dublin: IDA, 1977); O'Farrell, P.N. and O'Loughlin, B., *An Analysis of New Industry Linkages in Ireland* (Dublin: IDA, 1980). The export-gross output ratio for indigenous industry in 1979 is from the Telesis Consultancy Group, *A Review of Industrial Policy*, NESC paper No. 64 (Dublin: Stationery Office, 1982), p. 295.

17. OECD manufactured imports increased by a factor of 3.54 in 1966-73 in current (£ sterling) prices *(OECD Statistics of International Trade)*, while exports of industries in Ireland other than new foreign industry increased by a factor of 3.38.

18. The import penetration data in Table 1.2 show the average increase per annum in imports' percentage share of the Irish market; e.g. if imports held a 10 per cent share in 1967 and 22 per cent in 1979, the table would show they gained an extra 1 per cent per annum. Job losses are defined as the decline in employment over the period, in *each firm* where employment declined, summed up for all such firms; the rate of job loss is total job losses over the period, as a percentage of employment in the initial year; and the rate of job loss *per annum* is the rate of loss presented as an annual rate.

19. Export-gross output ratios, by sector, for industries other than new foreign industry, are calculated by subtracting exports and gross-output data for new foreign industry from national totals. Unfortunately the last year for which such data are available by sector is 1973, from McAleese, *op. cit.*

20. 'Irish Companies 1978', *The Irish Times*, 1 and 2 January 1979.

21. Fitzpatrick, Jim, *Industrialisation, Trade and Ireland's Development Co-operation Policy* (Advisory Council on Development Co-operation: Dublin, 1981).

22. The largely non-traded nature of small firms in indigenous Metals & Engineering is indicated by the fact that the small size categories were enjoying quite a boom in the 1970s, yet exported little. The Telesis report to the NESC, *op. cit.* p. 113, finds that over 600 new (mainly small) firms were established since 1967 in Metals & Engineering, but their total exports in 1979 were only £11 million — about 2 per cent of all indigenous manufacturing exports.

23. The *Irish Business* ranking is done according to sales, but employment data are also provided. Some companies ranking quite high in terms of

sales have very low employment, indicating rather small manufacturing activity in terms of employment or value-added. Thus it was decided to include in the top 100 referred to in this chapter only those above a minimum employment level. The figure of 145 workers was chosen as the minimum because the sales of the 100th ranked firm corresponded to employment of 145, given the average sales/employment ratio of all 100 firms.

24. Telesis report to NESC, *op. cit.,* p. 349.
25. 'Irish Companies 1979', *The Irish Times,* 29 December 1979.
26. The following suggestions owe something to a National Board for Science and Technology discussion document, 'Technology and Industrial Policy', 1983, in the preparation of which the author worked with NBST staff.
27. White Paper on Industrial Policy (Dublin: Stationery Office, July, 1984).

2
Small-Scale Industry In Ireland

Kieran A. Kennedy and Tom Healy

In the past decade or so, economic analysts and policy-makers in all countries have devoted increasing attention to small-scale industry. For long, the subject was of little interest in the industrialised countries. This neglect arose from a number of factors. The general assumption was that large-sized firms were more efficient due to economies of scale. While small industrial firms were far more numerous than large firms in all Western countries, they nevertheless accounted for only a small share of total manufacturing output or employment — and this share was declining, at least up to the early seventies. Moreover they were, and still remain, poorly organised as a pressure group.

The increasing interest in recent years in small-scale industry also derives from a number of sources. For some, it stems from concern about the centralisation and concentration of power in a relatively small number of large units, often operating across national boundaries and not readily amenable to control by national governments. For others, it arises because of fears about the process of innovation should the large enterprises become stultified by their own ever-increasing bureaucracy. The intractable combination of unemployment and inflation since the early 1970s has convinced others that new industrial structures need to be developed, in which smaller-scale, participative, industrial units would figure more prominently.

In underdeveloped countries, the relatively greater interest in small industry is substantially focussed on development needs. New indigenous enterprise, in the private sector at least, must initially tend to be on a small scale. Ireland also, despite its comparatively high level of income *per capita,* exhibits significant features of underdevelopment, including an apparent shortage of native industrial enterprise; and the development of such enterprise is the chief reason underlying the attention to small industry in this country.

Unfortunately, despite the generally increasing interest in small industry, the subject remains, as the Bolton Report in the UK put it, 'little researched and poorly documented'.[1] An undue proportion of the literature on the subject tends to be uncritically promotional, so that the former position of comparative neglect has been transformed into one where exaggerated claims abound. In this chapter we aim to provide a realistic assessment of the problems and potentialities of small-scale industry in Ireland.

For this purpose, it is necessary first to discuss briefly the key definitional and measurement problems that arise. The following section gives a picture of the quantitative significance of small-scale manufacturing industry in Ireland and other countries, and how this picture has been changing over time. Then we examine the general advantages and disadvantages attaching to this form of enterprise, before considering the evolution of industrial policy for small firms in Ireland and the results of this policy. Finally, we present our conclusions in relation to the future policy perspectives.

DEFINITION AND MEASUREMENT

When speaking of small industry, the question immediately arises as to what is the appropriate unit of observation. Although there are several possibilities, the literature on the size distribution of industry generally concentrates on two — the *establishment* and the *firm*. The establishment is the unit of production of a homogeneous activity; while the firm is the unit of ownership or control of one of more establishments, and is often taken as synonymous with the term *enterprise*. The appropriate unit of observation differs depending on the subject under examination, so that, ideally, one would wish to have data on both establishments and firms. Unfortunately, reliable and comparable data on industry classified by firm size are much more rare than data by establishment size. The Census of Industrial Enterprises undertaken in Ireland in each year since 1975 in response to EEC directives covers only those with 20 or more employees. Consequently, it omits much of the data relevant to an analysis of small firms.

There is no one denominator of scale that is wholly satis-factory. In comparisons of the size structure of industry over time and across countries, employment is by far the most commonly used scale denominator, and indeed often the only one for which data are generally available. While it has several advantages, its limitations should not be overlooked. Persons do not constitute homogeneous units of labour. To classify as the same size, two establishments each with 100 workers could give rise to obvious anomalies where one consisted largely of highly-skilled technologists, while the other consisted mainly of juveniles and unskilled workers. Moreover, labour as an input can be substituted for by other factors of production, and the degree of substitution depends on forces which vary over time and between countries. Thus, the scale (in terms of other denominators such as output or capital employed) of an estab-lishment employing 100 workers today may be vastly different from one employing the same number 50 years ago.

In establishing a dividing line between small and large establishments, practice differs between countries and even among different agencies within the same country. In Ireland the Industrial Development Authority (IDA) defines 'small' as relating to establishments with up to 50 persons engaged, though there is an additional limit in terms of the amount of fixed asset investment. The Small Firms' Association — a group established within the Confederation of Irish Industry (CII) to represent the interests of small firms — caters for firms employing up to 100 persons. In the UK, the Bolton Report measured as small those manufacturing firms or establishments with less than 200 persons engaged. The legal definition of small firms in Japanese manufacturing relates to those employing up to 300 persons.[2] In Austria, Belgium, France, Sweden and Switzerland, small firms are usually taken to mean those with less than 50 workers, while Germany and Italy normally include in that category firms with up to 100 workers.[3] In the US, the Small Business Administration (SBA) varies its definition for different purposes, in some cases going as high as 1,500 workers.

For analytical purposes it is not necessary to establish a single dividing line, and indeed it is more useful to consider gradations of size. For administrative convenience, however, it is often necessary to have simple and consistent dividing lines. To accord with IDA practice in Ireland, we shall reserve the term 'small' for establishments with less than 50 persons engaged. We shall also be interested, however, in other ranges of size, but to simplify data presentation we limit the number of categories to four, labelled and divided as follows:

		Persons engaged
(1)	Small	Less than 50
(2)	Small-medium	50 - 199
(3)	Medium-large	200 - 499
(4)	Large	500 and over

The data actually available in relation to small manufacturing industry, particularly the very small establishments, often leave much to be desired. Part of the problem is that there are so many very small establishments, consisting of only a few people, that they are sometimes hard to locate and that they often have difficulty in giving satisfactory statistical returns. For this reason, many countries adopt a cut-off point and exclude the very small establishments from their industrial inquiries. The Irish Central Statistics Office (CSO), for instance, does not attempt to cover establishments with less than three persons engaged, though it is clear that some such establishments do enter the Census of Industrial Production (CIP).

The separation of manufacturing from other economic activities is often difficult in the case of small establishments, and practice differs between countries. For example, in Germany, *Handwerk* activities carried out in conjunction with a retail establishment (such as shoe repairs, silver-smiths, baking, sausage-making, upholstery, etc.) are treated as manufacturing, whereas in Ireland or the UK these would be included in the distribution sector or other service trades.

The foregoing discussion of conceptual and measurement problems should suffice to show that great care must be taken in interpreting data on small industry, especially when comparisons across countries are involved.

THE QUANTITATIVE SIGNIFICANCE OF SMALL INDUSTRY

The data on the size structure of Irish manufacturing industry used here are derived from the CSO data in the Census of Industrial Production and the IDA data in the Annual Employment Survey. A Census of Industrial Production is carried out each year, and an analysis of the data by size has been published at intervals. The IDA Annual Employment Survey started only in 1973 but gives a more up-to-date picture than the CSO data. Unfortunately, the two sets of data differ in important respects, and in particular the CSO data are less complete in relation to very small establishments.[3a] Since the two sets of data cannot readily be combined, they are presented separately.

Table 2.1 summarises the available CIP data on the number of establishments and employment in various size classes in

Table 2.1: Size Distribution of Irish Manufacturing Industry 1929-1975 (CSO data)

Establishment Size[1]	1929	1938	1946	1958	1968	1975
		No. of establishments				
Small	1912	2716	2376	2511	2305	2464
Small-medium	263	425	384	452	576	661
Medium-large			83	112	142	143
Large	11	15	21	31	51	52
Total	2,186	3,156	2,864	3,106	3,074	3,320
		Employment nos ('000)				
Small	22.2	32.8	32.5	37.5	38.2	39.8
Small-medium	32.0	53.4	34.7	42.3	56.5	63.8
Medium-large			23.9	32.4	42.1	43.1
Large	11.8	14.2	18.9	29.6	47.2	48.1
Total	66.1	100.2	110.0	141.8	183.9	194.8
		Employment shares (%)				
Small	33.6	32.7	29.5	26.4	20.8	20.4
Small-medium	48.5	53.2	31.5	29.8	30.7	32.8
Medium-large			21.7	22.8	22.9	22.1
Large	17.9	14.2	17.2	20.9	25.7	24.7
Total	100.0	100.0	100.0	100.0	100.0	100.0

1. The size ranges covered by each of these categories are given in the text.
Source: Census of Industrial Production for 1958, 1968 and 1975. The figures for 1938 and 1946 are taken from T. P. Linehan, 'The Structure of Irish Industry', *Journal of the Statistical and Social Inquiry Society of Ireland,* Vol. XX, Part V, 1961/62. The figures for 1929 are estimates based on the data available for the number of establishments in each size range in these years: the average employment in each size range was taken to be the same as in 1938, except for the 500 + class which was derived residually as the difference between total manufacturing employment and the estimated total of employment in the other sizes. The figures for 1946 and earlier years have been adjusted for comparability with later years.

Irish manufacturing industry for selected years from 1929-1975. The total number of establishments in CIP manufacturing was 52 per cent higher in 1975 than in 1929. The big increase came in the period 1931-1938, when extensive protectionist measures were adopted with a view to developing Irish manufacturing. During the Second World War there was a decline in the number of establishments to a low point of 2,800 in 1942, but there was a rapid increase in the immediate post-War years to a peak of 3,359 in 1952. Subsequently, the numbers declined to 3,074 in 1968, but recovered again to 3,320 in 1975.

Using the criterion of less than 50 persons engaged as designating small establishments, then the vast bulk of Irish establishments must be classified as small — 74 per cent in 1975. While small establishments dominate numerically, their importance in total employment is quite different, accounting for only 20 per cent in 1975. At the top end of the size range, establishments with 500 or more persons engaged accounted in 1975 for nearly 25 per cent of total employment, although they represented less than 2 per cent of establishment numbers.

The relative importance of small establishments has changed considerably over time. In 1929, they accounted for 34 per cent of manufacturing employment, but since then their share has declined in all of the years shown in Table 2.1. The employment share of establishments in the size ranges from 50 to 500 employees has been remarkably stable between 1938 and 1975. The outstanding long-term change has been the gain in the share of establishments with more than 500 workers at the expenses of those with less than 50 workers. Although the employment *share* of establishments with less than 50 workers has fallen substantially, the *absolute* numbers of workers was nearly 80 per cent greater in 1975 than in 1929. The big increase in numbers came in the 1930s, however, and since then there has been only a slight rise. The data suggest, however, that after 1968 the relative decline in employment in small establishments was arrested — a feature evident in other countries,[4] and which is confirmed for Ireland by the more up-to-date IDA data, to which we now turn.

Table 2.2: Size Distribution of Irish Manufacturing 1973 and 1980 (IDA data)

Establishment Size[1]	No. of Establishments		Employment (000)		Employment Shares (%)	
	1973	1980	1973	1980	1973	1980
Small	3913	4451	50.7	57.4	23.3	23.7
Small-medium	686	836	66.2	81.6	30.4	33.6
Medium-large	170	180	51.1	54.0	23.5	22.2
Large	60	61	49.7	49.5	22.8	20.4
Total	4829	5528	217.8	242.5	100.0	100.0

1. See Table 2.1.

Source: IDA *Annual Employment Survey.* The 1973 data for small establishments in Dublin were originally based on a sample of such establishments which was later found to have defects. As a result, there may be some degree of understatement in the 1973 figures for small establishments, and, if so, some overstatement of the employment increase from 1973-80. Also, the data for establishments with only 1 or 2 persons employed is somewhat erratic, but this would not affect the employment position much because of the small aggregate employment involved.

Table 2.2 presents the IDA data for 1973 and 1980. The IDA data include many more establishments than the CIP. Comparison of the two sets of data for 1973, however, shows that the vast bulk of the difference is accounted for by small establishments: of the overall difference of 1650 establishments, all but 30 had less than 50 persons engaged. In terms of employment, however, the distribution is not greatly altered, because small establishments are much less significant in terms of employment than in terms of establishment numbers. Looking at the changes over the period 1973-1980, the IDA data indicate a considerable upsurge in the absolute number of small establishments. Moreover, their share in employment also rose slightly, reversing the secular decline outlined earlier. Perhaps the most significant change, however, in this period relates to large establishments (500 plus) where employment fell, both absolutely and as a percentage of the total.[5] The largest gain in employment was in the small-medium class, where employment rose by nearly one-fourth.

The difficulties of making international comparisons regarding the relative importance of small industry are notorious, and the main problems have been outlined in the previous section. The problems are particularly acute as regards establishment numbers. It is safe to say, however, that, no matter which data classification is used, in all countries the great majority of establishments fall into the category of small — on any reasonable definition of small. Moreover, because the establishments that give rise to comparability problems usually have low employment, international comparisons of the size structure based on employment are less seriously affected by the differences in definition and coverage.

Table 2.3 gives data for a number of countries for the most recent available year on manufacturing employment, divided into the four size classes already specified. The employment share of small establishments varies considerably across countries from as low as 11½ per cent in the UK and West Germany,[6] to as high as 42½ per cent in Japan. Ireland with 23½ per cent comes about mid-way in the range, but nevertheless has a considerably lower share than some of the other small economies like Israel (38½ per cent), Switzerland (38½ per cent), New Zealand (32½ per cent) and Norway (31 per cent).

There are some theoretical arguments and empirical evidence supporting the view that establishment size differences between countries are positively influenced by the size of the domestic market. Though Ireland has a very small domestic market, the data in Table 2.3 suggest that it does not have a particularly high concentration of employment in small manufacturing industry. This impression is confirmed by the data in

Table 2.3: Manufacturing Employment in Various Countries, Divided into Establishment Size Classes*

Country and Year	Small		Small-Medium		Medium-Large		Large		Total
	No. '000	% of Total	No. '000	% of Total	No. '000	% of Total	No. '000	% of Total	No. '000
United States (1972)	2,682.7	14.9	5,020.6	27.8	2,784.7	15.4	7,546.4	41.8	18,034.4
Japan (1966)	4,384.0	42.6	3,437.0	33.4			2,470.0	24.0	10,291.0
United Kingdom (1973)	865.6	11.4	1,224.4	16.1	1,244.1	16.3	4,281.7	56.2	7,616.1
West Germany (1976)	853.0	11.5	1,465.1	19.8	1,343.9	18.2	3,739.3	50.5	7,401.3
Italy (1971)	1,041.1	26.1	1,071.1	26.8	655.6	16.4	1,222.2	30.6	3,990.1
Canada (1975)	306.6	17.3	473.6	27.2	362.8	20.8	605.5	34.8	1,748.5
Belgium (1970)	275.1	23.5	265.9	22.7	200.0	17.1	429.3	36.7	1,170.3
South Africa (1972)	135.5	12.0	273.7	24.2	252.3	22.3	469.6	41.5	1,131.1
Switzerland (1975)	366.5	38.4	241.4	25.3	138.7	14.5	207.1	21.7	953.7
Netherlands (1976)	158.3	17.0	256.2	27.5	168.6	18.1	349.1	37.5	932.8
Sweden (1975)	168.0	18.1	209.8	22.6	157.6	17.0	391.3	42.2	926.7
Norway (1975)	118.4	31.1	108.7	28.6	153.7	40.4			380.8
Denmark (1976)	91.4	24.4	112.2	30.0	69.7	18.6	100.7	26.9	374.0
New Zealand (1975/76)	93.2	32.5	82.6	28.8	45.0	15.7	66.1	23.0	286.9
Israel (1972/73)	104.4	38.5	166.5	61.5					270.9
Ireland (1980)	57.4	23.7	81.6	33.6	54.0	22.2	49.5	20.4	242.5
Northern Ireland (1977)	20.8	14.8	35.0	24.9	33.0	23.4	52.1	36.9	140.9

*The size classes are as follows with the exception of the US: *Small*, less than 50 persons engaged: *Small-medium*, 50-199; *Medium-large*, 200-499; *Large*, 500 or more. For the US, the small-medium class covers 50-249 persons engaged, and the medium-large class 250-499.

Sources: US: *Census of Manufacturers, General Summary*, Table 8.

Japan: OECD (1971), Table II and MITI (1971), p. 69.

UK: 'Report on the Census of Production 1973, Summary Tables', *Business Monitor*, PA 1002, Table 6.

West Germany: *Statistisches Jahrbuch 1978*. Data relates to 'betriebe'.

Italy: *Annuario Statistico Italiano 1977*, Table 163. Data relates to 'unita locali' and exclude 536, 131 units (1, 311, 800 workers) of 'artigiane'.

Canada: *Manufacturing Industries of Canada: Types of Organisation and Size of Establishments, 1975*.

Belgium: *Recensement de l'Industrie et du Commerce 1970*, Tome 1, Table 1. Data includes mining as well as manufacturing.

South Africa: *South African Statistics, 1978*.

Switzerland: *Statistisches Jahrbuch, 1978*.

Netherlands: *Overdruk uit Maandstatistich van Industrie*, September 1977, Table B.01.06. Data cover only establishments with 10 or more persons engaged.

Sweden: *Industri 1975*, Del 1, Table 2. Data cover mostly only establishments with 5 or more persons engaged.

Norway: *Statistik Arbok, 1978*.

Denmark: *Industristatistik 1976, Statisticke Meddelelser 1978*: 2. Data relate to establishments with 6 or more persons engaged.

New Zealand: *Census of Manufacturing Series A, General Statistics Bulletin No. 1, 1974-75 and 1975-76*.

Israel: *Statistical Abstract of Israel 1975*. Data include mining as well as manufacturing, but the mining component is very small.

Ireland: IDA, *Annual Employment Survey*.

Northern Ireland: Department of Manpower Services.

Table 2.4: Average Size of Establishment in Manufacturing, Various Countries

Country and Year	Establishments with 10 or more persons engaged (1)	Establishments with 20 or more persons engaged (2)	Establishments with 500 or more persons engaged (3)
United States (1972)	114	154	1,349
Japan (1975)	52	93	1,385[1]
United Kingdom (1973)	155	225	1,621
West Germany (1976)	n.a.	186	1,548
Italy (1971)	58	99	1,364
Canada (1975)	97	133	1,305
Belgium (1970)	86	129	1,301
South Africa (1972)	127	161	1,134
Switzerland (1975)	58	96	1,204
Netherlands (1976)	80	126	1,290
Sweden (1975)	98	146	1,349
Norway (1975)	66	100	n.a.
Denmark (1976)	69	100	1,158
New Zealand (1975/76)	59	90	918
Israel (1972/73)	61	106	n.a.
Ireland (1980)	74	100	849
Northern Ireland (1977)	115[2]	n.a.	1,446

1. Figure relates to 1966.   2. 11 + .

Sources: As for Table 2.3.

Table 2.4 giving details of average size of manufacturing establishment for the countries listed in Table 2.3. Because of the serious incomparabilities that arise in the case of the very small establishments, the averages are calculated first excluding all establishments with less than 10 persons engaged and then excluding those with less than 20 persons engaged.

Whether we consider the average for establishments with 10 or more employees, or with 20 or more employees, Ireland emerges with a relatively high average size of establishment for a country of its size. Ireland is the second smallest of the 17 countries (as measured by total employment in manufacturing) in Table 2.4 but it ranks tenth in terms of average size of establishment (with 10 or more employees).[7] What is most notable about the Irish situation is the high concentration of manufacturing employment in middle-sized establishments, and the low average size of its large establishments. As may be seen from Table 2.3, Ireland has the highest combined share of any of the countries listed in the two middle-sized classes — small-medium and medium-large. On the other hand, it ranks lowest in terms of the proportion of its manufacturing employment located in large establishments. This point is reinforced by Column 3 of Table 2.4 which shows that Ireland has by far the lowest average size of establishment with 500 or more persons employed.

To sum up, small-scale establishments, defined as those with less than 50 persons engaged, represent the vast bulk of manufacturing establishments in Ireland, accounting for about three-quarters of the total. This position is not unusual by international standards. Their share of employment in Ireland, however, is somewhat less than one-quarter of the total, well below the share in several other countries. By international standards, while Irish manufacturing does not have a particularly high share of employment in small establishments or a particularly low overall average size of establishment, it also has relatively few large establishments and their average size is low. More so than in most countries, employment is concentrated in middle-sized establishments (from 50 to 500 workers). Although the longer-term trend in Ireland up to the early seventies has been towards a decline in the relative importance of small establishments, the IDA data suggest that there may have been some reversal of this trend in the 1970s. Whether or not the new trend continues, the share of total manufacturing employment engaged in small industry is likely to remain large enough to justify studying the special features of such establishments, particularly if some have potential for substantial growth.

CHARACTERISTICS OF SMALL FIRMS

Small industry performs a number of important functions. One of the most important is in providing a training and testing ground for the emergence of larger enterprise. As the Bolton Report put it: 'Almost all the present large firms started off as small firms and grew, in one way or another, to their present size.'[8] Second, small-scale production is the optimal arrangement where, for example, a specialist product or service is required for which the market is small, or where logistic factors (such as transport costs) are of decisive importance to a firm's competitive position. Thus, the possibility of sub-contracting some activities to smaller firms can increase efficiency and flexibility of supply in large firms. Third, small firms play an important role in technological progress in that they are a significant source of inventions, even though the exploitation of these inventions may require a much larger scale of operation. And fourth, the large variety of small firms can increase economic welfare in a number of other ways. It provides an outlet for those who do not wish to work as employees due to a desire for greater independence or for other personal reasons; it permits greater regional diversification of industry; it provides competition for larger firms; and it increases the range of choice and of personalised service available to consumers. We will explore some of these issues further before going on to consider the major disadvantages facing small firms.

The data presented earlier indicate that employment in small establishments in Irish manufacturing rose by 13.2 per cent from 1973-1980 as against a rise of 11.3 per cent overall.

This relative increase in small industry does not, however, tell us whether small establishments were growing more rapidly than large, since the establishments that appear in one size group in any year are not necessarily those that appear in the same size group at a later year. Some will have grown to a larger size range, some will have declined, some will have closed down, and some new ones will have entered. It is possible, however, to elucidate the issue by considering the fate of the establishments which existed in 1973. Of the establishments with less than 50 engaged in 1973, 47.1 per cent had maintained or expanded employment between 1973 and 1980, as against 38.6 per cent in the case of establishments employing 50 or more. Of the establishments which declined, almost half of the small establishments had gone out of business altogether as against a quarter of the larger establishments. The corresponding figures for employment changes are given in Table 2.5. These show that small establishments fared better overall than others. There was scarcely any net change in employment from 1973 to 1980 in the small establishments existing in 1973 as against a net decline of 16 per cent in larger establishments. The components of the net changes also illustrate the greater volatility of small industry, where gross gains and gross losses both exceeded those in larger industries. Furthermore, the data indicate that closures form a much higher proportion of job losses in small establishments than in large.[9]

The data indicate clearly, however, that many of the small establishments have a capacity for growth, and that the aggregate contribution to employment resulting from this growth is quite considerable. In absolute terms, of the total increase of 37,092 jobs from 1973 to 1980 in expanding establishments, 16,695 (or 45 per cent) were in establishments with less than fifty persons engaged in 1973. There was also a total of 51,790 jobs in 1980 in establishments that entered after 1973, and of this total, 31,662 (or 61 per cent) were in establishments which started with less than 50 employees. On this reckoning about 55 per cent of total gross gains in manufacturing employment from 1973 to 1980 occurred in small establishments. In interpreting these figures, however, it must be borne in mind that many new establishments may in their initial year begin with only a fraction of the planned employment level. Also, since new entrants are by definition those with no employment in 1973, and since employment cannot be negative, all new entrants are recorded as gains. Nevertheless it is significant that middle and large-scale industry contributed relatively little to the increase in employment and that the job-generation process depended heavily on new establishments.[10]

Table 2.5: Percentage Changes[1] in Employment in 1973-1980 in Establishments Existing in 1973

Establish-ment size in 1973	Net Change	Gross changes			
		Gains	Closures	Con-tractions	Total losses
	%	%	%	%	%
Small	− 0.1	32.9	− 22.3	− 10.7	− 33.0
Other	− 16.1	12.2	− 13.0	− 15.4	− 28.4
Total	− 12.4	17.0	− 15.2	− 14.3	− 29.4

1. The various components of employment change are calculated as a percentage of total 1973 employment in the relevant size class.

Source: IDA, *Annual Employment Survey.* Relocations appear above as closures (and as new entrants in Table 2.8 below) and arguably inflate somewhat the figures for closures (and for new entrants) depending on the reasons for relocation.

There is little evidence on the contribution of small manufacturing firms in Ireland to the progress of technology. The evidence for other countries suggests that while very many small firms are not innovative, nevertheless small firms are not insignificant in promoting technological advance. They invest relatively less in research and development than larger firms,[11] but their share in innovation activity tends to be higher than their share in R & D expenditure.[12] In general their importance tends to be greater at the inventive stage, which can often be accomplished relatively cheaply, in contrast with the development and test marketing of products which often requires very large resources. The importance of small firms in technology advance varies considerably with the type of industry. There are major sectors where small firms are now of no consequence, such as aerospace, motor vehicles, many chemicals and cement; while their role is greater in activities such as scientific instruments, electronics, textiles and timber.[13]

Looking at the matter from the other viewpoint, the impact of technology on efficient scale of plant, a common conclusion of studies up to recently was that economies of scale were increasing over time due, in part, to the nature of technological advance. Developments in the seventies, however, have raised questions whether this conclusion, if once valid, continues to be relevant. Bollard, for instance, argues that 'electronic technologies appear to be most suitable for small scale operation, while certain aspects of automation can also be used to advantage'.[14]

If productivity is measured in terms of value of net output per person engaged, then it will generally be found that productivity is lower in small establishments than in large. Table 2.6 shows the distribution of Irish manufacturing establishments in different size categories in terms of net output per head in 1975. It may be seen that over one-half of the small establishments had a net output per head of less than £3,000 in that year, as against only 15 per cent of large establishments (500 +). At the other end, only 27 per cent of small establishments had a net output per head of £4,000 or more as against two-thirds of the large establishments. The average net output per head in small establishments, at £4,400, was 17 per cent below the average for all manufacturing. A chi-square test of the data showed a highly significant relationship between size and net output per person.

The generally lower productivity levels in small establishments indicated by these figures, however, does not necessarily imply that they are less efficient, since efficiency must have regard not only to the level of productivity but also the cost of achieving that level. For one thing, wage levels are generally lower in small establishments. This is shown in Table 2.7 for Irish manufacturing in 1968 (the earnings data are not available for 1975), which shows that salaries and wages per head are considerably lower in small establishments. This finding is not peculiar to Ireland. Among the explanations suggested as to why workers are prepared to accept a lower wage are the smaller degree of unionisation and the greater satisfaction which some find in working in a smaller organisation. Another possibility is that small establishments may draw on less skilled or lower quality workers. Whatever the explanation, it is clear from Table 2.7 that the degree to which small establishments fall short of the average in remainder of net output (a very crude proxy for gross profits) per head is absolutely much less than in the case of net output. A further reason why lower labour productivity in small establishments cannot be taken as an indication of lower efficiency is that capital per worker is generally much lower in small establishments. In fact, the Bolton Report concluded that there was no way of saying with confidence that small firms were more or less efficient than large. What could be said was that there was far greater variability in profitability among small firms than among large — both across firms and over time.

It should be recalled that efficient scale of operation is not determined by technology alone but by all the factors affecting costs, and that the optimum scale is not the same for all dimensions of cost. There is evidence, for instance, that the incidence of industrial disputes increases with the scale of operation. Prais[15] found in the UK that 'the burden of strikes in large plants is thus heavier in all three respects: the chance of having a strike-free year is lower; the expected number of strikes per year is greater; and the number of days lost per

Table 2.6: Distribution of Establishments in Different Size Classes in terms of Net Output per Head, Irish Manufacturing, 1975

Establishment size	Net Output per Person (£000 current prices)					Total %	Abso-lute no. of estabs.
	< 2 %	2 − 3 %	3 − 4 %	4 − 7 %	7 + %		
Small	31.7	24.3	16.9	18.9	8.2	100	2,464
Small-medium	10.6	25.6	20.7	28.0	15.1	100	661
Medium-large	2.8	13.3	23.8	41.3	18.9	100	143
Large	1.9	13.5	19.2	42.3	23.0	100	52
All manufacturing	25.8	23.9	18.0	22.0	10.3	100	3,320

Source: Irish Statistical Bulletin, Supplement, September 1981.

Table 2.7: Average Net Output and Wages per Head in Different Size Classes, Irish Manufacturing, 1968

Establishment size	Net output per head £	Salaries and wages per head £	Remainder of net output per head £
Small	1,370	660	710
Small-medium	1,575	719	856
Medium-large	1,748	798	950
Large	1,939	959	980
All manufacturing	1,664	786	898

Source: Irish Statistical Bulletin, Supplement, March 1973.

employee is greater'. Prais explained these results not in terms of different patterns of individual behaviour in large plants as against small, but rather as a pure diseconomy of scale, summed up in the principle 'the bigger the crowd, the greater the chance of a fight'.

PROBLEM AREAS FOR SMALL-SCALE INDUSTRY

There are, however, other major dimensions of business activity where scale factors impair the competitiveness and inhibit the expansion of small firms, which we now examine. Even where a small firm can compete in terms of production costs, it may still face large barriers in marketing. These may arise even when access to the market is not artificially restricted because of heavy overhead expenses in acquiring market information or in establishing contact with distributors, especially in distant markets. In addition, in industries where there is a high degree of monopolistic or oligopolistic concentration, access to the market may be restricted in a variety of ways. The extent of these constraints varies considerably from industry to industry as well as from one country to another.

A particular problem facing small firms in Ireland lies in the smallness of the home market. The record of industrialisation in many countries indicates that new enterprises often acquire experience first by operating on the home market where familiarity, ease of access and transport costs facilitate the establishment of a competitive advantage. In larger economies, small firms are able to attain a position of viability by supplying an extensive local or domestic market, whereas Irish small firms are often hampered by the limited home market opportunities. For some, in order to be viable, it would be necessary to launch into export markets, but they may lack the financial and marketing expertise to undertake this step. It is possible, however, that for some activities the rise in energy costs may stimulate more decentralised local production, which would improve the prospects for small firms in such industries.[16]

It is widely recognised in all countries that small enterprises are hampered in their efforts to start-up or expand business because of difficulties in obtaining finance. They are too small and insufficiently well known to raise capital on the stock exchange. Conventional lenders, such as the banks, tend to cast a jaundiced eye on their loan applications because they often offer little security, have no track record, and are unfamiliar with the niceties of presenting a good financial case. Furthermore, small industry is always in a state of flux with many new entrants and many closures, so that the risk of failure in any one case is quite correctly seen by lending agencies to be high. The difficulty cannot be adequately met by charging higher interest rates to such borrowers to cover the greater risk (although small firms often have to pay more for credit due to the higher handling costs of smaller loans). Paradoxically the higher the interest rate the greater the prospect that the business cannot start-up at all or will fail, since little or no operating profit may be made in the first couple of years.

It was precisely to meet this 'finance gap' that venture capital institutions developed in the United States. These institutions generally take equity holdings in a portfolio of firms, which are thought to have strong growth potential. It is recognised that, in the event, there will be many failures and only a limited number of 'high-flyers'; but the expectation is that the small number of high-flyers will secure an adequate overall rate of return. Although there has been a considerable growth in awareness among financial institutions in Ireland of the finance problem facing small firms, the venture capital market is as yet comparatively undeveloped. The obstacles to the development of venture capital for small enterprises do not lie solely with suppliers of finance, but also in the aversion of small firms to yielding any of their independence to outside equity participation.[17]

In very small firms the owner/manager of an enterprise will typically combine in himself all functions of management, as well as perhaps spending some of his time working on the factory floor. This can have undoubted advantages in keeping overhead costs down. But it can give rise to many problems, since the manager may be expert in one or two key areas but quite inexperienced in other aspects of business. These deficiencies are difficult to overcome since the manager is often so vital to the day-to-day functioning of the firm that he cannot take time off to attend even short-term management courses, assuming he were aware of such services and conscious of his need for them. In fact, there is evidence of a marked lack of awareness among Irish small firms of the services available to them from different agencies, public and private.[18]

As the very small firm grows, the need arises for a more delegated managerial structure with professional input in areas where the owner/manager is less skilled. Many small firms fail to overcome this hurdle — for serveral reasons. The manager may fail to identify the need, he may lack the knowledge of how to cope with it, or he may even be unwilling to move from essentially one-man control. There is also a reluctance on the part of good quality middle management to accept employment in the small firm, which often offers less security and prospect for promotion than larger corporate structures.

THE IDA SMALL INDUSTRY PROGRAMME

The main thrust of industrial policy in Ireland in relation to small manufacturing firms operates through the IDA Small Industries Programme (SIP). To qualify for aid under this programme, only projects which employ less than 50 persons, and which have a fixed asset investment of less than a maximum figure (£500,000 in early 1983), are eligible. The main type of assistance available to small firms under the SIP is in the form of non-repayable cash grants towards the cost of fixed assets. These grants are negotiable up to 60 per cent of the value of eligible fixed assets in designated areas (mostly in the western half of the country) and up to 45 per cent in other areas. Grants are also provided under the SIP towards the training of personnel and towards the rent of factory accommodation. There is an advance factory construction programme for small firms. Following grant approval, contact is maintained between the firm and IDA by means of the regional office of the IDA and/or the County Development Officer to ensure adequate after-care service. Since 1978 the Shannon Free Airport Development Company has been responsible for the promotion of indigenous small industry in the mid-west and similar aid is available for small establishments to that provided by the IDA in the rest of the country.[19]

The SIP was initiated in 1967 and has grown rapidly since then. The Dublin area was not fully incorporated into the programme until 1977. Grant payments to indigenous industry[20] under the SIP have accounted for 11 per cent of all payments to indigenous industry over 1970 to 1979, rising from 11 per cent on average in 1970-72 to 18 per cent in 1977-79, although the percentage fell to 9 per cent in 1973-76. In 1979-81, a record number of approvals was made. Approvals of manufacturing projects under the SIP and SFADCo schemes averaged 870 per annum in 1979-81, compared with an average of 140 in 1973-75. In addition to the SIP, the IDA also operate an Enterprise Development Programme, which is aimed at first-time entrepreneurs with background experience in technical or commerical work. Under this scheme, the IDA provides loan guarantees on working capital, interest subsidies and in some cases equity participation. Job approvals for small firms in 1980-81 under all IDA schemes (including the Enterprise Development Programme and International Services Programme) accounted for over 25 per cent of total jobs approved by the IDA, compared to 13-14 per cent in the mid 1970s.

Table 2.8: Components of Employment Changes in Various Types of IDA Grant-aided and Non-IDA Grant-aided Industry (1973-1980)

| | 1973 total employment | 1980 total employment | Gross Changes | | | | | |
| | | | Gains | | | Losses | | |
			New Entrants	Employment increases	Total gains	Closures	Employment decreases	Total losses
IDA Small Industry	12,000	24,246	9,658	5,649	15,307	1,880	1,181	3,061
IDA New Industry								
—Irish	49,624	50,820	5,115	9,258	14,373	6,500	6,677	13,177
IDA New Industry								
—Foreign	35,566	58,954	24,567	9,259	33,826	5,593	4,845	10,438
Other Small	31,711	33,683	6,825	6,382	13,207	7,538	3,697	11,235
Other Large	88,858	74,815	5,625	6,544	12,169	11,529	14,683	26,212
TOTAL	217,759	242,518	51,790	37,092	88,882	33,040	31,083	64,123

Note:

'Other Small' represents establishments which employed between one and 49 persons in 1973 (or in the first year of entry subsequently) and which did not receive a small industry or a new industry grant.

'Other Large' represents establishments with employment of 50 or more persons in 1973 (or in the first year of entry subsequently) and which did not receive a small industry or a new industry grant.

'New entrants' are those establishments which had no employment in 1973 but had in 1980. New entrants which did not receive a new industry or a small industry grant were included in 'Other Small', where they began with less than 50 persons engaged; otherwise they were included in 'Other Large'.

'Increases' refer to employment changes in establishments in existence in both 1973 and 1980 and where the 1980 employment was greater than or equal to the 1973 level.

'Closures' refer to job losses in establishments which were in employment in 1973 but had closed by 1980.

'Decreases' refer to employment changes in establishments in existence in both 1973 and 1980 and with lower employment in the latter year.

Source: IDA *Annual Employment Survey 1980.* See qualifications mentioned in Tables 2.2 and 2.5

In Table 2.8, data are given for 1973 and 1980 for different types of grant-aided establishments, and Table 2.9 shows the percentage changes over the period 1973 to 1980.[21] The general picture that emerges from Table 2.9 is that there has been very rapid growth in both IDA small industry and foreign-owned IDA new industry. As a proportion of total employment in manufacturing, IDA small industry's share has risen from 5½ per cent to 10 per cent between 1973 and 1980. The proportion of employment in IDA small establishments with less than fifty persons to total employment in all establishments with less than fifty persons rose from 21 per cent in 1973 to 31 per cent in 1980. It is impossible to say, however, how many projects would have gone ahead in the absence of IDA assistance.

The bulk of IDA small industry is indigenous, with foreign firms accounting for less than 9 per cent of the employment in 1980. The performance of IDA small industry is in marked contrast to that of indigenous IDA new industry which showed only a marginal employment increase. Similarly, the performance of small establishments not aided under the new or small industry programmes was rather poor by comparison with IDA small industry, though not as bad as in large establishments not aided under the new or small industry programmes

Whereas only 20 per cent of the grants paid to indigenous firms under the New Industries Programme (NIP) went to non-traded industry, the corresponding figure for SIP firms was 51 per cent.[22] This is not altogether surprising, however, since many establishments are small due to transport costs or logistic factors, and hence may be unsuited for export markets anyway. The SIP has been mainly concentrated on three broad industrial sectors — metals and engineering, wood and furniture, and miscellaneous manufacturing (which includes rubber and plastics). Together, these three sectors accounted for 68.3 per cent of total employment in 1980 in IDA small industry. With the exception of wood and furniture, these

Table 2.9: Percentage Change in Employment in Various Types of Industry (1973-1980)[1]

| | Total net change in employment 1973-1980 | Gains | | | Losses | | |
		New Entrants	Employment increases	Total gains	Closures	Employment decreases	Total losses
	%	%	%	%	%	%	%
IDA Small Industry	102.1	80.5	47.1	127.6	15.7	9.8	25.5
IDA New Industry							
—Irish	2.4	10.3	18.7	29.0	13.1	13.5	26.6
IDA New Industry							
—Foreign	65.8	69.1	26.0	95.1	15.7	13.6	29.3
Other Small	6.2	21.5	20.1	41.6	23.8	11.7	35.4
Other Large	−15.8	6.3	7.4	13.7	13.0	16.5	29.5
TOTAL	11.4	23.8	17.0	40.8	15.2	14.3	29.4

1. % changes in employment are in all cases expressed relative to total employment in each category in 1973.
Source: As in Table 2.8.

sectors grew at a very rapid rate over 1973-1980. Many of the firms in metals and engineering are sub-supply firms catering for purchasers of engineering and tool equipment or parts. It has been estimated[23] that 39 per cent of total IDA grant payments to indigenous SIP firms went to sub-supply businesses compared with 19 per cent in the case of NIP indigenous firms.

It is interesting to compare the various components of net employment change over 1973-1980 for different categories of industry as shown in tables 2.8 and 2.9. For total manufacturing industry, the net increase in employment was 11.4 per cent — made up of a gross gain of 40.8 per cent and a gross loss of 29.4 per cent, where all percentages relate to the base year (1973). It is clear that new entrants are the major factor behind the large net employment increase in IDA small industry, as well in IDA new industry. Even leaving aside new entrants, however, and focusing only on establishments which already existed in 1973, employment in IDA small industry grew by 21.6 per cent, whereas it declined for all other categories of industry. The overall rate of loss is relatively uniform across different categories: it is highest in other small industry, and lowest in IDA small industry at 25.5 per cent. In spite of the general tendency, referred to in the last section, for small establishments to have a high failure rate, the rate of closures in IDA small industry is close to the average for all manufacturing.

A problem in using information supplied in IDA annual reports is that grants approved and jobs anticipated in connection with a project may not actually materialise for a number of years following the approval, if indeed they materialise at all. SIP grants are approved and paid in stages which may stretch over a number of years. Some or all of the stages of investment planned by a firm may be cancelled or deferred due to changing economic circumstances. Even when grants are actually paid, there is no guarantee that jobs approved at the time of the initial grant approval will be translated into net additional employment for the project. From the data supplied by the IDA, it is not always possible to link specific stages of grant payments to preceding grant approvals, since there may be a series of grant approvals to the same firm over a period of years. In the case of job approvals, it is impossible to determine accurately how many of these were translated into actual jobs, since the employment level in the firm may be rising or falling due to factors other than the investment programme of the firm.[24]

To date, there has been limited analysis of the rate of conversion of job approvals into actual jobs for different IDA grant schemes. The IDA has stated on the basis of surveys of NIP firms carried out in the 1970s, that 60 per cent of expected jobs, on average, were translated into actual jobs within five years, while a further 15 per cent of all jobs approvals were in projects which did not proceed. The IDA has also stated that small industries brought jobs on stream more quickly than NIP firms. The Telesis Report estimated that only 24 per cent of all jobs approved in IDA-assisted foreign projects between 1973 and 1980 were still in place by January 1981.[25] In other words, only one in four jobs approved were actually sustained. For indigenous industry (new and small combined) the conversion rate was even lower at one in six jobs.

It is useful to compare the estimates of job conversion made in the Telesis Report with estimates we have prepared from data on the SIP. Any estimate of jobs converted is somewhat arbitrary since it is based on assumptions regarding the appropriate time horizon over which to measure the impact of approvals on actual employment. The 'jobs ratio' in Table 2.10 is calculated by dividing the actual increases in employment between year of first approval and 1 January 1979 by total approved employment in all SIP projects first approved in the period 1973-1977. This estimate allows for a time lag in job conversion, and includes job approvals not realised due to closures, cancellations or deferments. Of the 9,197 jobs approved in projects first aided in 1973-1977, 3,592 had

Table 2.10: Ratio of Approved to Actual Jobs and Grants for all Establishments First Approved for a SIP Grant in 1973-1977.

Status of establishment at at year of first approval (YFA)	Jobs ratio[1]	Payments ratio[2]
	%	%
Existing	28.1	56.5
New entrant	41.3	48.1
Total	39.1	51.5

1. The jobs ratio is calculated as the sum of net employment increases between YFA and 1 January, 1979, divided by the sum of jobs approved in 1973-1977 for all establishments first approved in 1973-1977.
2. The payments ratio is calculated as the sum of total grant payments over 1973-1978 divided by total grant amounts approved over 1973-1977 in all establishments first approved in 1973-1977.
Source: IDA Project Information File.

actually materialised by 1 January 1979, giving a conversion rate of 39.1 per cent — rather higher than in NIP projects.

The 'payments ratio' in Table 2.10 is calculated by taking the ratio of total grant payments over 1973-1978 to total grant amounts approved for all SIP projects first aided in 1973-1977. Training and other incentive grants are included in these figures. The payments ratio was 51.5 per cent for SIP projects, compared to an estimated payments ratio of 46 per cent for indigenous IDA small and new industry.[26]

Establishments which were already in existence before receiving their first approval ('existing') are distinguished in Table 4.10 from those which were not ('new'). It may be seen that job approvals made for new establishments were converted into actual jobs at a much higher rate than for existing establishments, and that this would appear to be unrelated to differences in the proportion of approved grants that were actually paid out.

From an administrative viewpoint, a key magnitude at the approval stage is the proportion of fixed-asset investment to be financed by capital grants, referred to here as the 'approved grant rate' (C/FA). The highest permissible value which C/FA can take for SIP firms is 60 per cent in designated areas. The size of approved grants is determined also, however, by the anticipated employment (E). The ratio C/E indicates the anticipated grant cost per job, while the ratio FA/E shows the anticipated capital intensity of the project. These three ratios are related as follows:

$$\frac{C}{E} = \frac{C}{FA} \cdot \frac{FA}{E}$$

The values of these three ratios are given in Table 2.11 for both the SIP and NIP schemes covering the period 1977-1981. Despite the fact that the approved grant rate was much higher for SIP than NIP firms, the approved grant cost per job was less than half. The reason is that anticipated capital intensity was about three times as great for NIP projects as for SIP projects. A more surprising fact is that in both NIP and SIP projects, there has been no upward trend since the late seventies in the real values of anticipated capital intensity and grant cost per job.

From an economic point of view, however, the actual values of these variables are of greater interest. Table 2.12 compares the anticipated and actual values for all SIP projects first approved in 1973-78 and which also received at least one grant payment in the same period. The anticipated grant rate did not vary much from the actual grant rate. However, actual capital grant cost per job was 25 per cent greater than anticipated (£3,636 compared to £2,904), and actual capital intensity similarly was higher. These differences are mainly

Table 2.11: Approvals Data for the Small Industries and the New Industries Programmes, 1977-1981 (in constant 1981 prices)

Year	Capital Grants/ Fixed Assets (C/FA)		Fixed Assets/ Jobs Approved (FA/E)		Capital Grants/ Jobs Approved (C/E)	
	NIP	SIP	NIP	SIP	NIP	SIP
	%	%	£	£	£	£
1977	30.7	42.9	22,704	6,443	6,966	2,763
1978	37.2	46.5	19,037	7,370	7,073	3,425
1979	39.0	47.6	20,622	8,383	8,048	3,993
1980	30.0	50.9	22,411	7,934	6,732	4,038
1981	29.6	51.3	25,216	7,221	7,474	3,702

Source: IDA Annual Reports.

due to shortfalls in job creation. For the same reason, the grant cost per job emerged as substantially higher for SIP projects involving existing firms than for SIP new entrants. Compared with the estimates that have been made for the NIP, it would appear that the actual grant cost per job in the SIP is substantially lower — by at least 40 per cent, depending on which estimate is used for the NIP.[27]

It may be argued that the grant cost per job tends to be lower in small industry because such industry is comparatively labour intensive. Hence, labour intensive large firms may generate as much, if not more, employment per pound of grants as small firms in general. However, in practice, size and capital intensity are negatively related to each other. As regards the relationship between the grant rate (per unit of capital) and capital intensity, analysis of the data for SIP firms showed a negative though weak relationship. Similarly, McAleese[28] found a non-significant inverse relationship for IDA new industry, while the findings of Ruane[29] for new industry were also inconclusive.

Table 2.12: Capital Grant Cost per Job (in constant 1981 prices) for all SIP Projects (1973-1978)[1]

	Anticipated Values			Actual Values		
	Existing	New	Total	Existing	New	Total
Capital grants ÷ Fixed assets (%)	39.6	41.1	40.5	37.7	39.2	38.5
Fixed assets ÷ Employment (£)	6,736	7,588	7,178	13,438	7,378	9,444
Capital grants ÷ Employment (£)	2,669	3,119	2,904	5,068	2,895	3,636

1. All projects included in this table were first approved in 1973-1978 and received at least one grant payment in the same period.

Note: Nominal amounts are deflated using an average of the wholesale price index applicable to transportable capital for use in industry as well as the Building and Construction Capital Goods Index (*Source: CSO Irish Statistical Bulletin*).

Source: IDA Project Information File.

It emerges from this review that the Small Industry Programme provides a relatively successful and less capital intensive way of providing jobs compared to other IDA programmes. As with other IDA schemes, however, the SIP shows a significant, though smaller, divergence between anticipated and actual performance. Moreover, the capital grant cost per job and the number of jobs directly created cannot be taken as providing a global estimate of the costs and benefits of the SIP. To measure total costs and benefits, data would be needed on the cost of other incentives and of IDA staff resources used by the Small Industries Division, taxation, output, balance of payments effects, etc. — not to mention non-tangible benefits such as a more balanced industrial structure.

THE FUTURE INDUSTRIAL ENVIRONMENT IN IRELAND

Policy for small industry should properly be considered in the context of general industrial policy, which in turn must be framed with regard to the overall economic environment. In the years ahead the growth of domestic and foreign markets is likely to be sluggish. A satisfactory growth of manufacturing output can be achieved, therefore, only by increasing market share, particularly in export markets. This in turn implies that progress depends on exploiting more effectively whatever competitive advantages Ireland has, and in improving these competitive advantages. Moreover, the aggregate volume of mobile international projects may be reduced, and there is likely to be intensified international competition for such projects. These circumstances suggest the need to concentrate relatively more than in the past on the development of domestic enterprise.

Yet, though the prospects for growth in manufacturing output and employment are less favourable, the need for such growth is in no way diminished. The growth in the labour force is likely to be of the order of 17,000 per annum. Agricultural employment will probably fall by about 3,000 per annum on average, so that if unemployment is not to rise further above the present intolerable levels, an annual increase in employment of the order of 20,000 would be needed. If we postulate that one-third of this should be sought in manufacturing, this would call for growth in manufacturing employment of the order of about 7,000 per annum (or 3 per cent). On the basis of past relationships, such an increase would require a growth in manufacturing output of 9 per cent per annum, or nearly double the rate achieved for 1973-1979 before the onset of the current recession.

Industrial strategy, however, must also look beyond the pressing needs of the years immediately ahead. A major re-orientation of strategy cannot be accomplished overnight. The broad framework must remain in place for a considerable time, and cannot be chopped and changed every few years if clear signals are to be given to firms, and if the development agencies are to market and exploit it to best effect. Moreover, the environment for industry is strongly influenced by general policy measures as well as those specific to industry itself. These general measures relate to such matters as the improvement of development facilities (e.g. education, infrastructure), macro-economic policies affecting profitability (e.g. incomes policy), the influence of taxation on risk-taking and work effort, the rewards for saving, the ease of access to investment funds, and even the climate of social attitudes towards risk and failure. There is always a temptation to pick on industry-specific measures as a palliative for failure to tackle broader environmental deficiencies, some of which have been created by defective general policies.

These considerations are particularly relevant in approaching the question whether there should be a special policy approach to small industry over and above that applying to the rest of industry. Discrimination in favour of small industry is warranted only where there are problems particular to small industry, *and* where particular benefits accrue from measures to overcome these problems. Thus, for example, the fact that small firms have to pay more for their purchases is not in itself a cause for concern if it simply reflects the fact that smaller orders are more costly to handle. Though it is a differential cost penalty to the small firm, it does not provide a justification for intervention unless corresponding differential benefits can be expected to accrue to the society from such intervention.

For these reasons, a number of studies in other countries have come out against any special discrimination in favour of small firms other than to remove general disadvantages that were not justified by market forces.[30] In our opinion, however, such recommendations, while largely justified in well-established industrial countries, are not fully appropriate to less developed or semi-developed economies. We believe that in Ireland's situation of late industrialisation in free trade conditions, there are grounds for a more specific degree of intervention in favour of small industry. We develop this point in the next section, after first considering here the likely future shape of general industrial development strategy in Ireland.

Beginning in the late 1970s the National Economic and Social Council sponsored a series of studies of Irish industrial development policy. In the context of future policy directions the key study is the Telesis Report, which proposed certain modifications to the prevailing industrial strategy and the addition of new strategic dimensions. The general intent of these proposals is to concentrate on the development of indigenous industry and those foreign companies with characteristics relevant to the long-term strength of Irish industry. The emphasis would be on developing enterprises producing traded goods that would be large enough to serve world markets. Non-traded activities would be less favoured then heretofore, except in the case of high-skilled, sub-supply activities. As regards type of industry, the prime focus would be on 'complex factor cost businesses' where the key to competitive success lies in skill levels, innovation, marketing, etc. rather than in low wages or in logistic factors.

In developing a suitable corporate shell to undertake a selected activity, Telesis would favour a more directive approach on the part of the development agencies. Existing companies would be encouraged to rationalise and combine, joint ventures might be arranged, or holding companies formed. There would be a more active dialogue between government policy-makers and large companies about investment plans, and sticks as well as carrots might be used. Policy instruments would be designed to address specifically whatever cost penalties had to be overcome in each selected enterprise — whether they related to product or process technology, overseas marketing, skill development, working or fixed capital, etc. The instruments would also seek to develop capabilities in firms rather than in the developing agencies.

The White Paper, *Industrial Policy,* which was published in July 1984 outlined the Government's intentions about the future direction of industrial policy. While it endorses many of the views of Telesis, there are substantial differences between the two documents, at least in emphasis. Of course, it was evident from the start that much more work would need to be done to translate the Telesis strategy into operational programmes,[31] and only time can tell to what extent it will be implemented in practice. It seems to us, however, that there is much merit in the Telesis stress on the development of selected large indigenous companies. Irish manufacturing has relatively few large firms and their average size is small by reference to international experience in developed countries. Thus, it seems sensible to stress, as the strong right arm of industrial strategy, the building of large companies that would eventually be able to engage on their own in the full range of functions needed for success in world markets. We now turn to the question whether there is scope for a second arm focusing on small firms.

FUTURE STRATEGY FOR SMALL INDUSTRY IN IRELAND

The Telesis Report is rather ambivalent on the policy approach to small firm development. While its whole thrust is towards 'the building of fewer larger companies with strong internal capability', it goes on to say that this is not regarded as a substitute for the development of small industries but rather 'as a supplement in those cases where the business opportunity is large and the chances for success are great'.[32] Though the Report is strongly critical of the extent of the 'hand-holding' activities by the development agencies, it nevertheless suggests that strong regional offices could maintain some of the intensive 'hand-holding' functions of the Shannon Free Airport Development Company (SFADCo.), which went beyond most of the other development agencies. It is clear, however, that the Report favours the handling of small industry projects 'as part of an integrated indigenous development charter' to build structurally strong firms and to foster linkages, rather than dealing with them through a specific agency or division.[33]

For the following reasons we believe there is a danger that in such an approach the development of small industry would play second fiddle, and that its potential contribution would not be given adequate weight or attention. First, it will take a lot of time and effort to operationalise the new strategy, and it would seem only sensible to keep in place the main elements of the present strategy until new approaches have been worked out. Second, the need for jobs is very pressing in the next five to ten years, and we have shown that the SIP has been a significant contributor to employment at a relatively low capital cost. No doubt some of the projects were not ideal from a long-term point of view and will not remain viable. But it remains to be demonstrated in practice that an alternative approach would yield better results, and until this has been shown at least through pilot experiments, it would be risky to forego the achievements of the present approach. Third, the Telesis Report pays no attention to the important issue of regional policy, in regard to which we have already pointed out that small firm projects can play an important role. Fourth, Ireland already has many small firms, a significant proportion of which, while surviving, will not necessarily grow large. Nevertheless, the improvement in efficiency in such small firms is an important consideration, and poses different issues from larger firms.

Finally, and perhaps most important, the outlook and the instruments needed to build the structurally strong firms are substantially different from those required to nurture new first-time enterprise. The development staff responsible for building strong firms will not normally begin with new entre-preneurs: rather they will look to the existing medium and larger-sized firms and a limited number of the established small enterprises which have clearly shown a potential for successful growth over at least a few years. It will be helpful to these staff to be able to select from a reasonably wide range of promising small firms. But a lot of their energies would be dissipated if they were also responsible for building from scratch the pool from which they were drawing.

Given the very substantial resources that will be committed to each of the firms selected for enlargement, it would seem best also that the selection be done by a separate set of personnel from those responsible for bringing the firm to that level, and who could be, quite understandably, less detached in their assessment. Moreover, the expertise and the instru-ments required to build a diversified pool of small new firms are different in many respects from those involved in the development of the limited number of strong firms. For example, the Telesis Report regards it as vital that the strong firms be encouraged to provide their own capabilities in research, marketing, etc., something that would neither be feasible nor economic in new firms until they had reached a reasonable scale.

The need to give specific attention to the development of new enterprise seems to us to be supported by the relatively low take-up of new industry grants by domestic enterprises. The package of industrial incentives has been available equally to Irish and foreign firms; Irish firms are better placed to know about them; and Irish firms as a matter of course have a variety of knowledge about the social and economic background, which has to be acquired at some expense by foreign firms. Yet according to McAleese's study, 60 per cent of the total employment arising from the IDA New Industry Programme occurred in foreign firms.[34] It also appears that the vast bulk of the domestic projects assisted under the New Industry Programme represented expansions in firms surviving from the tariff-protected era, and only a small part represented wholly new undertakings.

We would accept that it is not necessary or desirable to establish a new agency for small firms, but rather that the relevant existing agencies preserve a section or division with the two-fold objective of encouraging new small enterprises and raising efficiency in the existing ones. We now turn to the question whether there are any modifications that might be made in the existing range of policy measures applicable to small industry.

In comparison with the funds allocated through tax relief and capital grants and subsidies, the amounts devoted directly to overcoming technological and marketing barriers have been relatively small. Yet these often constitute the most formidable barriers to indigenous development. The acute marketing problems facing new ventures in a free trade environment have been outlined in a previous section. Given the nature of these problems, the volume of new small enterprise would be less than desirable if, as the Telesis Report seems to suggest, assistance were confined to traded goods and skilled sub-supplies.

Greater marketing grants would be of limited effectiveness for small firms. An institution which could be re-examined is the industrial marketing board, exploited with such success in Japan, where a large proportion of exports are centrally handled by a few large selling organisations. The basic advantages of industrial marketing boards would be in supporting selected firms to reach a viable scale of operation, in sharing the advantages of economies of scale in selling and purchasing, and in the spreading of risks. True, the first effort to apply this idea in Ireland, the Irish National Trading Corporation, failed after a short time with significant losses. But the idea might be worth reviving, taking due note of the causes of failure in the first instance, and studying the pre-conditions for success as demonstrated by Japanese experience.

Another institution also exploited with particular success in Japan has been that of sub-contracting by the large firms. Such contractual links tend to be on a long-term basis, and greatly simplify the marketing problem for the new or small business, as well as improving the security of the market. The recent establishment by SFADCo. of a 'matchmaker service' is a step in this direction. Shannon Development acts as a broker between small firms and large enterprises and maintains a permanent exhibition in Limerick of small industry products. Similar links might also be considered in relation to the purchases of public bodies, under which the buying agencies would use their purchasing power as a lever to develop these firms. This could be done in association with other development agencies like the IDA and IIRS by, for instance, laying down standards in relation to quality and design, and providing technical advice to the firms to help them meet these standards. The White Paper, *Industrial Policy,* announced a number of initiatives in regard to the development of linkages, sub-supply and co-operative trading, which will be tested first on a pilot basis.

In regard to technology, what is most needed in the case of small firms is not necessarily more R and D grants, but easier access to the advisory services and to laboratories offering design experimentation or prototype facilities. The establishment of the Innovation Centre and the National Microelectronic Applications Centre in Limerick, may go some way to overcoming the latter difficulty. In regard to the former, there may be a case for treating small industry in a parallel manner to agriculture by providing an extension service akin to that offered to Irish farmers by the agricultural institutions. Rather than waiting for firms to seek information and advice, the advisers would call on the firms. Such a service to small firms has been operated with considerable success in Israel by the Productivity Institute there.[35] In general, a movement towards more regional organisation of support for small firms is welcome, but care should be taken to ensure within each region that there is adequate co-ordination between the different agencies offering services, including where possible a common location.

In regard to capital constraints, the Telesis Report favoured the greater use of loans, loan guarantees and equity participation in preference to capital grants. This approach has much to recommend it and might be extended to working capital, which is generally not grant-aided at present, and which can be a serious barrier to the entry and expansion of small firms. The efforts to encourage the development of a range of private venture capital facilities should also continue. One of the advantages of the wider development of equity participation both by State and private interests lies, not only in the injection of finance provided, but also in the pressure for expansion that such outside interests would be likely to exert on a proprietor who might otherwise rest content at a modest scale.

CONCLUDING REMARKS

The development of small firms poses a variety of problems, many of them quite distinct from those involved in building large firms. There is a good case, in our view, for continued specialised attention to small firms within the major development agency, the IDA, and also in some of the other development agencies. The focus of attention should not simply be on those with outstanding growth prospects, the high-flyers, but also on encouraging the formation of new small enterprise and increasing efficiency in those which survive but never grow large.

Nevertheless, there is a danger that the great diversity in the experience of small firms, and in the problems facing them, could lead to a continuous accretion of services. Thus a service introduced to meet problems particular to one class of firms may be demanded even by those in less need of that service. Some safeguards can, however, be suggested. First, all programmes should try to establish clear objectives and criteria. Second, to facilitate this process and to ensure that programmes are as effective as possible, there should be more pilot experimentation with any new service or incentive before it is introduced generally. Third, each of the programmes should be subject to regular review by the parent government department rather than by the agency responsible for the programme. Finally, the aggregate of services and incentives offered by the various agencies should be subject to independent overall evaluation at periodic intervals, not only to ensure adequate co-ordination but also to re-assess the scale of subsidisation in relation to benefits. Such reviews should assess whether in the changing economic environment the need for specific attention to small industry remained.

NOTES AND REFERENCES

1. Bolton, J. E., (Chairman), *Small Firms: Report of the Committee of Inquiry on Small Firms* (London: HMSO, 1971), p.xv.
2. Bannock, G., *The Small Business in Britain and Germany* (Farnborough: Wilton House Publications, 1976).
3. OECD, *Problems and Policies Relating to Small and Medium-Sized Businesses* (Paris, 1971).
3a. Since going to press, the CSO has published an extended coverage of the 1979 CIP results. The number of establishments engaged in manufacturing in 1979 has been increased by 683 to 4,589 compared with the former coverage. The vast majority of the additional establishments are very small, with nearly three-fifths having less than 10 persons engaged. The general effect of the extension in coverage is to bring the CSO data much closer to the data shown in Table 2.2.
4. Beckler, D., *Small and Medium-Size Firms in the OECD Countries — Trends and Policy Issues:* paper given at International Symposium on *Industrial Policies for the 1980s* (Madrid, 1980, May 5-9).
5. It is possible that this fall may reflect forces special to the 1970s rather than a long-term trend. These forces include the impact of free trade on the older Irish import-substituting industries, the world depression following the oil crisis of late 1973, and factors peculiar to particular firms such as the closure of the Ferenka plant, employing about 1,500 persons, in late 1977.

6. If *Handwerk* activities were included, however, the share of employment in small establishments in West Germany would be much higher.

7. Previous research suggests that in practice differences in the structure of manufacturing among countries is not an important determinant of the differences in overall average size. *Vide* Linehan *op. cit.* and Pryor, F. L., 'The Size of Production Establishments in Manufacturing', *The Economic Journal*, Vol. 82, No. 326 (June 1972), pp. 547-66.

8. Bolton Report, *op. cit.*, p.29.

9. These findings on the volatility of small industry are borne out by studies in other countries. *Vide* Hymer, S. and Pashigian, P., 'Firm Size and the Rate of Growth', *Journal of Political Economy*, Vol. 70 (1962); Birch, D. L., *The Job Generation Process* (M.I.T. Report, 1979); Boswell, T., *The Rise and Decline of Small Firms* (London: Allen and Unwin, 1972); and Mansfield, E., 'Entry, Innovation and the Growth of Firms', *American Economic Review*, Vol. 52, No. 5 (December 1962).

10. For similar findings in relation to the United States over the period 1969-76, see Birch, *op. cit.* A quite different perspective on the US experience, however, is given for a more recent period in Armington, C. and Odle, M. 'Small Business — How Many Jobs?' *The Brookings Review*, Winter 1982. It should be noted in the case of the Irish data that some of the small establishments were branches of larger firms, and it might be thought that very different results would arise if the data were given on a firm or enterprise basis. While it is not possible to establish satisfactorily how many of the small establishments were independent enterprises, a check through the names of establishments in the IDA Annual Employment Survey indicated that less than about 10 per cent of employment in small industrial establishments was located in the obvious branch establishments of larger firms. More important, however, the employment performance in these branches of larger firms was not superior to that of the independent establishments.

11. In Ireland, data collected by the National Board for Science and Technology showed that in 1979, 28 per cent of establishments employing 100 or more persons were engaged in R. and D., compared with only 1 per cent of establishments with less than 50 workers — *Irish Science and Technology Statistics* (Dublin 1982).

12. Bolton Report, *op. cit.*, p. 54.

13. Freeman, C., *The Role of Small Firms in the United Kingdom Since 1945*, Report to the Bolton Committee of Inquiry on Small Firms (London, 1971).

14. Bollard, A., 'Technology, Economic Change, and Small Firms', *Lloyds Bank Review*, No. 147 (January 1983).

15. Prais, S., 'The Strike-Proneness of Large Plants in Britain, *Journal of the Royal Statistical Society*, Series A., Vol. 141, Part 3 (1978).

16. Bollard, *op. cit.*

17. National Board for Science and Technology, *Innovation in Small Manufacturing Firms — An Irish Research Study* (Dublin 1982).

18. *Ibid.*, and Confederation of Irish Industry, *Small Firms Report* (Dublin 1978).

19. Various other agencies also provide assistance to small firms. These include AnCO, the Industrial Training Authority; Údaras na Gaeltachta which caters for small industry in Gaeltacht areas; and a number of agencies offering specialised marketing, managerial or technological services to small firms (e.g. Coras Trachtala Teo., the Irish Productivity Centre, the Institute for Industrial Research and Standards, and the Irish Management Institute). Various financial institutions are also active in catering for the financial requirements of small firms.

20. An indigenous industry is defined as one whose main headquarters is located in the Republic of Ireland.

21. All establishments approved for a small industry grant in any year up to end 1979 are included under IDA Small Industry in the tables. Some of these establishments would have grown to such an extent as to qualify for a new industry programme grant before 1980. Out of a total of over 24,000 employees in IDA small industry in 1980, over 4,000 were in establishments which were approved for a new as well as a small industry grant. IDA new industry in the tables comprises those establishments which were approved for a new industry grant but not a small industry grant. Foreign new industry firms are those with a parent headquarters located outside the Republic of Ireland. The remainder of manufacturing employment was allocated between small and large firms, depending on their level of employment in 1973.

22. Telesis Consultancy Group, *A Review of Industrial Policy* (Dublin: National Economic and Social Council (No. 64) 1982), p. 407. A non-traded industry is defined as one in which the key to competitive success lies in factors such as transport or logistic costs.

23. *Ibid.*

24. Furthermore, a number of small firms aided under the SIP would have also received assistance under the NIP and hence not all of the actual change in employment could be ascribed to the effect of SIP grants alone. Those firms, however, account for only one-sixth of total employment in IDA small industry.

25. Telesis Report, *op. cit.,* p.188.

26. *Ibid.,* p.188

27. For estimates in relation to the NIP, see McAleese, D., *A Profile of Grant-Aided Industry in Ireland* (Dublin: IDA, 1977), and NESC, *Policies for Industrial Development: Conclusions and Recommendations,* Paper No. 66 (Dublin 1982), p. 27.

28. *Ibid.*

29. Ruane, F., *Trade, Fiscal Policy and Industrialisation in the Small Open Economy: The Irish Experience*, B. Phil. Thesis, Nuffield College, Oxford, 1976, and *Government Policy and Resource Allocation in Semi-developed Countries with Special Reference to the Republic of Ireland*, D. Phil. Thesis, Nuffield College, Oxford, 1978.

30. *Vide* Bolton Report, *op. cit.* and Beckler, *op. cit.*

31. For further details, see Kennedy, K. A., 'The Design of a New Industrial Strategy', contributed to Symposium on Industrial Development,

Journal of the Statistical and Social Inquiry Society of Ireland, Vol. XXIV, Part V, 1982/83, forthcoming.

32. Telesis Report, *op. cit.,* p. 234.
33. *Ibid.*
34. McAleese, *op. cit.*
35. Kennedy, K. A., 'Impressions of Israel', *Administration,* Vol. 24, No. 4 (Winter 1976). It may be noted that AnCO has recently announced an initiative which goes part of the way in this direction in the form of a special business training advisory service, a small firms' information 'hot-line', a retired executives counselling service and computer-based training packages. Small firms will be directed as appropriate to other agencies for more specialised advice.

3

The Import Dependence of the Irish Economy: Implications for Industrial Policy[1]

Alan W. Gray and John H. Kelly

Ireland is one of the world's most open economies. Imports and exports together were equivalent to almost 120 per cent of Gross National Product (GNP) in 1983, a level exceeded only by Belgium/Luxembourg within the OECD area.[2] A consequence of this openness is that foreign products compete freely with the output of domestic industry on both home and foreign markets. Changes in the volume and composition of industrial imports are, therefore, of interest as a reflection of the performance of manufacturing industry in Ireland. A growing import share in domestic demand in many cases reflects an increasing inability of industry to meet the challenge of foreign competition which, in the absence of corrective measures, may lead to firm closures and job losses.

In one of the first studies of the relationship between imports and economic growth in Ireland, Leser[3] pointed out that 'in the economic development of any country, except for very large and almost self-contained units, imports assume a key role and the trend in imports demands constant attention'. Over the years, Irish imports have indeed received considerable attention from economic researchers and a number of useful empirical studies have been produced. The most widely used approach adopted in such studies has been to view the level of imports as a function of relative prices and an activity variable such as real income. Models constructed in this manner were used by McAleese, Sloane and Kelleher, Boylan, Cuddy and O Muircheartaigh and Fitzgerald,[4] with estimates of the relationship between the variables being derived for total imports and for number of sub-categories. More recently, a similar approach was adopted by Lynch[5] in the first study of import demand to use Quarterly National Accounts data. From the point of view of industrial policy, a major disadvantage of these studies is that it has been impossible to capture the effects of structural change in the industrial sector. Thus, while measures of capacity utilization, cyclical developments and trend factors have been employed, none of these can be said to have adequately taken account of the significant structural changes which have taken place in Irish industry since the mid 1970s.

The analysis of imports presented in this chapter differs from previous studies in two important respects. First, import data classified according to the NACE system are employed so as to allow for direct comparison with Irish industrial production statistics. This enables a detailed examination of developments in imports at a twenty-sector level of disaggregation to be undertaken. Second, rather than attempting to estimate precise relationships between variables, trends in the level and growth of imports are highlighted. The explanation of these trends and the implications for industrial policy formulation are seen as of primary importance.

In order to provide a context for the later sectoral anaysis, in the first section of this chapter the role of imports in the Irish economy is discussed and the trend in imports over the period 1963-82 in relation to both GNP and Final Domestic Expenditure (FDE) is examined. The second section then deals with the response of Irish industry to demand expansion over the period 1977-80 and looks at growth in the level of imports by sector.

The reasons for the level of and the movements in import penetration which occurred are analysed by examining separately industries with high levels of import penetration and industries with low levels of import penetration. This constitutes the subject matter of the third and fourth sections. In the fifth section attention is turned to the policy implications of the earlier findings while some conclusions are presented in the final section.

THE ROLE OF IMPORTS IN THE IRISH ECONOMY

One characteristic of the Irish economy is a high marginal propensity to import. The marginal propensity to import measures the increase in imports associated with a given increase in GNP. In the Irish case, the marginal propensity to import has been estimated to be of the order of 0.8[6] This implies that for every increase of £100 in aggregate demand there is a tendency for imports to increase by £80.

This high marginal propensity to import gives rise to two related problems for government economic policy in Ireland. First, demand management policy is seriously constrained as a means of stimulating the economy since a large proportion of any extra demand will 'leak' out of the economy through increased imports. Second, the balance of payments position of the economy may from time to time act as a brake on policies designed to promote faster economic growth.

The import leakage flows through two channels. As domestic incomes rise, Irish people spend a greater proportion of their total income on imported goods and services. In addition, there is a high imported input content in domestic production. As a result, fiscal multipliers in Ireland are low, on average not much above unity,[7] and fiscal actions to increase aggregate demand are blunted. This is not to deny that there may be some scope for short-term demand management, especially if it can be applied to selected sectors with relatively low import contents,[8] but from the point of view of longer-term industrial development, the best that can be said is that successful demand management policies may facilitate growth. This point will be pursued in more detail in the following section where the response of individual industrial sectors to demand

Table 3.1: Growth of Irish Imports, 1963-82

Year	Imports of Goods and Services	Gross National Product	Imports as % of GNP
1963	889.8	2,378.4	37.4
1964	1,004.7	2,513.2	40.0
1965	1,116.1	2,559.4	43.6
1966	1,155.5	2,583.6	44.7
1967	1,199.2	2,711.1	44.2
1968	1,386.7	2,893.4	47.9
1969	1,573.2	3,020.5	52.1
1970	1,610.0	3,104.1	51.9
1971	1,685.1	3,202.0	52.6
1972	1,770.3	3,393.4	52.2
1973	2,107.3	3,530.8	59.7
1974	2,059.1	3,681.0	55.9
1975	1,814.0	3,738.4	48.5
1976	2,074.5	3,792.7	54.7
1977	2,344.0	4,022.4	58.3
1978	2,710.0	4,226.5	64.1
1979	3,108.1	4,349.2	71.5
1980	2,970.2	4,491.4	66.1
1981	3,023.0	4,542.0	66.6
1982	2,889.0	4,480.0	64.5

Data in IR£ millions at constant 1975 prices.

Source: National Income and Expenditure, 1981, and Economic Review and Outlook, Summer 1983

expansion is examined. Before proceeding to this more detailed analysis, however, trends in total imports of goods and services over the past two decades are considered briefly.

The growth of imports, both in real terms and as a proportion of GNP, over the period 1963-82 is shown in Table 3.1

below. Two major features of imports are readily apparent from the table; their importance as a proportion of GNP and their rapid growth, in real terms, over the two decades.

The most pronounced growth in imports took place over the decade to 1973, as world trade expanded rapidly and as Ireland pursued a policy of tariff reduction in preparation for EEC membership. Over this period the real value of imports more than doubled while the ratio of imports to GNP rose from 37 per cent to 60 per cent. The import ratio subsequently declined in 1974 and 1975, as a quadrupling of oil prices during 1973 contributed to the substantial 44 per cent rise in Irish import prices during 1974. Between 1976 and 1979 the import ratio resumed its upwards trend, reaching a high of 72 per cent of GNP in 1979 before falling back to an average level of some 66 per cent in the three years to 1982. The data also show that the volume increase in imports of goods and services was of the order of 225 per cent over the twenty-year period while GNP increased by less than 90 per cent. This underlines the growth in import penetration which took place.

The comparison between imports and GNP presented above is influenced by movements in exports which are one of the constituents of GNP. An alternative approach is to express imports as a percentage of Final Domestic Expenditure (FDE), which is defined as GNP minus exports, plus imports. An examination of the data in Table 3.2 reveals a similar trend to that in Table 3.1, with imports growing at a faster rate than domestic demand. From these results it is obvious that the principal factor behind the rise in imports which has taken place is not the increase in demand but rather the increase in the share of demand supplied by imports.

In considering the high level of import dependence of the Irish economy, it should be noted that some 70 per cent of imports are made up of either producer capital goods or materials for use in industry. More remarkably, despite the more than twofold volume increase in imports between 1963 and 1982, the share of such imports remained relatively

Table 3.2: Irish Imports as Percenage of
Final Domestic Expenditure

Year	Final Domestic Expenditure	Imports of Goods and Services as a % of FDE
1963	2,533.1	35.1
1964	2,724.4	36.9
1965	2,810.4	39.7
1966	2,781.5	41.5
1967	2,854.9	42.0
1968	3,123.3	44.3
1969	3,393.0	46.4
1970	3,460.3	46.5
1971	3,581.8	47.0
1972	3,811.4	46.4
1973	4,138.2	50.9
1974	4,229.6	48.7
1975	3,933.4	46.1
1976	4,116.8	50.4
1977	4,370.4	53.6
1978	4,694.7	57.7
1979	5,061.0	61.4
1980	5,917.6	60.4
1981	4,980.0	60.7
1982	4,680.0	61.7

Data in constant 1975 prices

Source: National Income and Expenditure 1981, and Economic Review and Outlook, Summer 1983.

constant. In 1963 imports of producer's capital goods and materials for further production in industry constituted 73.5 per cent of total imports. Fourteen years later, in 1979, these two categories amounted to exactly the same proportion of the total, although by 1982 their contribution had declined somewhat to 68.7 per cent.[9]

In general, imports of capital goods and raw materials have been viewed as an important source of non-available products which are 'essential to industrial growth'[10] However, just what proportion of imports satisfy demands which it is impossible to meet from domestic resources has been a subject of much discussion and in a number of studies attempts are made to differentiate between competing and non-competing imports.[11] It is clear that a continued supply of non-competing imports are important to employment maintenance and job creation. It is on the other category of imports, those products which compete with domestic production, that the debate regarding the desirability of imports focuses. Some aspects of this question will be touched on in a later section dealing with policy questions.

No attempt, however, is made in this chapter to distinguish between those imports which compete with domestic production and those which do not. There are two main reasons for this. First, as Matthews[12] has pointed out, the usefulness of categorizing imports as 'non-competing' and 'competing' is diminished by the fact that the distinction is largely subjective. Second, over a period when rapid industrial change is taking place the distinction becomes extremely blurred. New firms are established whose products previously were classified as non-competitive imports while some older-established firms go out of business, leaving no Irish manufacturer of a particular product. This problem is particularly acute in dealing with industries such as chemicals and electrical engineering, where technological advances add to classification difficulties.

THE RESPONSE OF IRISH INDUSTRY TO DEMAND EXPANSION

In order to gain greater insight into the extent to which Irish industrial output is influenced by an expansion in domestic demand, movements in manufacturing output and home market demand for manufactured goods over the period

1977-80 are examined. The years 1977 to 1980 are chosen as the study period for a number of reasons. First, this chapter is primarily concerned with developments in imports. As shown in Table 3.1, imports as a proportion of GNP were at their highest in these years. Second, following five years of transitional arrangements with respect to tariffs on trade in industrial products, Ireland moved to free trade with other EEC countries in 1978. Any increase in import penetration which may have come about as a result will, therefore, be contained in the 1977-80 period. Third, volume of production indices for manufacturing industries are available on a consistent basis only from 1977 onwards, when a revision on the basis of the results of the 1977 (amended) and 1978 Censuses of Industrial Production was made. As described below these indices are used to derive estimates of production for later years where published data were not available. Finally, the period is not extended beyond 1980 as demand was either static or falling in later years.

A problem facing any attempt to compare imports with industrial output is that official publications from the Central Statistics Office (CSO) classify Irish trade data on a different basis from that used for production. Production data, as provided by the annual Census of Industrial Production, have, since EEC entry, been classified on the NACE* basis. Irish trade data is classified by the CSO on the SITC basis. The problem has been overcome in this study by utilising Eurostat NACE trade data. These data were obtained in European units of Account and were converted into Irish pounds using an average of EUA/Irish pound quarterly exchange rates.[13]

Production data were taken from the Census of Industrial Production 1977 and updated using price and volume indices. As there are frequently large revisions in production data, it is likely that the output figures are the main determinant of any errors which may exist in the estimates. In addition, the existence of transfer pricing may lead to an undervaluation of

*Nomenclature General des Activities Economiques dans les Communautes

imports and in consequence an underestimation of import ratios. However, as it is broad trends rather than precise movements in the aggregates which are relevant to policy formulation, these imperfections are not seen as serious. In the tables presented below, home sales are calculated as a residual of output minus exports. Home sales combined with imports give total home market demand.

Table 3.3: Import Penetration, 1977-80 (Current Prices)

Year	Total Manufacturing (£ million: current prices)				
	Output	Home Sales	Manufacturing Imports	Home Market	Import Penetration %
1977	4,849.5	2,621.5	2,701.8	5,323.3	50.8
1978	5,729.9	3,064.5	3,378.9	6,442.9	52.4
1979	6,796.8	3,624.3	4,331.4	7,995.7	54.4
1980	7,454.8	3,691.7	4,821.7	8,513.4	56.6
% increase 1977-80	53.7	40.8	78.5	59.9	

Movements in these variables, in current prices, together with a measure of import penetration are shown in Table 3.3. From this table, it can be seen that while manufactured output increased by some 54 per cent in value terms, imports of manufactured goods increased by as much as 78 per cent, thus giving rise to an increase of almost 6 percentage points in the import penetration ratio. Furthermore, as the growth of domestic demand slowed down during the year 1979-80, the value of imports increased by 11.3 per cent while home sales grew by less than 2 per cent in value, reflecting a substantial volume decline.

Volume changes in domestic output and imports in response to changes in domestic demand are presented in Table 3.4 below. This table shows that the rapid expansion in domestic demand of 10.3 per cent in 1978 and 9.9 per cent in 1979 had a minimal impact on Irish manufacturing industry, with domestic sales rising by less than 4 per cent per annum. The expansion in demand did, however, have a significant influence on imports, although, as will be shown below, there was considerable variance between industries. The decline in real domestic demand during 1980 led to only a marginal decline in the volume of imports, while the volume of domestic sales by Irish manufacturers fell by almost 8 per cent. As a result, import penetration in manufactures increased still further during 1980, although, as has been shown in Table 3.1, the overall ratio of imports to GNP declined in that year.[14].

The small proportion of growth in home market demand for manufactured goods which is supplied by manufacturing industry in Ireland is noteworthy. Although demand expansion has never been regarded as a specific component of industrial policy, it has been widely agreed that the more rapid expansion of domestic demand since the late 1950s has been important to industrial growth. In examining economic growth during the 1960s, Kennedy and Dowling[15] have drawn attention to the beneficial effects for industrial growth arising from demand expansion, while McAleese,[16] among others, has noted similar effects in the early 1970s. While not refuting the basic point that demand expansion may have a beneficial effect on industrial growth, the data presented here suggest that the magnitude of this effect is small. The implication for policy formulation is, therefore, that macroeconomic policies aimed at an expansion of aggregate demand are an extremely inefficient means of stimulating industrial output.

Table 3.4: Import Penetration, 1977-80 (Constant Prices)

| Year | Total Manufacturing (£ million: constant 1977 prices) | | | | |
	Output	Home Sales	Imports	Home Market	Import Penetration %
1977	4,849.5	2,621.5	2,701.8	5,323.3	50.8
1978	5,256.8	2,725.1	3,144.5	5,869.0	53.6
1979	5,577.5	2,822.4	3,631.6	6,454.0	56.3
1980	5,516.1	2,609.1	3,506.4	6,115.5	57.3
% increase 1977-80	13.7	− 0.5	29.8	14.9	

Nevertheless, a fact concealed by the aggregate figures is that certain sectors of industry tend to rely quite heavily on domestic demand. This is particularly true of the more sheltered manufacturing activities where logistics costs prevent effective competition from overseas but it is also true of the more traditional unsheltered industries where older established firms predominate. Looking at the period 1965 to 1973, Matthews[17] found growth of home demand to be an important source of expansion for certain sectors of manufacturing. The ability of firms which have traditionally served the domestic market to compete with imports is, therefore, critical to their survival prospects.[18] Future industrial strategy must have regard to the problems facing such firms, and in this context an examination of developments in imports and in demand by industrial sector can be of assistance in identifying sectors which are particularly at risk.

The differential impact of demand expansion on the major industrial sectors from 1977 to 1980 is considered in Table 3.5 below, together with the growth of imports by sector. In columns 4 to 6 changes in domestic demand for manufactures are shown as a percentage of the previous year's level, while similar percentage changes for imports are presented in columns 1 to 3.

The data in Table 3.5 highlight the wide variations between sectors which are concealed by the aggregate figures. While no consistent overall relationship is readily apparent, some correspondence between changes in imports and movements in demand in certain industries can be observed. First, and most important, it is possible to identify a group of industries where import growth has consistently exceed growth in domestic demand and where sharp increases in import penetration have consequently taken place. Clothing, plastics, leather, motor vehicles and non-metallic mineral products are the best examples of such industries, but timber and wooden furniture and electrical engineering might also be included in this group. Second, there are a number of industries where growth

Table 3.5: Impact of Demand Expansion on Major Industrial Sectors, 1977-80

(£ current prices)	% Change in Imports			% Change in Domestic Demand		
	77/78	78/79	79/80	77/78	78/79	79/80
Non-metallic mineral products	56.3	36.6	11.7	28.0	28.3	11.6
Chemicals (incl. man-made fibres)	36.5	23.8	0.5	34.4	27.9	1.4
Manuf. of metal articles & mechanical engineering	32.4	22.3	6.4	35.9	19.5	2.4
Electrical engineering	27.8	26.5	26.4	22.6	17.6	26.3
Manuf. of assembly of motor vehicles and parts	55.3	10.6	− 3.0	39.0	0.1	− 2.6
Textile industry	5.3	13.5	2.6	4.4	20.8	− 7.1
Leather & leather goods & footwear	34.8	33.0	13.1	21.0	14.4	4.8
Clothing	38.9	43.5	17.7	16.2	25.6	12.3
Timber & wooden furniture	24.4	36.6	4.1	15.1	26.4	—
Paper and paper products	15.2	28.5	17.3	5.7	21.9	18.9
Processing of rubber	27.1	13.8	22.2	22.9	29.9	20.2
Processing of plastics	17.4	35.4	13.2	3.6	30.5	− 10.4
Drink	44.0	23.6	− 3.0	15.1	20.5	22.4
Tobacco	12.7	22.5	5.5	10.4	17.0	33.3
Foods of which						
Slaughtering & preserving of meat	14.1	26.4	43.1	27.6	32.0	− 22.2
Manuf. of dairy products	14.9	6.9	35.5	23.4	4.0	2.3
Processing and preserving of fruit & vegetables	26.9	29.9	16.6	3.8	30.0	10.1
Grain milling & manuf. of animal & poultry food	44.5	59.1	1.1	13.9	25.3	− 5.0
Bread, biscuits & flour confectionery	26.3	36.1	32.7	23.9	8.6	20.3
Manuf. of sugar & cocoa choco & sugar confectionery	13.5	24.2	33.8	15.7	− 4.5	25.0

in domestic demand is approximately paralleled by import growth and where, as a result, no significant change in import penetration has taken place. This group is best exemplified by chemicals, textiles and mechanical engineering. Third, some extremely high growth rates in imports are observed in most sub-sectors of the food industry. While a considerable degree of volatility exists here, in general, import growth has been well in excess of growth in domestic demand. The result, as with the industries in the first group, is a notable increase in import penetration which is of concern. Finally, a word of caution with respect to the interpretation of demand and import trends in the drink sector. A doubling of the excise duty on beer and spirits between 1975 and 1980 makes trends in current price data difficult to interpret, as declining volumes of consumption are masked by price increases caused by the increase in taxation. However, it must be stressed here that the primary aim of this chapter is to identify broad movements in import penetration which are relevant to industrial policy and not to become over-involved in attempting to explain precise changes in individual sectors.

The sectoral trends in import penetration identified from Table 3.5 by themselves provide only limited information for industrial policy formulation, since they give no indication of the overall importance of imports in each of the sectors. Thus, in sectors where import penetration is relatively low, small changes in import quantities may result in quite large percentage changes, while the opposite applies in high import penetration sectors. In order to examine the relationship between imports and domestic demand more fully, it is also necessary to look at the share of domestic demand accounted for by imports in each sector. This information is provided in Table 3.6 below.

The import penetration ratios shown here for twenty industries are the average of the annual ratios over the four years 1977-80. The industries are listed according to the magnitude of their import ratios with 50 per cent being chosen as the cut-off point between 'high' and 'low' import ratio sectors. Twelve industries fall into the high imports category, with imports accounting for 70 per cent or more of demand in two-thirds of the cases. Of the low import industries, three-quarters had import ratios below 13 per cent. The low import category is mainly comprised of sectors of the food industry together with drink, tobacco and non-metallic mineral products.

Table 3.6: Imports as a Percentage of Domestic Demand

Industry sectors with high import ratios	Average 1977-80
Electrical engineering	90.3
Metal articles & mechanical engineering	70.9
Chemicals	77.5
Manuf. & assembly of motor vehicles & parts	73.7
Processing of plastics	70.9
Textile	69.5
Rubber	68.3
Leather & leather goods and footwear	65.5
Clothing	64.9
Paper	58.3
Timber & wooden furniture	57.5
Processing of fruit & vegetables	51.5
Industry sectors with low import ratios	
Sugar, chocolate, etc.	27.7
Non-metallic mineral products	19.2
Bread, biscuits and flour	12.9
Drink	10.2
Grain milling and animal poultry food	9.8
Slaughtering of meat	7.2
Tobacco	5.6
Dairy products	2.3

Before considering the policy implications of the developments in imports described in this section, it is necessary to explore the reasons behind both the level of imports and their movements as a share of domestic demand. Do the high import sectors, for instance, have common characteristics which help explain their level of import penetration? Why have certain sectors experienced very high growth in imports during the four years under review? What can be learnt about likely future developments in imports from the experience of this period? To facilitate this analysis, industries with high levels of import penetration and industries where imports supply only a small proportion of domestic demand are dealt with separately.

INDUSTRIES WITH HIGH IMPORT PENETRATION

Imports as a percentage of domestic demand for those industries with high levels of import penetration are shown in Table 3.7. From the annual data it can be seen that in the case of ten out of the twelve industries, imports accounted for a higher market share in 1980 than in 1977. It is clear, therefore, that in examining the reasons behind the import penetration ratios it is necessary to consider explanatory factors for both the level of and the movements in the share of domestic demand accounted for by imports.

Table 3.7: Imports as a Percentage of Domestic Demand: High Import Penetration Industries, 1977-80.

Industry sector	1977	1978	1979	1980
Electrical engineering	84.3	87.9	94.5	94.6
Processing of plastics	59.1	67.0	69.5	87.8
Metal articles & mechanical engineering	81.4	79.3	81.1	84.3
Manuf. & assembly of motor vehicles & parts	64.3	71.9	79.4	79.1
Leather & leather goods and footwear	54.5	60.7	70.6	76.3
Chemicals	78.1	79.3	76.7	76.0
Clothing	51.9	62.1	71.0	74.4
Textile	69.3	70.0	65.8	72.7
Rubber	70.8	73.2	64.1	65.2
Timber & wooden furniture	51.5	55.7	60.2	62.7
Paper	53.3	58.1	61.2	60.4
Processing of fruit & vegetables	43.4	53.1	53.1	56.2

In seeking to explain the trends which are evident in Table 3.7, it is useful to look at both developments in international trade and changes in the structure of Irish industry. Four factors in particular are chosen for consideration here:

(1) Industrial specialisation and intra-industry trade.
(2) The international competitiveness of Irish industry.
(3) The import content of industrial purchasing.
(4) The structure of Ireland's industrial base.

It is to be expected that the importance of each of these factors will vary considerably between sectors. Developments in appropriate sectors will, therefore, be used to illustrate the impact of the various factors. In addition, it should be noted that the above factors are not mutually exclusive; some or all may help explain developments in each industrial sector. Changes in the structural composition of a sector, for instance, may amplify the effects of some of the other factors.

(1)   Economists have developed a wide variety of theories to explain the determinants of international *specialization* and trade in manufactured goods. Much of the discussion about specialization has been focused on the distinction between inter-industry and intra-industry specialization. The Heckscher-Ohlin[19] theory was at one time widely regarded as affording a satisfactory explanation of the sources of comparative advantage and hence of the observed pattern of trade. According to this theory, the transition from protection to free trade will involve greater inter-industry specialization with resources moving from protected import-competing sectors to export-oriented sectors in accordance with comparative advantage.

The opportunity to test the empirical validity of the Heckscher-Ohlin theory was provided by the steady momentum towards trade liberalization during the 1960s and 1970s.[20] The results of empirical studies have, however, been at variance with the predictions of the theoretical model. Trade liberalization, it was found, has tended to bring about increasing industrial specialization and a streamlining of production at an individual plant level. Since the specialization takes place within rather than between sectors, this process is known as intra-industry specialization.

The causes of intra-industry specialization have been extensively discussed by Grubel and Lloyd and Giersch, among others.[21] In a comprehensive analysis by Grubel and Lloyd, the importance of economies of scale, product differentiation and imperfect competition, all factors excluded by the assumptions of the Heckscher-Ohlin model, are stressed. Following the dismantling of protective tariffs, a firm faced with intensified foreign competition responds by narrowing its product range in order to gain economies of scale, by engaging in sharper product differentiation and by selling to a narrower section of both home and export markets. In the case of large multinational corporations, the movement towards greater freedom in world trade has resulted in specialization taking place between different plants of the same firm in different geographical locations. Where these plants are dispersed between countries such intra-firm trade will have the effect of increasing both the import and export ratios of the countries concerned.[22]

An empirical study of the industrial sectors of the Republic of Ireland and Northern Ireland by McAleese[23] provides evidence that the move to free trade in the Republic between 1964 and 1971 resulted in an increase in intra-industry specialization. While some increase was observed in inter-industry specialization, the effects here were found to be small in comparison to the increase in intra-industry trade, which the author concluded represented 'increased levels of intra-plant and intra-firm specialisation' which 'appear in trade and production statistics in the form of higher export and import ratios'.[24]

Increased specialization and the growth of intra-industry trade has, therefore, been important in contributing to the marked increased in total imports since 1963, observed in Table 3.1. But how significant a factor is it in explaining the level and growth of imports since 1977 shown in Table 3.7? First, as the level of imports is itself the outcome of past growth rates, then intra-industry specialization during the earlier period of rapid growth and liberalization of trade flows is an important factor in explaining this. Second, with regard to the growth of imports between 1977 and 1980, intra-industry trade remains important, especially in the newer and more rapidly developing sectors. The effects of reduced protection were still evident in this period as it was not until 1979 that the Tokyo Round of multilateral trade negotiations was completed, while up to 1978 certain tariffs still existed on Irish trade in manufactures within the EEC. Since 1980, however, it is likely that the influence of specialization on import growth has been reduced.[25]

Electrical engineering, the sector with the highest import penetration ratio, serves as a good example of a sector where the effects of increased specialization have been important. The sector, which includes the electronics industry, is primarily a high technology one and the high import ratio reflects, *inter alia,* the highly specialized nature of much of its output. Thus, while import penetration ratios were large and growing over the period, exports as a percentage of output were increasing at an even faster rate and rose from 78 per cent in 1977 to 91 per cent in 1980.[26]

(2) The issue of competitiveness has been a recurring one in discussions of the performance of Irish industry. As early as 1923 the Fiscal Inquiry Committee drew attention to the 'competitive disabilities' of Irish industry, among which figured high wages relative to our main trading partner, the United Kingdom.[27] In more recent years, the 'competitiveness' of Irish industry has again been to the forefront of economic policy discussions, with the need to curb increases in labour costs receiving particular attention in the quarterly economic

commentaries of both the Central Bank and the Economic and Social Research Institute. But despite over sixty years of concern, no totally satisfactory measures of industrial competitiveness are available. Problems arise because all of the factors which are important to the competitiveness of an industry can not be readily quantified, and also because differences exist regarding the interpretation of trends in those variables which are easily measured.

From the point of view of manufacturing industry, competitiveness may be defined as a measure of the ability of a particular industry to retain a strong position in domestic and foreign markets. Indices of manufacturing competitiveness centre upon relative prices and relative costs. The relative price approach compares specific prices in a particular country with a weighted average of such prices in other countries. The relative cost approach makes a similar comparison of domestic and foreign costs, usually concentrating on some measure of relative wage costs. The respective merits and theoretical underpinnings of price indices and cost indices as measures of competitiveness are dealt with in detail by O'Leary[28] and O'Malley.[29] A persistent rise in a country's price or cost index relative to the indices of trading competitors indicates a weakening of its competitive position and may be expected to lead to both increased import penetration and a decline in export markets. Difficulties of interpretation arise when a country's price and cost indices show conflicting trends.

Both price and cost indices, however, suffer from the fact that there are a wide range of qualitative influences on competitiveness, none of which they are capable of taking into account. Manufacturing industry embraces a wide diversity and changing mix of products, technologies and forms of business organization. Statistical measures based on either price or cost trends cannot allow for product, technological or organization innovations. Over periods of time, therefore, during which structural changes may have taken place, changes in competitiveness cannot be reliably assessed by simple appeal to such indices. Some of today's most dynamic inustries were scarcely beyond their research stage a decade ago and, as a result, are unlikely to be adequately represented in official statistics. These caveats must be borne in mind in discussing the impact of changes in competitiveness on import penetration.

Movements in the prices of imports and domestically produced goods between 1977 and 1980 are shown in Table 3.8 below, where figures for the wholesale price index and the import price index for these years are presented. From this table it is not possible to find any strong association between price movements and the increase in import penetration which took place. Although domestic prices rose somewhat faster than import prices in 1978 and 1979, over the four-year period average import prices rose by over 40 per cent compared with a rise of about 35 per cent in domestic wholesale prices.

Table 3.8: Import and Wholesale Price Movements, 1977-80

Year	1977	1978	1979	1980
Wholesale price index	140.1	152.6	171.2	189.2
Import price index	139.3	146.2	165.9	195.6

Source: Economic Review and Outlook, Summer 1983

In the *Report of the Committee on Costs and Competitiveness*[30] three indices of relative Irish costs were calculated. The first was based on economy-wide unit labour costs, the second on hourly earnings in manufacturing industry and the third on hourly earnings adjusted for average productivity gains. All three indices showed a steady deterioration in the Irish economy's labour-cost competitive position in the period 1977-80. This evidence accords with the observed increase in import penetration during the period, but, for the reasons described above, it might be dangerous to infer too close a causal relationship. Indeed, the authors of the study themselves noted 'that for many services and industrial products, it is quality factors and marketing effectiveness that essentially determine sales levels, and that the relationships of these with cost trends is complex and indirect'.

However, as the structure of wage bargaining in Ireland during the late 1970s led to wage increases being relatively uniform across industrial sectors, it would be reasonable to assume that if wage increases were a significant factor in contributing to increased import penetration, then those sectors where labour accounted for a higher proportion of value-added would be most affected. To test this hypothesis some statistical tests were carried out on the relationship between the growth of import penetration between 1977 and 1980 and labour's share in value added by sector.[31] No close correlation was found to exist between these two variables for the twelve industrial sectors in Table 2.7. Controlling for the effect of changes in demand on changes in import penetration produced slightly better, but still statistically insignificant, results. However, when observations for the rubber sector were excluded, a small but significant positive relationship between growth in import penetration and labour intensity was discovered.[32] While the statistical validity of excluding a 'nonconforming' sector is questionable, the practical implications are that labour intensity has been a factor in explaining import growth in most sectors. The fact that there is considerable variance among firms within each sector as to the share of labour in value added also causes problems. Differences in productivity between sectors will also affect the outcome. However, it is noteworthy that the two sectors in Table 2.7 which show the highest growth in import penetration, clothing and leather and footwear, are also among the most labour intensive, and have been identified by Keenan[33] as sectors where productivity growth was insufficient to prevent unit wage costs from rising.

(3) The third factor of relevance in discussing the levels of import penetration shown in Table 3.7 is the import content of

industrial purchasing. The importance of this factor is seen from the distribution of imports according to main use, where, in 1980, 56.5 per cent of total imports were materials for further production in industry and 13.8 per cent were pro-ducers' capital goods. As a proportion of aggregate imports, both these categories have shown some decline between 1977 and 1980.[34] However, the magnitude of raw materials and components imports at over half of total imports makes this category, in particular, worthy of further examination.

The extent to which new grant-aided industry in Ireland is integrated with the rest of the economy has long been recognised as important for industrial development. As a result, over the past decade there have been a number of studies directed at measuring the extent to which new industry, and especially foreign-owned new industry, sources its input requirements of raw materials and components from within Ireland.[35] While these studies have identified considerable variation between industrial sectors, the low overall level of domestic purchases of raw materials and components as a percentage of total raw materials and components purchases (or backward materials linkages as they are more commonly called), in all sectors except food, has given rise to concern.

The most recent comprehensive analysis of backward linkages in Ireland is that by O'Farrell and O'Loughlin[36] and relates to industrial purchasing during 1976. The analysis in this study was carried out at a higher level of sectoral aggrega-tion than that used in this chapter but, nevertheless, some interesting facts emerge. First, the percentage of raw materials purchased in Ireland by firms in the metals and engineering sector, at 11.4 per cent, was found to be the lowest for any sector. This suggests that a large proportion of the very high import penetration levels for electrical engineering and metal articles and mechanical engineering shown in Table 3.7 are comprised of sub-assembly items and raw materials. Second, the sector which O'Farrell and O'Loughlin found to have the next lowest level of backward materials linkages was chemicals and plastics, at 19.6 per cent. Again, both the chemicals and plastics sectors appear in the top six sectors in Table 3.7, with import penetration ratios in excess of 70 per cent.

The high proportion of new overseas firms which belong to these sectors, and the specialized nature of their output, may provide an explanation for their low levels of domestic sourcing. A sectoral breakdown of direct foreign investment during the latter part of the 1970s reveals that investment in projects in the metals and engineering sector accounted for substantially more than one half of the total, while by 1979 the chemicals and plastics sectors had moved up to second and third places, respectively, in terms of volume of foreign investment.[37]

New overseas firms are frequently oriented towards high technology or specialized activities requiring inputs which are not available from domestic Irish producers. This was found to be particularly true of the metals and engineering sector by the Telesis review of industrial policy.[38] On the basis of 1976 purchasing patterns, Telesis found that in the metals and engineering sector, foreign firms purchase just over 8 per cent of their inputs in Ireland compared with 18 per cent for Irish owned firms. Foreign firms were found to import all of their raw materials and 90 per cent of their components. In electronics, the most rapidly growing sub-sector of metals and engineering, a 1981 study by Kelly found a similar low level of backward linkages among foreign firms. Over 60 per cent of foreign firms sourced less than 3 per cent of their total materials and components requirements from domestic producers during 1980, while about one half of these firms purchased no inputs whatever in Ireland.[39]

In assessing the domestic content of industrial purchasing, Telesis noted that 'Ireland's industry is only minimally meeting the supply requirements of foreign and domestic firms, and the proportion of necessary supplies bought in Ireland is increasing only marginally.'[40] Moreover, it was found that up to 1981 no Irish producer had succeeded in a skilled, traded, high-scale sub-supply business. The question of how Irish firms might more effectively exploit the market for industrial inputs will be returned to later in the chapter in the discussion of policy options.

(4) Finally, import penetration ratios may change because of a change in the structure of an individual sector. This may come about, for instance, when a number of new firms with a greater dependence on imported inputs come on stream or when a number of established firms which had an above-average reliance on domestic inputs go out of production. In the first instance, the increase in imports would normally be associated with increases in output and in exports, and consequently would not be of major concern. In the second instance, however, a decline in domestic output will result, and it is important that the precise reasons for closure be ascertained if further job losses are to be averted.

Looking at the output performance of the high import-penetration sectors, the overall picture is one of declining output volume. With the exception of chemicals and the engineering sectors, all of the remaining industry sectors showed a negative change in the average annual volume of output over the period 1977-81, as can be seen from Table 3.9. The table also shows that in many of these sectors import penetration grew strongly over the same period. In these cases, the growing import ratios reflect a displacement of domestic Irish sales. Leather and footwear, clothing and the processing of fruit and vegetables are the industries where this pattern is most apparent.

Certain of the factors behind the general rise in import penetration, such as declining competitiveness, are also relevant in explaining the output performance of these sectors, but it is likely that the reasons go beyond a simple decline in price competitiveness brought about by increases in labour and other costs. It is not possible here to explore these reasons in greater depth. A detailed analysis of developments in a

Table 3.9: Average Annual Change in Volume of Output

Industry Sector	Average Annual change in Volume of Output	Imports as a % of Domestic Demand	Change in Level of Import Penetration
	1977-1981	1980	1977-1980
Processing of plastics	− 1.0	87.8	28.7
Manuf. & assembly of motor vehicles	− 5.6	79.1	14.8
Leather & footwear	− 5.1	76.3	21.8
Clothing	− 2.1	74.4	22.5
Textile	− 2.1	72.7	3.4
Rubber	− 1.7	65.2	− 5.6
Timber & wooden furniture	− 3.6	62.7	11.2
Paper	− 1.5	60.4	7.1
Processing of fruit and vegetables	− 6.2	56.2	12.8

number of sub-sectors of the clothing industry by Fitzpatrick, contained in Chapter 4 of this book, provides further information regarding the source of competition in these areas. However, if future industrial policy is to be directed towards assisting such sectors, then a study of all the factors involved must be undertaken.

INDUSTRIES WITH LOW IMPORT PENETRATION

Developments in imports in the eight industry sectors which Table 3.6 showed to have average import penetration ratios of less than 30 per cent are presented in Table 3.10 below. While their levels of import penetration distinguish these sectors from those discussed in the previous section, it is interesting to note that even in industries where domestic production has held a dominant share of the market, imports share was, in general, greater in 1980 than it was in 1977. Two main issues are, therefore, addressed in this section. For what reasons do these eight sectors enjoy relatively low import ratios? Why have these import ratios increased during the four-year period under review?

Table 3.10: Imports as a Percentage of Domestic Demand: Low Import Penetration Industries, 1977-80.

	1977	1978	1979	1980
Sugar, chocolate etc	24.0	23.5	30.6	32.7
Non-metallic mineral products	15.9	19.4	20.7	20.7
Bread, biscuits and flour	11.0	11.2	14.1	15.4
Grain milling and animal poultry food	7.0	8.9	11.3	12.1
Slaughtering & processing of meat	6.6	5.9	5.7	10.5
Drink	9.0	11.2	11.5	9.1
Tobacco	5.7	5.8	6.1	4.8
Dairy products	2.2	2.0	2.1	2.8

Looking first at levels of import penetration, a number of characteristics common to most of sectors in Table 3.10 can be identified. First, certain activities in these sectors enjoy an advantage in the domestic market because logistics costs limit the degree of foreign competition to which they are exposed. Logistics costs refer primarily to the cost of transportation relative to the value of either raw materials or finished products or to the difficulties of distribution to a dispersed group of customers. As was pointed out by the Telesis Report,[42] when these costs are a high proportion of total cost a virtually non-traded business can be created as a result. A large part of agricultural-based industries fall into this category and it is notable that such industries have some of the lowest import penetration ratios shown in Table 3.10. A further instance of the importance of logistics costs may be found in the non-metallic minerals sector where the low value to weight ratio of most products limits competition from abroad.

Second, most of the eight sectors with low import ratios are involved in low value-added basic processing activities where proximity to the source of raw materials is an advantage. This is especially true of sectors of the food industry, where

O'Farrell and O'Loughlin[42] found that 94 per cent of all raw materials used were purchased in Ireland. Third, large, long-established domestic firms tend to predominate in certain of the sectors in Table 3.10. The market strength of these firms enables them to compete more effectively with imports while brand loyalty may also be a factor in limiting import penetration. This is especially true of the drink and tobacco sectors as well as in cement, which is a component of non-metallic mineral products.

In looking at the growth of import penetration, most of the factors discussed in the previous section are also relevant here. The detailed discussion of these is not repeated but sectors where particular factors have an impact are indicated. From the sectoral developments shown in Table 3.10, for instance, it can be seen that import ratios in the sugar and cocoa, chocolate and sugar confectionery sector have grown significantly since 1978. While the sugar industry is more analogous to other food sectors, confectionery is dominated by multinational firms who have, in recent years, reduced the number of product lines produced in Ireland so as to achieve economies of scale. Therefore, the increase in imports in this sector is due, in part, to increasing industrial specialization.

Although certain of the activities of the low import penetration sectors enjoy considerable protection from foreign competition, changes in competitiveness can have a marked impact on the less sheltered activities. Thus, while the production of bread is a virtually untraded activity, in the biscuit and flour industry as well as in the case of animal and poultry foods a decline in the competitiveness of domestic producers is likely to have contributed to the observed increase in imports. In such low technology industries, labour cost increases are likely to have contributed to a decline in market share, but a more fundamental problem may have been a failure on the part of some firms in these sectors to adapt their processes in line with developments abroad or to rationalize their activities in order to derive maximum benefit from scale economies.

The fact that increases in import penetration took place from a low base in the sectors shown in Table 3.10 means that most of these sectors continued to enjoy positive output growth during the period under review. The annual average change in the volume of output in all eight sectors is shown in Table 3.11 below, together with the change in the level of import penetration.

Table 3.11: Average Annual Change in Volume of Output*

Industry Sector	Average Annual Change in Volume of Output	Imports as a % of Domestic Demand	Change in Level of Import Penetration
	1977-1981	1980	1977-1980
Sugar, chocolate etc	− 3.0	32.7	8.7
Non-metallic mineral products	2.1	20.7	4.8
Bread, biscuits & flour	1.2	15.4	4.4
Grain milling & animal/ poultry food	1.0	12.1	5.1
Slaughtering and processing of meat	− 2.7	10.5	3.9
Tobacco	0.9	4.8	− 0.9
Dairy products	3.6	2.8	0.6

*The drink sector is omitted from this table as the incorporation of tax and excise duty in the value of output makes it difficult to calculate average annual changes in volume of production.

The almost total reliance of most sectors of the food industry on the agricultural sector as a source of raw materials leaves these industries vulnerable to fluctuations in agricultural output. The slaughtering and processing of meat is a sector which suffered from this dependence between 1977 and 1980 and much of the decline in growth shown in the above table as well as the associated increase in import penetration can be attributed to problems which the industry faced in obtaining raw materials from 1979 onwards. In addition to policies which improve their competitiveness, therefore, the low import sectors must be assured of guaranteed access to adequate supplies of raw materials if import penetration is to be contained. Awareness of the interdependence which exists between certain sectors of industry and Irish agriculture can help in the formulation of policies which are of benefit to the whole economy.

POLICY IMPLICATIONS

Macro-economic policy in Ireland is constrained by the tendency for increases in demand to 'leak' out of the economy by way of imports. Attempts to boost domestic demand are, therefore, likely to have their principal impact on the balance of payments. Import penetration rose to a particularly high level in the years 1977 to 1980 at a time when a rapid expansion of domestic demand took place. The analysis of developments during this period from the point of view of manufacturing industry revealed that as a result of increases in import penetration demand expansion had only a small impact on output growth in most sectors of industry. The implications are that macro-economic policies aimed at increasing aggregate demand constitute on extremely inefficient means of stimulating industrial growth. This leads to the conclusion that a more micro-economic approach to policy formulation is required. Industrial policy can form an important element of such an approach.

To highlight the important role of industrial policy is not new, as the wide discussion which surrounded the publication of the Telesis Report testifies.[43] However, despite the many assertions concerning the direction of future policy, the body of empirical evidence on which such policy must be based remains thin. Consequently, it is important that available evidence be used to the full to identify those approaches which must be rejected as well as those measures which should be pursued.

The discussion of industrial sectors with high import ratios in this chapter found three factors to be of particular significance in explaining the import growth which took place in the late 1970s; intra-industry specialization, changing competitiveness and industrial purchasing patterns.

The first of these, it was pointed out, has led to high levels of import penetration being associated with high levels of exports in several industrial sectors. Increased product specialization at individual plant level, which is one feature of intra-industry specialization, is in many cases likely to be the only hope for commercial viability. The higher degree of product differentiation, which intra-industry trade involves, may also be expected to reduce the price elasticity of demand for the goods concerned. This, in turn, reduces the vulnerability of firms to cost pressures. The main threat to Irish firms, producing specialised products for sale largely on export markets, comes from increased trends towards protectionism in world trade.

At an international level, the late 1970s have seen the emergence of new pressures to introduce restrictions on trade in certain products. This 'new protectionism'[44] largely operates through quantitative restrictions and 'voluntary restraint agreements' forced on exporters, rather than through tariff barriers, but its proliferation can have an equally stultifying impact on trade and output. In view of the rising unemployment and depressed growth prospects which many sections of Irish industry face, it is perhaps not surprising that quite a number of industries have called for various forms of import restriction in order to reduce their problems.[45] But a return to protectionism must not form any part of future industrial policy. While import restrictions may be perceived to have benefits for certain sectors, these are largely short-term. In the longer term the limitation of competition can only have a negative effect on efficiency in the industries concerned. In addition, the risks of retaliation or a more generalized adoption of restrictions by our trading partners threatens those sectors with strong export growth potential.

Firms and industry associations resort to demands for protection primarily because they find themselves unable to compete with imported products in existing circumstances. Table 3.8 showed that in most of the high import sectors growth in import penetration was coupled with a decline in the volume of domestic output, reflecting a displacement of home produced goods on the domesic market and/or a poor export performance. The most immediate task facing industrial policy, therefore, is to assist industry to adjust in a positive manner in order to become more competitive.

In looking at competitiveness in its broadest sense it is possible to distinguish between two types of developments; those which affect the short-term performance of existing industry and those which arise in the medium-term from a fundamental shift in comparative advantage away from producers in Ireland. The first type of competitive pressures originate largely from an increase in the cost of inputs to Irish industry. The second type arise as lower income countries engage in the production of products which are currently manufactured in Ireland. If an objective of industrial policy is to secure economic growth and higher standards of living, then the only response to such medium-term shifts in competitiveness away from certain industrial activities must be to assist industry to restructure into activities where firms in Ireland are less vulnerable to competition from low-income countries.

To date, in Ireland, most attention has focussed on short-run developments which affect the competitiveness of existing industry. Labour costs are an important determinant of the price at which a firm can sell its output and as the analysis presented in this chapter has shown, in general the more labour-intensive sectors have been the ones where import penetration growth has been highest. Control of relative labour costs is, therefore, important to the competitiveness of a large number of sectors. But it is also important that other relevant costs are considered in discussing competitiveness.

Energy costs are a case in point. Both electricity and petrol costs in Ireland are among the highest in Europe. In recent years, also, increases in social welfare contributions and other costs have led to an increasing gap between the cost of labour to the employer and the reward which the employee receives. The firm, however, is likely to be indifferent between the sources of cost increase; increases in the cost associated with employing labour have the same impact on competitiveness as wage increases. The contradictory effects of many government policies on industrial development have been pointed out by Ruane.[46] While conflicts between industrial policies and fiscal, energy, social and transport policies, will not be easily overcome, it is important to realize that industrial policy does not operate in a vacuum. Greater consistency between policies aimed directly at industry and other government policy must be attained, if progress is to be made. The figures presented here with respect to increasing import penetration add weight to the urgent need for action in this area.

To secure the competitiveness of Irish industry in the medium term, a restructuring in line with movements in comparative advantage becomes necessary. As Fitzpatrick shows in Chapter 4, a number of developing countries, collectively designated the newly industrialising countries (NICs), have during recent years developed a comparative advantage in the area of relatively simple, labour-intensive manufacturing and assembly operations. This advantage is particularly evident in the clothing sector as well as in consumer electronics, leather, toys and footwear. The data presented here show that the clothing and leather and footwear sectors in Ireland have shown declining output between 1977 and 1980 and that these sectors were also among the top three in Table 3.8 with respect to import penetration growth over the period. Such evidence can only give an indication that a problem exists in these sectors. All firms in the sectors will not be equally affected. Indeed, Fitzpatrick has shown that in the clothing industry the impact of NIC imports has been relatively small at the sectoral level but has been significant in a number of specific sub-sectors.

Consequently, a necessary first step is to identify the particular sub-sectors of Irish industry where shifts in comparative advantage have created competitiveness problems. The circumstances in each sub-sector will then indicate the appropriate response. In general, this will be either to assist manufacturers of the product concerned to adjust to a new technological level or to encourage them to move to new products in which they have some strategic advantage. A key ingredient of such a strategy to improve industrial competitiveness is the encouragement of innovation at product, process and organizational levels. Policy-makers could do worse than recall Schumpeters' famous passage outlining the need for 'the perennial gale of creative destruction' in which he stresses that it is not day-to-day competition but rather 'competition from the new commodity, the new technology, the new source of supply, the new type of organization . . .' which is really important.[47]

The third factor of importance to import growth is the input requirements of both new grant-aided and existing industry. Raw materials and components account for more than half of total imports, while those sectors where new foreign investment is most concentrated have the lowest backward linkages with the domestic economy. The beneficial aspect of imports as an information source on the type of inputs required has been pointed out by Corden.[48] 'The availability of imports', he states, 'carves out a market for new goods and so shows domestic producers what it is possible to sell in the country, reducing the risk element in developing products. Imports create the asset knowledge for the local producers. Knowledge that there really is a domestic market.' The problem, however, is greater than simply identifying the market. It is one of obtaining and holding the business for a sustained period.

In order to establish the reasons why sub-supply markets are not exploited more fully by domestic industry, a detailed investigation into the purchasing behaviour of a sample of 30 non-food grant-aided firms was undertaken by O'Farrell.[49]

This survey found that the 30 firms involved secured only 14 per cent of their materials and components in Ireland, but considered that about twice that amount could be provided by Irish firms without changes in the level of technology employed or increases in investment. The barriers to the realization of this potential, according to O'Farrell's study, were that purchasing managers of overseas firms, in particular, perceived Irish firms to compare unfavourably with foreign suppliers in terms of reliability, product quality, price and delivery speed, all criteria which they noted were of prime importance in selecting suppliers. In addition, about one-quarter of the respondents asserted that Irish suppliers compared unfavourably with overseas ones in terms of marketing expertize, with Irish firms being less professional at processing orders and slower in responding to requests for a quotation. Telesis further noted that many sub-supply firms in Ireland were in the very small size category and in many cases owner-managers had not the resources to undertake financial, marketing and technological functions necessary for success. As mentioned earlier, Telesis also found that up to 1981 no highly skilled sub-supply firm existed in Ireland.

There are, therefore, two broad areas where action is needed. The first relates to assisting existing sub-supply firms to secure a greater proportion of the market provided by the industrial sub-supply needs of other firms in Ireland. The second area relates to encouraging the development of new or existing firms to undertake the investment needed to enter highly-skilled sub-supply businesses. A number of specific policy proposals might assist in the achievement of these objectives. First, an efficient dissemination of the purchasing needs of industry would, at minimal cost, ensure that imports did indeed 'show domestic producers what it is possible to sell in the country'.[50] The size of the market for sub-assembly and components items currently sourced abroad suggests that there is scope for a widening of the dissemination process and an increase in the resources devoted to this. Second, efforts must be made to improve the marketing skills of firms in the sub-supply industries. An IMI Survey[51] conducted some years ago showed that only 26 per cent of medium-to-large Irish firms (100-499 employees) provided extensive training in selling techniques while a more recent study found that the marketing of Irish-made goods was perceived by industrial buyers in Ireland to be inferior to that of foreign goods.[52] This indicates that there is clearly room for policy to place a greater emphasis on marketing expertize. While marketing support services from state agencies may assist in this task in the short run the long-term objective should be to build up marketing skills within firms.

Third, expanded management training is required to promote the importance of high standards of product quality and fast and efficient service in competing for a share of the sub-supply market. Finally, policy measures to aid price competitiveness, discussed above, can have an impact although it must be noted that some of the price disadvantages which domestic firms suffer may arise from their being unable to benefit from the scale economies available to large international producers.[53] This raises the question of firm size. While there is no one appropriate firm size, it appears that many sub-supply firms may not have the size and structure necessary for competitive success. This has implications for assisting the development of new firms, especially in the highly-skilled areas of sub-supply where no firms exist at present, while it also indicates a need to improve the technical capabilities of existing sub-supply firms.

The data presented in this chapter show exceptionally high import ratios in the chemicals and the metals and engineering sectors, with the main reason for this being the high import content of the input requirements of these sectors. These two sectors have also demonstrated the strongest volume growth in output in recent years and are characterized by a very high net output per employee. This implies that the direct employment impact of the growth in these sectors has been significantly below the output/employment relationship evident in other industries. Given the increasing importance of these particular sectors in Ireland's industrial base, ways to increase the indirect employment impact of their output growth need to be urgently pursued. One way in which this might be done is by selecting certain sub-sectors which would serve as targets for a concentrated effort to develop sub-supply firms with the adequate size and technical capabilities to succeed. This approach to linkage development, however, must be carefully determined. The existence of sub-supply requirements in Ireland does not, in itself, ensure that production here will be economically viable. Only those sub-supply projects which conform to Ireland's comparative advantage can hope to enjoy long-term success.

In discussing the import content of industrial purchases in Ireland, we pointed out the importance of ensuring that adequate firm size was considered. The need to take account of the minimum scale of operation necessary for competitive success in all product areas receives further tentative support from the analysis of import levels in the low import penetration sectors. Here it appeared that in the drink and tobacco sectors, in particular, the market strength of large domestic firms may have enabled them successfully to resist the challenge from imports. The fact that by international standards most firms in Ireland fall into the very small category and the fact that some of the factors which appear to be associated with the high import ratios are related to firm size implies that there may be a need to re-examine industrial policy as it relates to the small firm sector. While proclaiming that small firms should be given priority may be politically desirable, we would advocate that increased attention should be given to the size of firms necessary for competitive success.

The data on import penetration indicated that firms in internationally traded sectors experienced very high import ratios. This is, of course, not surprising. What is more noteworthy is the fact that the results showed that some industry sectors such as timber and wooden furniture and paper, which are sectors where high logistics costs apply, are also only supplying a very small percentage of the domestic market. It is also of note that even in such sectors as metallic mineral products which are traditionally local industries, imports account for a significant proportion of the domestic market and have been growing rapidly in recent years. These developments confirm the Telesis view that in countries such as Ireland products which are non-traded in most developed countries are often imported.

The policy implication of this is that the potential for import substitution in traditionally non-traded sectors should not be overlooked by industrial policy. This is not to suggest that it is inappropriate for industrial policy to give priority to internationally traded sectors or that it may not be appropriate to reduce aid to non-traded industries. The priority and the mix of resources allocated to non-traded and internationally traded sectors should be determined by what is required to further the overall objectives of industrial policy. The relative risk/return prospects of each type of firm should be considered in determining the balance of resources to be allocated to such firms. The evidence in this chapter confirms that traditionally non-traded firms are exposed to import competition in Ireland, and we believe it would be a policy mistake to ignore this reality.

CONCLUSIONS

The four years 1977 to 1980 saw a rapid expansion of domestic demand in Ireland. This demand expansion, however, was associated with a much faster growth in industrial imports than in the output of industry. Although there was considerable variation in the responsiveness of individual industrial sectors to demand expansion, the examination of twenty industrial sectors in this chapter revealed that the strongest increase in import penetration took place in the more traditional sectors of industry such as clothing, leather and footwear, non-metallic mineral products and a number of sub-sectors of the food industry.

The progressive reduction of barriers to international trade during the 1970s contributed to the rise in Irish industrial imports through an increase in intra-industry trade. However, the large number of industry sectors which experienced losses in domestic market share and a decline in output points to a need to improve the competitiveness of industry in Ireland. Both short-run cost trends and more medium-term shifts in comparative advantage require attention in this respect. In the short-run, attention should not focus exclusively on developments in relative labour costs; energy and other infrastructural costs, as well as the effects of government policies in other areas, deserve greater attention. In the medium term, shifts of comparative advantage away from certain sectors of industry in Ireland must be recognized. It is inevitable that increasing import penetration in some sectors will result from participation in an international trading environment. However, the response to such developments is not to attempt to preserve employment in the affected sectors by artificial means, but rather to encourage a process of positive adjustment through the introduction of new technology and the encouragement of innovation.

The high proportion of imports accounted for by industrial inputs makes the sub-supply market an obvious target for import substitution. Policies aimed at the development of greater marketing and managerial expertize can be of assistance here, as can more efficient dissemination of the purchasing needs of existing industry. In many cases, however, simply identifying needs is not enough. Domestic firms must be assisted in improving their technical abilities, so as to enhance their chances of winning and retaining a greater portion of the sub-supply market. In encouraging the establishment of new enterprises in the sub-supply sector, the question of firm size is important. In many sub-supply activities scale-economies are essential to competitive success. In the future increased attention needs to be paid to this aspect of linkage development.

Finally, the growth of imports in sectors which enjoy a degree of protection through logistics costs or proximity to raw material sources or which are normally regarded as non-traded draws attention to the scope for import substitution in this area. Trends in competitiveness in such sectors are, therefore, as important as in the more exposed sectors. The fact that these sectors already enjoy some degree of natural protection increases the probability of success of policies aimed at maximizing their potential.

NOTES AND REFERENCES

1. The authors would like to thank Mr Philip Kelly, Senior Economist in Córas Tráchtála (The Irish Export Board), and Mr Fionan O'Muircheartaigh, Department of Industry and Energy, for helpful comments on an earlier draft. The authors are especially thankful for the extensive and invaluable suggestions made by Professor Dermot McAleese, Whatley Professor of Political Economy, Trinity College, Dublin. The usual disclaimer applies.

2. OECD Economic Survey, *Ireland* (December 1983).

3. C. E. V. Leser, *Imports and Economic Growth in Ireland, 1947-1961*, (Dublin, Economic and Social Research Institute, Paper No. 14, 1963.)

4. D. McAleese, *A Study of Demand Elasticities for Irish Imports* (Dublin, Economic and Social Research Institute, Paper No. 53, 1970); P. Sloane and R. Kelleher, *Import Demand Equations* (mimeo, Central Bank of Ireland, 1976); T. Boylan, M. Cuddy and I. O'Muircheartaigh, 'The Functional Form of the Aggregate Demand Equation: A Comparison of Three European Economies', *Journal of International Economics* (November 1980); J. Fitzgerald, 'The Determinants of Irish Imports', *Research Paper* (Department of Finance, 1979).

5. D. Lynch, 'Determining Irish Merchandise Imports', *Technical Paper No. 1/RT/84* (Research Department, Central Bank of Ireland, 1984).

6. D. McAleese, *op. cit.*

7. C. McCarthy, 'Economic Development and Economic Policy', *Administration*, Vol 27, No. 2 (1979).

8. This is argued by, among others, Kennedy and Foley and O'Connor, O'Malley and Foley. See K. A. Kennedy and A. Foley, 'Industrial Development' in B. R. Dowling and J. Durkan (eds), *Irish Economic Policy: A Review of Major Issues* (Dublin, Economic and Social Research Institute, 1978) and R. O'Connor, E. O'Malley and A. Foley. *Aspects of the Swedish Economy and Their Relevance to Ireland* (Dublin,

Economic and Social Research Institute, Broadsheet No. 16, 1979).

9. Data based on revised CSO series taking SITC, Rev 2, into account. Data for 1963 kindly estimated by CSO for the authors. Data for later years comes from *Economic Review and Outlook* (Summer 1983), Table 19.

10. J. O'Hagan and H. Neary, 'EEC Entry and Ireland's Balance of Payments', *Central Bank of Ireland, Quarterly Bulletin* (Autumn 1972).

11. Changes in the Irish market share of competing imports are dicussed by O'Malley in Chapter 1 of this book.

12. A. Matthews, 'Import Penetration and Job Losses', paper read to the *Dublin Economic Workshop Annual Policy Conference* (October 1980).

13. A similar approach to the analysis of imports has been used in the preparation of *A Statistical Review of Irish Industry* (Irish Goods Council, 1982). Data source: *Eurostat* microfiche trade data, SCE-2911.

14. The import penetration ratios shown in Table 3.4 are somewhat higher than those in Table 3.3. This divergence between current and constant price import ratios reflects a smaller rise in the price of imports than in the GNP price.

15. K. A. Kennedy and B. R. Dowling, *Economic Growth in Ireland: The Experience Since 1947* (Dublin, Gill and MacMillan, 1975).

16. D. McAleese, 'Outward-Looking Policies, Manufactured Exports and Economic Growth: The Irish Experience' in M. J. Artis and A. R. Nobay (eds), *Proceedings of the 1977 AUTE Conference* (Oxford, Basil Blackwell, 1978).

17. A. Matthews, 'The European Community's External Trade Policy: Implications for Ireland' (Dublin, European League for Economic Co-operation and Irish Council of the European Movement, 1980).

18. The importance of domestic demand for many Irish firms was indicated by a survey of 340 small manufacturing companies in the mid-west region. Of the 340 companies only 41 were engaged in exporting (16 at the initial stage of export prospecting and 25 at an advanced stage), 46 were not exporting but had potential to export, while the remaining 253 companies did not and for one reason or another could not export. See CTT survey quoted in *CII Industry Report 1980*. The survey was undertaken to test small firms' export servicing requirements. It should be noted that average employment was around 10.

19. See B. Sodersten, *International Economics* (London, MacMillan, 1971), Chapter 4, for a lucid statement of the Heckscher-Ohlin theory. For a comprehensive survey of trade theories and the results of empirical testing see, R. M. Stern, 'Testing Trade Theories' in P. B. Kenen (ed.), *International Trade and Finance: Frontiers for Research* (Cambridge, Cambridge University Press, 1975), pp. 3-49.

20. See, for instance, B. Balassa, *Trade Liberalisation among Industrial Countries* (New York, McGraw-Hill, 1967) and V. Curzon, *The Essentials of Economic Integration* (London, MacMillan, 1974).

21. H. G. Grubel and P. J. Lloyd, *Intra-Industry Trade* (London, MacMillan, 1975); H. Giersch (ed.), *On the Economics of Intra-Industry Trade* (Tubingen, JCB Mohr (Paul Siebeck), 1979); A. Aquino, 'Intra-

Industry Trade and Inter-Industry Specialisation as Concurrent Sources of International Trade in Manufactures', *Weltwirtschaftliches Archiv,* Vol 114, No. 2 (1979).

22. G. K. Helleiner and R. Lavergne, 'Intra-Firm Trade and Industrial Exports to the United States', *Oxford Bulletin of Economics and Statistics,* Vol 41, No. 4 (1979).

23. D. McAleese, 'Do Tariffs Matter? Industrial Specialisation and Trade in a Small Economy'. *Oxford Economic Papers,* Vol. 29 (1977); D. McAleese, 'Industrial Specialisation and Trade: Northern Ireland and the Republic', *Economic and Social Review,* Vol 7, No. 2 (1976).

24. D. McAleese, ibid, p. 158.

25. World trade stagnated between 1980 and 1982 before showing a small upturn in 1983. During this period also attempts to impose various forms of non-tariff protection have been evident. See, for instance, C. F. Bergsten and W. Cline, *Trade Policy in the Eighties* (Institute of International Economics, Washington DC, 1982).

26. A detailed analysis of the growth of both imports and exports for the electronics sector is provided in R. O'Brien, D. J. Cogan, J. H. Kelly, E. M. Lawless, E. Onyenadum and J. Wrynn, *The Irish Electronics Industry* (Science Policy Research Centre, UCD, July 1981).

27. B. M. Walsh, 'The Trading Environment', paper presented to the 30th National Management Conference, 1982.

28. J. O'Leary, 'Competitiveness Indices for Irish Manufactured Exports', *ESRI Quarterly Economic Commentary* (July 1981).

29. J. O'Malley, 'Changes in Manufacturing Cost Competitiveness', *Journal of the Institute of Bankers in Ireland,* Vol 84 (1982).

30. B. M. Walsh and D. F. McAleese and T. J. Baker, *Report of the Committee on Costs and Competitiveness* (Dublin, The Stationery Office, 1981).

31. Labour's share in value added was calculated by expressing Census of Industrial Production data for total labour costs as a percentage of gross value added less excise duty and other indirect taxes. Data source: Irish Statistical Bulletin (December 1982).

32. The correlation coefficient between the growth of imports and labour's share in value added was found to be statistically insignificant at 16.7. However, a regression of labour's share on import growth, controlled for demand changes, resulted in an R^2 of 48.6 and showed the relationship between the variables to be significant at the 10 per cent level when the rubber sector was omitted.

33. J. G. Keenan, 'Irish Manufacturing Industry — Recent Wage, Price and Productivity Developments', *ESRI Quarterly Economic Commentary* (December 1982).

34. *Economic Review and Outlook* (Summer 1983) Table 19.

35. See, for instance, P. J. Buckley, 'Some Aspects of Foreign Private Investment in the Manufacturing Sector of the Economy of the Irish Republic', *Economic and Social Review,* Vol. 5 (1974); D. McAleese, *A Profile of Grant-Aided Industry in Ireland* (Dublin, IDA, 1977); D. McAleese and D. McDonald, 'Employment Growth and the Development of Linkages in

Foreign-Owned and Domestic Manufacturing Enterprises', *Oxford Bulletin of Economics and Statistics* (1978); P. N. O'Farrell and B. O'Loughlin, *An Analysis of New Industry Linkages in Ireland* (Dublin, IDA, 1980); and J. C. Stewart, 'Linkages and Foreign Direct Investment', *Regional Studies,* Vol. 10 (1976).

36. P. N. O'Farrell and B. O'Loughlin, *op. cit.*

37. *IDA Annual Reports,* various years.

38. Telesis Consultancy Group, *A Review of Industrial Policy* (Dublin, National Economic and Social Council (Report No. 64) 1982).

39. J. H. Kelly, 'Backward Linkages in Electronics', report prepared for the National Board for Science and Technology, 1981.

40. Telesis Consultancy Group, *op. cit,* p. 116.

41. ibid.

42. P. N. O'Farrell and B. O'Loughlin, *op. cit.* Table 3.1.

43. Telesis Consultancy Group, *op. cit.*

44. A good discussion of the 'new protectionism' is found in G. K. Helleiner, 'The new Industrial Protectionism and Developing Countries', *Trade and Development, an UNCTAD Review,* Vol. 1 (1979).

45. A survey conducted by the CII among its members revealed 39 products from 30 countries against which import restrictions were sought. Quoted in A. Matthews, *op. cit.*

46. F. P. Ruane, 'Government Financial and Tax Incentives and Industrial Employment', *The Irish Banking Review* (June 1983).

47. J. A. Schumpeter, *Capitalism, Socialism, and Democracy* (5th edition, Allen and Unwin, 1977).

48. W. M. Corden, *Trade Policy and Economic Welfare* (Oxford, Clarendon Press, 1974).

49. P. N. O'Farrell, 'Industrial Linkages in the New Industry Sector: A Behavioural Analysis', *Journal of Irish Business and Administrative Research,* Vol 4, No. 1 (April 1982).

50. W. M. Corden, *op. cit.*

51. L. Gorman, G. Hynes, J. McConnell and T. Moynihan, *Irish Industry: How it is Managed* (Dublin, Irish Management Institute, 1975).

52. W. J. Glynn, 'Irish Industrial Buyers and their Attitudes towards Industrial Salesmanship and Marketing', *Journal of Irish Business and Administrative Research,* Vol 5, No 2 (October 1983).

53. This was found to be particularly true in the case of printed circuit boards and other electronic components, in a study of purchasing patterns in the electronics industry in Ireland. See J. H. Kelly, *op. cit.*

4

Competition from the Less Developed Countries and Irish Manufacturing Industry

Jim Fitzpatrick[1]

The 1970s was a decade which saw many major changes in the world economy, each with its own set of implications for Irish industrial policy. One such change was the emergence of a number of newly industrialising developing countries, or NICs, as prominent exporters of cheap manufactured goods. The present chapter describes this emergence and discusses its implications for Irish industry and industrial policy. The chapter has four parts. It begins by clarifying to which less developed countries the term 'NICs' is applied. It then looks at the role which this group of countries plays in world trade and in Ireland's foreign trade. The nature and extent of the import competition from these countries which Irish industry faces are then examined. Finally, the chapter reviews the response of the industrialised Western countries to such competition and it discusses the forms of response which Ireland's industrial policy-makers might consider.

WHO ARE THE NEWLY INDUSTRIALISING COUNTRIES?

In a 1979 Report on the impact of the newly industrialising countries on the world economy, the OECD defined the NICs as developing countries 'characterised by a fast growth of the level and share of industrial employment, an enlargement of export market shares in manufactures and a rapid relative reduction in the real per capita income gap separating them from the advanced industrial countries'.[2] In terms of other characteristics such as geographical size, location and features, population and GND per capita, countries fitting the OECD's description are a heterogeneous group. Consequently, despite the by-now considerable literature on the subject, there is no agreed list of NICs.[3] In the data in this chapter the term NIC generally refers to South Korea, Taiwan, Singapore, Brazil, Mexico and Yugoslavia.[4] These seven countries appear in most listings of NICs. They are the 'non-OECD' NICs as defined in the OECD's 1979 Report. However, it is recognised that other countries also are potential candidates. The OECD's definition is, of course, one into which Ireland itself might well fit. The 1979 report remarked that exclusion of Ireland from the NIC group was 'difficult to justify by macro-economic criteria alone'[4] and indeed it included three OECD member countries — Greece, Spain and Portugal — as NICs.

In terms of growth of manufacturing output, Ireland's performance over the 1970s was comparable to the rates achieved by the NICs; the share of manufacturing industry in Ireland's output, employment and exports is matched by most NICs and average Irish GNP per capita is similar to that of the better-off NICs such as Singapore, see Table 4.1 (also Annex 4.I). However, the NICs are most logically viewed as a relatively industrialised sub-group of the world's less developed countries (LDCs). Ireland's general living standards, geographical location, its political system, language and culture, together with membership of the EEC, can be said to place it firmly within the developed or industrialised nations of the West. Nevertheless, this is essentially a matter of classification to which there is no definitive answer but one which, fortunately, for present purposes is not fundamental.

Table 4.1: A Comparison of Selected Characteristics of the NICs (exc. Taiwan) and Ireland, 1981/82

	Singapore	Brazil	Mexico	Hong Kong	South Korea	Yugo-slavia	Ireland
Size ('000 sq. km)	1	8,512	1,973	1	98	256	70
Population (millions)	2.5	126.8	73.1	5.2	39.3	22.6	3.5
Population density (people per sq. km)	2,500	15	37	5,200	401	88	50
GNP per capita	5,910	2,240	2,270	5,340	1,910	2,800	5,150
Industry as percentage							
— GDP	37	—	38	—	39	45	38
— Labour force[1]	39	24	26	57	29	35	37
Manufactures as a percentage of merchandise exports[2]	56	41	—	97	90	79	62

1. 1980.

2. Exc. processed foodstuffs.   — not available.

Source: World Bank, World Development Report 1984.

137

THE ROLE OF THE NICs IN WORLD TRADE

The role in world trade of the NICs and of other LDCs has attracted considerable attention over the last decade. Yet, in the aggregate, these countries account for a relatively small share of world trade. In 1979, a quarter of the world's merchandise exports originated in the LDCs and one-fifth of the world's merchandise imports were bought by the LDCs. These shares represented an increase over 1970 of 7 per cent in the case of exports and 3 per cent in the case of imports. However, the oil-producing LDCs, including OPEC countries, accounted for most of this growth. Furthermore, the LDCs' aggregate share in world trade in 1979 was still about 5 per cent lower than it was some 30 years earlier in 1950 (see Annex 4.II).

For evidence of the increased role of the NICs, it is necessary to look at the trends in trade in manufactured goods. Table 4.2 shows the share of the LDCs as a whole in world manufacturing value-added and in world exports of manufactured goods in the years 1963, 1970 and 1982.

Table 4.2: The Percentage Share of Less Developed Countries in World Manufacturing Value-Added and Exports, 1963, 1970, 1982

	1963	1970	1982[3]
Value-Added[1]	8.1	8.8	11.0
Exports[2]	4.2	5.0	9.2[4]

[1]constant 1975 prices. [2]current prices. [3]estimates. [4]1981.

Source: UNIDO, *A Statistical Review of the World Industrial Situation 1980* (Vienna: UNIDO, 1981).

Between 1963 and 1982 the LDC's share in world industrial value-added increased from just over 8 per cent to 11 per cent. However, these countries' share in world exports of manufactured goods more than doubled over the 20 years, from 4.2 per cent in 1963 to 9.2 per cent in 1982. The vast majority of this growth is accounted for by the exports of the NICs. In 1976, the seven NICs listed earlier accounted for 78 per cent of all manufactured exports from less developed countries. This compared with a share of 42 per cent in 1963. It is, therefore, only a small exaggeration to say that a discussion of LDC manufactured exports is really a discussion of NIC manufactured exports. Of the major products in LCD manufactured exports, the NIC proportion of total OECD imports from LDCs in 1979 were as follows: clothing 79 per cent; textiles 45 per cent; leather, footwear and travel goods 68 per cent; wood and cork manufactures 69 per cent; electrical goods 82 per cent; miscellaneous manufactures 85 per cent.[5]

No single or simple explanation for the unusual export performance of the NICs is adequate. This performance has been the result of a combination of factors and varies as between one NIC and another. However, the NICs have one important explanatory feature in common with each other, and with Ireland. This is, that during the 1960s and 1970s they pursued industrial development policies of outward-looking, export-led growth.

For the NICs, a typical package of such policies includes some or all of the following elements: in trade and payments policy a liberal regime frequently involving tax-free exports and zero or low tariffs on the imported inputs of exporting industries; in exchange rate policy a single market-determined exchange rate; in industrial policy tax incentives to production for export such as accelerated depreciation allowances and tax-free export profits. Additional measures to encourage foreign investment such as the elimination of restrictions on foreign ownership and profit repatriation are also generally involved.[6] These policies contrast with the import-substitution approach more common to the majority of LDCs and which preceded current outward-looking policies in the NICs, apart from Hong Kong and Singapore. The latter have been free ports since the 1800s.[7] Again, in common with Ireland, the policy shift in the other NICs took place in the late 1950s or early 1960s. The degree to which outward-looking policies have been pursued by the NICs has varied with the two big Latin American economies, Brazil and Mexico, maintaining higher degrees of protection then the smaller Asian NICs.

Also evident is a broadly common pattern of the type of manufactured product in which the NICs, and some other LDCs, have become successful exporters. Table 4.3 shows the important manufactured exports of all non-oil-producing LDCs in the years 1963, 1970 and 1976. The role of simpler, labour-intensive manufacturing and assembly operations in which the NICs have developed a comparative advantage is evident. Concentrating on the most recent year shown, 1976, it can be seen that although fairly evenly spread across the three broad categories, LDC manufactured exports were heavily concentrated in a few specific product groups. Four — textiles, clothing, office/telecommunications/electrical and footwear/ toys/leather goods — accounted for 67 per cent of the total, while textiles and clothing alone accounted for 33 per cent. So, in Table 4.3, the 'old faithfuls' which keep cropping up in relation to NIC manufactured exports are evident.

Much of the explanation for the economic difficulties, real or perceived, which NIC competition has caused to industry in developed countries lies in this concentration of their manufactured exports in a few products. Added to this are two further features. First, a number of these products are the output of older, traditional industries in developed countries. Textiles, clothing and footwear are the outstanding examples. Second, even within the product categories shown in Table 4.3, NIC exports tend to be concentrated in even more specific items. Another important feature of Table 4.3 should be noted. This is the change which took place in the structure of LDC manufactured exports between 1963 and 1976. Most pronounced is the declining importance of semi-manufactures, mainly textiles, and the growing importance of engineering products,

Table 4.3: Main Manufactured Exports from Non-Oil Producing Less Developed Countries, 1963, 1970 and 1976 (% current value)

	1963	1970	1976
Semi-manufactures	60	41	35
of which: textiles	33	17	14
iron and steel	4	4	4
plywood and paper	3	4	2
other	20	16	15
Engineering products	13	26	29
of which: industrial machinery	4	5	6
office, telecommunications, other electrical equipment	7	17	18
transport equipment	2	3	5
Other finished products	27	33	35
of which: clothing	9	17	19
footwear, toys, leather goods, miscellaneous	18	16	16
All manufactures	100	100	100

Source: Blackhurst, R., *et al., Adjustment, Trade and Growth in Developed and Developing Countries* (Geneva; GATT, 1978), Table 7.

mostly in the office, telecommunications and other electrical equipment group.

This growth of the office, telecommunications and other electrical equipment sector in the NICs draws attention to a feature of their recent industrialisation which is shared with Ireland, namely, the role of foreign investment and of multinational companies (MNCs) in the NICs.

While most frequently thought of as the establishment of

local subsidiaries, MNC involvement with NIC manufactured exports can involve a whole range of relationships within the 'international subcontracting' framework. International sub-contracting refers to the system whereby all or part of a production process is contracted out to an overseas producer, the key feature being that marketing of the final product is done by the firm giving the contract.[8] In NICs, this system has been particularly suited to the labour-intensive assembly stage of clothing and electronic products. At one extreme is 'outward processing' or 'offshore assembly' operations in a wholly-owned subsidiary where the parent company supplies inputs and purchases outputs. At the other extreme is arms-length purchasing from independent local companies. In between, are numerous variants such as majority and minority shareholdings, offshore assembly-type operations in nominally independent local firms, and management and licensing contracts. Multinational firms involved in such activities need not themselves be manufacturing companies and are frequently multinational trading and buying groups.

It is widely accepted that the manufactured exports of the NICs are heavily dominated by MNCs in one form or other. However, the precise role of the MNCs in the manufacturing sector of the newly-industrialising countries is not clearly documented. Broadly speaking, direct foreign investment in manufacturing production and exports is more important in the Latin American NICs, Brazil and Mexico, than it is in Asia.[9] Table 4.4 brings together some indicators of the role of direct investments in the NICs, excluding Yugoslavia. It points to the larger role of foreign-owned subsidiaries in Brazil and Mexico than among the Asian NICs, but Singapore appears to be an exception among the latter. This generalization must also be tempered with two facts. First, there is a tendency towards foreign minority ownership in Asian NICs and this is not easily captured in data such as that in Table 4.4. Second, and also statistically illusive, is the importance of multinational trading and buying groups in Asian exports.[10]

Table 4.4: Selected Indicators of the Role of Direct Foreign Investment (DFI) in Manufacturing Industry in Six Newly Industrialising Countries

		Brazil	Mexico	Hong Kong	Taiwan	Singapore	South Korea
Stock of manufacturing DFI (1975/6):	$M	6889	3670	1952	0.5[1]	2217	742
	% all DFI	76	77	100	—	59	80
Country of origin of all DFI as a percentage (1975/6)[3]	US	32	69	47	55	33	17
	Japan	11	1	22	19	14	66
MNC share in manufactured exports as a percentage (various years 1969-1974)		43	25	10	20	70	15
Percentage of manufactured exports to US which was 'related party' trade, (1977)[4]		38	71	18	20	83	20
Employment in Export Processing Zones (1978)		27,300	70,000	59,600[2]	77,400	105,000	120,000

1. 1971   2. Employment in industrial estates   3. Stock of DFI in all sectors   4. Trading companies related by at least 5 per cent ownership in either direction.

Sources: United Nations, *Transnational Corporations in World Development: A Re-Examination* (New York: UN, 1978), Table 111-50; Cohen, B., *Multinational Firms and Asian Exports* (New Haven: Yale University Press, 1975), pp. 56-60; Nayyar, D., 'Transnational Corporations and Manufactured Exports from Poor Countries', *Economic Journal*, 88(349), 1978, 59-84, Table 1; Currie, J., *Investment: the Growing Role of Export Processing Zones* (London: EIU, 1979), Table 4.7; OECD, *North-South Technology Transfer, The Adjustments Ahead* (Paris, 1981), Table 6.

THE NICS AND OTHER LDCS IN IRELAND'S FOREIGN TRADE

Table 4.5 shows the origin and destination of Ireland's foreign trade in percentage terms for the years 1962, 1977 and 1984. This includes all merchandise trade, both raw materials and manufactured goods, and percentages are of current value. It can be seen that the share of the less developed countries in this trade was about one-tenth of exports and one-twentieth of imports in 1984. This is small by comparison with these countries' role in world trade as a whole (see Annex 4.II). Their share in Irish exports increased over the 1970s. However, their share in imports has declined.

Table 4.5: Origin of Irish Imports and Destination of Irish Exports, 1962, 1977 and 1984 (as a per cent of current value)

	Imports			Exports		
Area	1962	1977	1984	1962	1977	1984
UK	50	48	43	74	47	34
Other EEC	16	20	22[1]	6	29	34[1]
Total EEC	66	68	65[1]	80	76	68[1]
EFTA	4	5	5	1	3	5
USA/Canada	10	9	18	9	8	11
Other developed countries	4	5	4	1	3	4
State trading countries	2	2	2	0	1	1
Less developed countries	11	8	6	3	8	9
Unclassified	3	1	0	6	1	2
Total	100	100	100	100	100	100

[1] EEC of ten, other years are EEC of nine.

Source: Central Statistics Office, *External Trade Statistics,* 1965/66, and *Trade Statistics of Ireland,* Dec. 1978 and 1983 (Dublin: Stationery Office).

In 1980, Ireland's imports from the less developed countries as a whole was divided among sub-groups of LDCs as follows: OPEC accounted for 50 per cent; the NICs for 15 per cent; and all other LDCs accounted for 35 per cent. Both the OPEC and NIC shares had increased over the previous decade; OPEC from 40 per cent in 1970 and the NICs from 7 per cent in 1970. The share of all other LDCs fell from 53 per cent in 1970. In the case of Ireland's total exports to LDCs in 1980 the shares of the three sub-groups of countries were: OPEC 44 per cent; the NICs 15 per cent; and other LDCs 41 per cent. The OPEC share grew rapidly over the decade from 17 per cent in 1970, while that of 'other LDCs' fell from 66 per cent in the same year. The NICs export share remained relatively static.

The product composition of Ireland's trade with the NICs and with all LDCs combined is shown in Table 4.6 for the year 1978. Three product groups are shown: food, drink and tobacco; raw materials and fuels; and manufactured goods.

Table 4.6: Product Composition of Ireland's Trade with Less Developed Countries, 1978 (as a per cent of current value)

Product category	Imports		Exports	
	NICs[1]	All LDCs	NICs[1]	All LDCs
Food, drink, tobacco	23	28	45	54
Raw materials, fuels	8	49	0	1
Manufactures[2]	69	23	55	45
	100	100	100	100

[1]Brazil, Mexico, Hong Kong, Taiwan, Singapore, South Korea, Yugoslavia
[2]excludes food

Source: Central Statistics Office computer tabulations.

It can be seen that the bulk of imports from the NICs (69 per cent) were manufactured goods with the other two product categories accounting for only 31 per cent. This is the reverse

of the pattern of Ireland's imports from LDCs in general.
These are dominated by raw materials and fuels (principally
crude-oil) and by foodstuffs which together accounted for 77
per cent of imports in 1978. Ireland's exports to the NICs and
to all LDCs are of a more similar pattern. In each case, they
were roughly divided half-and-half between foodstuffs and
manufactured goods in 1978.

The remaining sections of this chapter will concentrate on
issues surrounding Ireland's imports from the LDCs. However,
in doing so it is important to bear in mind that trade with the
LDCs is a two-way process involving both imports and exports.
The trends in percentage shares presented in Table 4.5 show
that the LDCs, as a whole, were one of Ireland's fastest
expanding export markets over the 1970s, though from a very
small base. Table 4.7 presents Ireland's balance of trade with
the LDCs in 1980.

Table 4.7: Ireland's Balance of Trade with Less Developed Countries, 1980

	Trade balance	*Trade deficit as percentage of total national deficit*
	IR£m	
NICs	− 14.0	1.1
OPEC	− 62.4	4.8
Other LDCs	+ 5.4	—
All LDCs	− 71.0	5.5

Source: Central Statistics Office, *Trade Statistics of Ireland, December 1980* (Dublin: Stationery Office, 1981).

Ireland had a balance of trade deficit of IR£71m with the
LDCs as a whole in 1980. Of this, trade with the seven NICs
accounted for £14m or 18 per cent, while trade with the OPEC
countries accounted for 82 per cent. Ireland had a small trade
surplus of £5m with other LDCs. The total deficit with LDCs

was equivalent to 5 per cent of the total national deficit for all foreign trade in 1980. The NIC deficit accounted for 1 per cent of this national trade deficit.

IMPORT COMPETITION FROM THE NICS

Imports of competitively priced or 'low-cost' manufactured goods is the aspect of trade with the NICs which attracts controversy. These, it is argued, seriously displace Irish sales and consequently put Irish workers out of jobs. Table 4.8 shows those categories of manufactured goods of which the LDCs supplied 10 per cent or more of total Irish imports in 1978. It also shows the percentage of these imports originating in the NICs.

Table 4.8 illustrates a number of important points. First, the list included all the well-known cases of products of which the LDCs have become prominent exporters — textiles, electrical goods, footwear, travel goods, wood products and light engineering items. Second, it is clear that Irish imports of these from LDCs were dominated by the NICs with NIC shares in imports from LDCs running as high as 100 per cent for portable radios. With regard to LDC shares in total imports of these products, a 30 per cent share was exceeded in only one case listed — again that of portable radios. These are, therefore, product categories where the LDCs have captured large, but not dominant, import shares.

A large LDC share in total imports of a manufactured product does not, however, in itself constitute or indicate a major low-cost competitive threat. For this, two further features are required. First, the affected domestic sector must be a significant one in terms of output and/or employment.[12] Second, imports from NICs must have achieved a significant proportion not just of total imports but of all domestic sales, that is a high level of 'import penetration'. It is in this light that the amount of attention given to low-cost competition in the textiles and clothing industries must be seen. In Ireland, and

Table 4.8: Manufactured Products of which Less Developed Countries Supplied 10 per cent or more of Irish Imports in 1978

Product	Imports from LDCs as % total imports	NICs' %[1] share in total imports from LDCs
Organic chemicals	18	2
Antibiotics	27	19
Cork/wood manufactures (except furniture)	17	66
Cotton yarn	24	57
Cotton fabric	19	55
Black & White TVs	12	91
Portable radios	40	100
Recording/reproducing equipment	19	98
Electrical components	14	94
Travel goods, handbags	23	77
Footwear	10	62
Watches, clocks	15	82
Baby carriages, toys, sporting goods	12	81

[1] Brazil, Mexico, Hong Kong, Taiwan, Singapore, South Korea, Yugoslavia.
Source: Central Statistics Office computer tabulations.

traditionally in most Western economies, these industries have been important, particularly as employers. For example, in September 1982 the Irish textiles and clothing industries combined employed nearly 25,600 people or 13 per cent of the workforce in manufacturing industry.[13] Comparative figures for some other sectors affected by low-cost competition were: footwear, 3100 employees (1.5 per cent of manufacturing employment); leather goods, 1100 employees (0.5 per cent of manufacturing employment); timber/furniture, 6800 employees (3.4 per cent of manufacturing employment). Textiles and clothing are, therefore, the comparatively big 'threatened' sectors. This, together with the fact that textiles and clothing are consistently an early LDC industrial export success, goes a long way towards explaining the prominence of these industries in international debate and controversy about low-cost competition (see also Appendix 4.III).

Table 4.9: Percentage Share of Less Developed Countries in Ireland's Textile and Clothing Imports 1970-1980 (per cent of current value)

	Textiles	Clothing
1970	2.5	1.4
1971	2.3	0.8
1972	3.0	0.9
1973	3.9	1.3
1974	6.2	2.7
1975	4.9	2.9
1976	6.7	4.9
1977	6.9	5.0
1978	5.4	6.5
1979	5.7	8.8
1980	6.0	8.3

Source: OECD, Trade by Commodities, Series B, various issues.

Table 4.9 shows the percentage share of the LDCs in Ireland's imports of textiles and clothing over the ten years 1970 and 1980, inclusive. This share grew substantially, increasing by a factor of 2.5 in the case of textiles and by a factor of 6 in the case of clothing. However, this growth was from a very small base and remained well below 10 per cent of total imports in 1980. As is the experience internationally, the NICs and a small number of other LDC producers dominated

Table 4.10: Percentage Share of the Irish Market for Cotton Textiles, Knitwear and other Clothing Held by Various Producers in 1974 and 1980

	1974	1980
Cotton textiles		
All sources	100	100
Irish	39	33
Imports	61	67
of which:		
developed countries	40	46
state trading countries	3	3
less developed countries	18	18
Knitwear		
All sources	100	100
Irish	62	21
Imports	38	79
of which:		
developed countries	37	72
state trading countries	0	0
less developed countries	1	7
Other clothing		
All sources	100	100
Irish	71	32
Imports	29	67
of which:		
developed countries	29	62
state trading countries	0	0
less developed countries	0	5

Note: 0 = less than 0.5%.

Source: Author's estimates based on Central Statistics Office trade and production statistics (see Annex 4.V).

these imports. In 1978, 15 countries accounted for approximately 90 per cent of Ireland's textile and clothing imports from LDCs (see Annex 4.IV).

The relatively small overall impact of imports from the

LDCs is also illustrated in Table 4.10. This estimates the market shares of the developed, state trading and less developed countries in Irish sales of cotton textiles, knitwear and other clothing in 1974 and 1980.[15] These are the three textile and clothing sub-sectors in which the LDCs have been most successful. The market, or annual consumption, is calculated as domestic Irish production minus exports, plus imports, of the product in question. Foreign shares are calculated from import statistics and domestic sales by Irish manufacturers are estimated as local production less exports. The data used in the calculation are, therefore, gross output, imports and exports for each of the three product groups for 1974 and 1980. Central Statistics Office trade data were cross-classified with the industrial categories in which output figures are available. The latter are taken from the annual Census of Industrial Production. Gross output for 1980 was estimated using output and price indices (see Annex 4.V for actual data).

In 1980, the largest LDC market share (18 per cent) was in cotton textiles. However, this had remained static over the period since 1974. The LDCs' market shares in knitwear and other clothing grew between 1974 and 1980. However, this was a growth from a negligible share in 1974 to shares of 7 per cent and 5 per cent, respectively, for knitwear and other clothing in 1980. The major growth in import penetration in these two products over the years 1974 to 1980 originated in the developed countries, principally the UK and other EEC countries.

Table 4.10 has a number of limitations which must be noted. First, it deals with the Irish domestic market only. Ireland's exports also face NIC competition on overseas markets and this is not analysed here.

Second, in the case of cotton textiles, the period is too late to capture most of the impact of low-cost competition which had had its effect in the 1960s.

Third, a proportion of Ireland's imports of textiles and clothing from LDCs may be recorded in trade statistics as imports from an EEC country, particularly the UK, thereby distorting the data somewhat.[16]

Fourth, there are well recognised methodological limitations to the use of import penetration ratios as an indicator of the effects of low-cost competition on industrial production and employment. For example, import penetration ratios can over or underestimate the losses in domestic output depending on the price-responsiveness of domestic supply and demand in the industry in question. Also, the various pressures for change on an industry (foreign competitiveness, shifts in demand and changes in technology) are generally inter-related, making the singling out of the one such as import competition difficult.[17]

Finally, the sectoral level at which the analysis is carried out does not identify the much larger impact of LDCs at the level of more specific products. For example, clothing items of which LDCs were major sources of Ireland's imports in 1978 were: men's and boys' cotton trousers (55 per cent); women's/girls' cotton underwear (40 per cent); jerseys and cardigans (73 per cent). Table 4.8 already pointed to similarly high LDC import shares at the level of specific product items in other industries.

The picture which emerges from this evidence is, therefore, twofold. The LDCs in general, and the NICs in particular, have made major inroads into the Irish market for many individual manufactured goods. However, these inroads have been heavily concentrated in specific product lines. Even in sectors such as textiles and clothing, the aggregate impact of the LDCs is still relatively small by comparison with that of our industrialised competitors.

THE INTERNATIONAL RESPONSE TO COMPETITION
FROM THE LDCS

Ultimately, Western industrialized countries face two opposing choices in their response to competition from the NICs and other LDCs. One option is to stave off such competition by the erection of trade barriers. The alternative option is to adjust their industries to this competition. This adjustment can involve either a shift of productive resources out of products which have lost their competitiveness vis-a-vis the LDCs, what the OECD have labelled 'positive adjustment'[18], or attempts to regain competitiveness through investment in new plant and technology, so-called "defensive restructuring". In practice, the developed countries' response has involved elements of all three approaches with the emphasis differing between countries[19]. However, as the general economic growth of the 1960s and early 1970s has given way to recession, Western countries have turned increasingly to protection to save industries and jobs seen to be threatened by import competition. The official rhetoric of 'free trade' has turned increasingly to calls for 'fair trade'. As far back as 1977, the Secretariat of the General Agreement on Tariffs and Trade (GATT) reported that protectionist pressure had 'reached a point at which the continued existence of an international order based on agreed and observed rules may be open to question'.[20]

Despite the post-Second World War free-trade ideals embodied in the GATT, international trade in manufactured goods even among Western countries has always been subject to numerous exceptions. However, the 'new protectionism'[21] of the 1970s and 1980s has caused concern because it differs from the earlier experience in a number of important respects.

First, it is generally not motivated by overall balance of payments considerations but by product-specific 'market disruption'. Second, it is discriminatory in that it is usually directed at specific exporters or groups of exporters of the product in question. Third, it contravenes both the letter and spirit of the GATT Treaty, operates outside the normal GATT framework, and is subject to little or no multilateral surveillance. Fourth, there has been a clear move away from tariff to non-tariff trade barriers. These are mostly quantitative import controls in the form of quotas unilaterally imposed by the importing countries or 'voluntary export restraints' agreed to by the exporting country at the importer's insistence. There was a rapid proliferation of voluntary export restraints and other non-tariff barriers during the second half of the 1970s.

It must be said that this new protectionism is not directed exclusively at the NICs. Much of this type of measure has its origins in continuing efforts by Western countries to stem the growth of Japanese exports. Trade with the Eastern Bloc and EEC-US trade has also seen a growth in this form of protection.

Of the various manufactured products exported by the NICs, the new protectionism has reached its most sophisticated and institutionalised form in the case of textile and clothing. Industrialised countries' imports of textiles and clothing from the NICs and other LDCs are regulated under the arms of Multifibre Textile Arrangement (MFA). The MFA first came into operation in 1974, but its origins go back to similar earlier arrangements governing trade in cotton textiles and first signed in 1961.[22] The MFA ran initially from 1974 to 1977, inclusive. It was then renewed for the years 1978 to 1982 and the current second renewal covers the period 1983 to mid-1986. Although designed, like its predecessors, to facilitate a gradual growth in the LDCs' share of world textile and clothing exports, the importing countries have come to rely on the MFA's mechanisms as a protective device for their own textile and clothing sectors.

The EEC is a party to the MFA. Under the terms of the Arrangement, which itself is a broad umbrella agreement, the Community has bilateral voluntary export restraint agreements with 26 'low-cost' MFA signatories.[23] Additional low-cost producers are restrained under formal agreements outside the MFA,[24] under informal gentlemen's agreements with EEC preferential trading partners[25] and unilateral quotas.[26] Altogether, therefore, the exports of both the NICs and of all other significant exporters of low-cost textiles and clothing (i.e. other LDCs, state trading countries and southern Europe) are subject to some form of quantitative limitation. These place

Table 4.11: Quantitative Ceilings on Irish Imports of the Eight 'Super-Sensitive' MFA Textile and Clothing Products[1], from MFA Signatories, China and Taiwan in 1981.

Country[2]	Category 1 tonnes	Category 2 tonnes	Category 3 tonnes	Category 4 000 pieces	Category 5 000 pieces	Category 6 000 pieces	Category 7 000 pieces	Category 8 000 pieces
Argentina	59	–	–	–	–	–	–	–
Brazil	1,410	607	–	45	–	8	–	–
Columbia	316	204	204	–	–	–	–	–
South Korea	3	20	30	121	222	58	12	60
Hong Kong	20	448	125	145	46	70	26	53
India	346	373	–	42	–	–	105	181
Mexico	67	68	–	–	–	–	–	–
Pakistan	397	779	–	23	9	–	10	34
Peru[3]	1	16	–	–	6	–	–	–
Romania	28	55	6	18	20	7	0	12
Yugoslavia	44	11	4	14	4	1	1	8
Egypt	–	21	–	–	–	–	–	–
Hungary	–	38	4	3	15	0	0	1
Malaysia	–	10	157	23	5	9	3	5
Poland	–	100	79	7	8	1	–	5
Singapore	–	21	27	94	46	21	37	51
Thailand	–	124	124	23	77	2	8	12
Macao	–	–	–	15	15	19	4	5
Phillipines	–	–	–	2	32	96	9	35[6]
Sri Lanka	–	–	–	13	8	17	14	27
China[4]	89	495	52	21	26	34	20	38
Taiwan[5]	0	45	39	13	26	8	2	4
Total	2,780	3,435	851	542	565	264	251	531

Note: 0 means no imports allowed. – means no restraints in force.

1. Category 1 = cotton yarn; Category 2 = cotton fabric (excluding terry); Category 3 = woven synthetic fabric; Category 4 = knitted shirts, vests, light pullovers; Category 5 = jerseys, pullovers; Category 6 = trousers, slacks; Category 7 = blouses; Category 8 = shirts.
2. Five further MFA signatories are not subject to restraints.
3. Excludes Tanguis and Prima type.
4. Restrained under a bilateral agreement outside the MFA
5. Restrained under unilateral quotas.
6. New 'basket extractor' restraint.

Source: Official Journal of the European Communities, L 149 18/6/79, L 354 13/12/79, and L 317 10/11/78.

annual absolute limits on imports into the Community (broken down by Member State) from these exporters and allow new controls to be introduced as required. Consequently, such controls are in operation on imports of most textiles and clothing (over 200 items in all) from any NIC, LDC or other low-cost producer who exports these in any significant quantity. This control is effected through a system of import licences. As a result, such imports of textiles and clothing are now the subject of a system of administrative controls which are normally associated with a centrally planned rather than a free trade economic system.

Ireland, as a Community member, is part of the controlled EEC market. In the case of each Community-wide import ceiling, a proportionate ceiling is allocated to Ireland. An impression of the extent of the resulting series of import controls can be gauged by examination of Table 4.11. This shows the quantitative ceilings on Ireland's imports of eight MFA products from low-cost countries in 1981. The products shown are the eight categories where NIC competition has been perceived to be greatest, i.e. 'super-sensitive' products in MFA terminology. These are cotton yarn; cotton fabric; woven synthetic fabric; knitted shirts; jerseys and pullovers; trousers and slacks; blouses; shirts. In all, 122 individual import ceilings are listed for these products alone. Added complexities are surveillance of imports from LDCs not currently subject to controls and monitoring of intra-EEC trade. No comparable controls exist on imports from our EEC partners nor on most textile and clothing imports from other industrialised countries.

IRELAND'S RESPONSE TO NIC COMPETITION

The arguments for and against the MFA and the appropriate response of the West to the NICs' competitiveness in textiles and clothing constitute a long-running debate and are not in themselves the focus of this chapter.[27] The relevance of the textiles and clothing case here is that it is illustrative of the general issue of NIC competition in manufacturing industry. However, it is clear from the evidence of earlier parts of this chapter that these sectors are not unique. Other industries, too, will face continuing low-cost competition. The issue is whether the textile and clothing approach is to provide the model for the response to this competition.

As with other Western countries, Ireland's policy-makers face a basic choice in their reaction to low-cost industrial competition from less developed countries, that is whether to try to protect Irish industry against such competition, to try to help ailing sectors to regain competitiveness vis-a-vis the LDCs, or to move out of product lines in which competitive advantage has shifted to the NICs and other LDCs.

To date, no clear choice among these alternatives is evident. In practice, policy towards low-cost competition has involved elements of all three approaches. Ireland, represented by the Department of Industry, Trade, Commerce and Tourism has been among the EEC countries which favour a protectionist approach towards the MFA, whereas some other Community countries, notably Germany and the Netherlands, favour a more liberal policy line.[28]

The IDA, on the other hand, have pursued a policy broadly in line with positive adjustment. It has encouraged the establishment of newer, more competitive export-oriented industries and has been reluctant to give grants to indigenous firms perceived as facing serious low-cost competition. The NESC review of industrial policy also came down in favour of a positive adjustment approach.[29] However, the subsequent White Paper on Industrial Policy did not address the issue.[30] Some of the services which State agencies such as the IIRS and AnCO provide could, in the case of traditional sectors, also be seen as defensive restructuring, i.e. attempts to help firms in these sectors regain their competitiveness in the face of low-cost competition. So, in practice, a consistent policy approach has not been followed.

One reason for the mix of approaches is that, whatever their preferred intentions might be, policy-makers find arguments and pressure in favour of a protectionist response very difficult to resist. However, in the case of a small trade-dependent economy such as Ireland, a protectionist policy, alone or in combination with defensive restructuring, needs especially careful consideration. This is so for a number of reasons. First, any drift towards greater protectionism internationally is unlikely to be in Ireland's own interests as an exporting nation. Second, heavy reliance on protection against low-cost competition is an unreliable safeguard for threatened firms or sectors. This is so because Ireland, as an EEC member, has very limited independent influence or control over the degree of such protection since external foreign trade policy is determined jointly by the Community. Third, Ireland's close trading links with its larger neighbours, particularly the UK, make any tight system of import controls very difficult to operate from a purely administrative viewpoint.

Defensive restructuring also faces serious limitations as a policy response to low-cost competition. It is not really an alternative to protection since a considerable period of protection is usually required during which such restructuring can take place. The experience of other countries with such policies does not provide a great basis for optimism. Major attempts to revitalise sectors such as the UK textiles industry have generally failed.[31] Industries like textiles and clothing, where most technology is of a non-proprietary nature, also face the problem that the latest cost or labour-saving methods are as available to the NICs as they are to Ireland.

Pursuit of a positive adjustment approach by Irish policy-makers would involve decisions in two areas, namely foreign trade policy and domestic industrial policy. The former is largely an EEC matter, the latter is largely determined nationally. With regard to *trade policy* the option open to Ireland is membership of the liberal rather than the protectionist group of Community countries on EEC trade relations with the

LDCs. In the field of *industrial policy* the need would be not for new policy instruments but for an appropriate orientation and co-ordination of the wide range of instruments which already exist in the areas of grant-assistance, manpower, technology and other industrial aids and services.

The evidence of this chapter points to the feasibility of adopting such a positive approach to low-cost LDC competition. It is evident that this competition, while significant and growing, is not as sweeping or dramatic as may sometimes be supposed. It is limited to a small number of identifiable industrial sectors. Within these, it is concentrated in a range of products and is not threatening to 'wipe out' entire industries. The chapter also shows that examination of data such as that on international trade patterns allows the extent of such competition to be assessed and should make a degree of early warning possible. If an active industrial policy involves attempts to "pick winners", the corollary is that it must also be able to identify the losers.

NOTES AND REFERENCES

1. Thanks are due to Dr Helen O'Neill, Centre for Development Studies, Department of Political Economy, UCD, who supervised the research on which this chapter is based.
2. OECD, *The Impact of the Newly Industrialising Countries on Production and Trade in Manufactures* (Paris: OECD, 1979).
3. For a comparison of lists see Fitzpatrick, J. 'Trade Between a Newly Industrialised and Newly Industrialising Countries: The Case of Ireland', *Administration*, Vol. 31, No. 2 (1983).
4. OECD, *op. cit.*, p. 22. This is also discussed in Durkan, J. and Gormley, P.J., *Some Aspects of Trade in Manufactures between Developed and Less Developed Countries* (Dublin: Economic and Social Research Institute, 1981, mimeo).
5. Figures from OECD *op. cit.* and from OECD, *The Impact of the Newly Industrialising Countries on Production and Trade in Manufactures, Updating Selected Tables from the 1979 Report* (Paris: OECD, 1981).
6. For detailed descriptions see Donges, J.B., 'A Comparative Survey of Industrialisation Policy in Fifteen Semi-industrialised Countries',

Weltwirtschaftliches Archiv, Vol. 122, No. 4 (1976) and Balassa, B. *Development Strategies in Semi-industrialised Economies* (Baltimore; Johns Hopkins University Press, 1982).

7. Singapore did operate a degree of import substitutions through selective tariff protection prior to 1960.

8. See Sharpston, M., 'International Subcontracting', *World Development,* Vol. 4, No. 4 (1976).

9. This was concluded in Nayyar, D., 'Transnational Corporations and Manufactured Exports from Poor Countries', *Economic Journal,* Vol. 88, No. 349 (1978).

10. On this see Hone, A., 'Multinational Corporations and Multinational Buying Groups: Their Impact on the Growth of Asia's Exports of Manufactures — Myths and Realities', *World Development,* Vol. 2, No. 2 (1974).

11. Ireland's trade with LDCs is also discussed in Matthews, A., *The European Community's External Trade Policy: Implications for Ireland* (Dublin: European League for Economic Co-operation and Irish Council of the European Movement, 1980).

12. The extreme case is that of 'non-competing' imports where there is no domestically produced substitute, e.g. oil. Importing countries then worry about high, not low, import prices.

13. All figures from the Central Statistics Office, *Industrial Employment, Earnings and Hours Worked,* quarterly.

14. For example, see Apparel Industries Federation, *The Future of the Irish Clothing Industry in the 1980s* (Dublin: Confederation of Irish Industry, 1980).

15. Other discussions of the effects of trade with LDCs on Ireland are given in Matthews, *op. cit.,* and in McAleese, D. and Carey, P., 'Employment Co-efficients for Irish Trade with extra-EEC Countries: Measurement and Implications', *Economic and Social Review,* Vol. 12, No. 2 (1981). Regarding the NICs see Teeling, J. and Lynam, J., 'Irish Industrial Development Policy: A Review', *Irish Journal of Business and Administrative Research,* Vol. 2, No. 2 (1980).

16. This would be most likely to occur where Ireland is treated as part of a UK distribution system. However, Irish trade statistics are intended to show countries of ultimate origin of imports, not the country of immediate consignment.

17. On this, see Martin, J. P. and Evans, J. M., 'Notes on Measuring the Employment Displacement Effects of Trade by the Accounting Procedure', *Oxford Economic Papers,* Vol. 33, No. 1 (1981).

18. OECD, *Positive Adjustment Policies, Managing Structural Change* (Paris: OECD, 1983).

19. See Wolf, M., *Adjustment Policies and Problems in Developed Countries* (Washington D.C.: World Bank [Staff Working Paper No. 349], 1979).

20. GATT, *International Trade 1976/1977* (Geneva: GATT, 1977), p. 22.

21. This is discussed in Helleiner, G. K., 'The New Industrial Protectionism and Developing Countries', *Trade and Development, an UNCTAD Review*, Vol. 1 (1979).

22. The origins and operations of the MFA are described in Keesing, D. and Wolf, M, *Textile Quotas Against Developing Countries* (London: Trade Policy Research Centre, 1981).

23. Sri Lanka, Pakistan, Peru, Uruguay, Thailand, Poland, Czechoslovakia, Bangladesh, Bulgaria, Haiti, Romania, Hungary, Guatemala, Egypt, Yugoslavia, India, Colombia, Mexico, Philippines, Malaysia, Singapore, Brazil, Indonesia, Hong Kong, Macao, Korea.

24. China and Yugoslavia.

25. Cyprus, Egypt, Malta, Morocco, Spain, Tunisia, Turkey, Portugal.

26. Taiwan and Argentina.

27. On the international situation, see for example Cable, V., *An Evaluation of the Multifibre Arrangement and Negotiating Options* (London: Commonwealth Secretariat, 1981).
On Ireland, see Fitzpatrick, J., *Industrialization, Trade and Ireland's Development Co-operation Policy* (Dublin: Advisory Council on Development Co-operation, 1982).

28. EEC member state's positions on MFA renegotiations were described in Stevens, C. (ed.), *EEC and the Third World, A Survey 3, The Atlantic Rift* London: Hodder and Stoughton, 1983), Ch. 6.

29. National Economic and Social Council, *Policies for Industrial Development: Conclusions and Recommendations* (Dublin: NESC, No. 66), p. 37.

30. White Paper on Industrial Policy, (Dublin, The Stationery Office, 1984).

31. See Wolf, *op. cit.,* also Finger, J. M., *Industrial Country Policy and Adjustment to Imports from Developing Countries* (Washington D.C.; World Bank [Staff Working Paper No. 470], 1981), and Shepherd, G., *Textile Industry Adjustment in Developed Countries* (London, Trade Policy Research Centre, 1981). Also OECD, *Textile and Clothing Industries: Structural Problems and Policies in OECD Countries* (Paris: OECD, 1983).

Annex 4.I: Real Annual Average Growth Rates in Newly-Industrializing, in Other Country Groups and in Ireland

	GNP per Cap (1960-78)	GDP (1970-80)	Manufacturing output (1970-78)	Merchandise exports (1970-78)
Brazil	4.9	9.2	9.5	6.0
Mexico	2.7	5.0	6.2	5.2
Hong Kong	6.5	8.2	5.6	4.8
South Korea	6.9	9.7	18.3	28.8
Taiwan	6.6	8.0	13.2	9.3
Singapore	7.4	8.5	9.2	9.8
Yugoslavia	5.4	5.6	9.3	4.8
All NICs	4.9[2]	7.7	7.9	9.8
Low Income LDCs[2]	3.6	4.2	− 0.8	
Middle Income LDCs[2]	5.7	6.8	5.2	
Industrialised Countries	3.7[2]	3.2	3.3	5.7
Ireland	3.3	3.4	−	8.4

Source: World Bank, *World Development Report*, 1980, Annex, various tables.
1. Excludes major oil exporters, includes Southern Europe.   2. Weighted averages.

Annex 4.II: Percentage Share in World Exports (E) and Imports (M) 1950 to 1979, all LDCs and Selected Sub-Groups (per cent current value)

		1950	1955	1960	1965	1970	1975	1979
All LDCs	E:	30.8	25.5	21.5	19.6	18.1	24.3	25.0
	M:	26.7	24.3	22.2	19.0	17.1	20.9	20.1
Major Petroleum Exporters[1]	E:	6.2	7.1	6.8	6.4	6.2	13.7	13.4
	M:	4.1	4.4	4.6	3.7	3.3	6.1	6.2
Fast Growing Exporters of Manufactures[2]	E:	7.8	5.0	3.9	3.5	3.4	3.5	4.7
	M:	7.3	5.7	4.9	3.6	4.3	4.9	5.5
Other LDCs	E:	16.9	13.4	11.0	9.7	8.3	7.1	6.9
	M:	15.3	14.2	12.7	11.6	9.4	9.7	8.3

Source: UNCTAD, *Handbook of International Trade and Development Statistics*, Supplement 1980, tables 1.9 and 1.10.
1. Algeria, Angola, Bahrain, Brunei, Ecuador, Gabon, Indonesia, Iran, Iraq, Kuwait, Libya, Nigeria, Oman, Qatar, Saudi Arabia, Trinidad and Tobago, United Arab Emirates, Venezuela.
2. Argentina, Brazil, Hong Kong, South Korea, Mexico, Singapore.

Annex 4.III: Import Penetration Ratios and Shares in Irish Manufacturing Employment for Twenty-Five Industry Groups, 1976[1]

Industry Group[2]	Gross Penetration[3] Total	Gross Penetration[3] LDC	Net Penetration[4] Total	Net Penetration[4] LDC	% share[5] in Emp.
Chemicals					
basic industrial chemicals (inc. fertilizers)	90.5	1.8	− 48.7	+ 9.5	1.5
pharmaceutials, other industrial chemicals	55.6	2.0	+ 14.2	+ 18.7	1.7
Metals					
foundry products	41.8	1.2	− 24.4	+ 0.9	0.4
other finished metal articles	71.1	2.0	− 35.5	+ 2.8	2.3
Office and Data Processing Machinery	73.7	2.9	+ 25.7	+ 17.6	0.8
Electrical Engineering					
electrical machinery	85.9	1.1	− 52.8	+ 5.9	1.1
radios, T.V.s, sound equipment	72.5	4.0	− 24.2	+ 4.4	1.2
Food, Drink and Tobacco					
margarine, fats, oils	60.9	11.5	− 56.3	+ 1.1	0.2
processed fruit, vegetables	40.4	5.4	− 20.6	− 3.8	1.3
flour	7.3	1.7	− 6.7	− 1.6	0.9
miscellaneous foodstuffs	57.6	12.6	+ 31.4	+ 0.2	0.7
sugar	31.3	15.4	+ 3.0	− 15.4	1.0
cocoa, chocolate, confectionery	24.2	4.2	+ 29.2	+ 2.7	2.7
spirits	62.8	2.5	− 22.1	+ 17.8	0.2
Textiles					
textile fabric	81.1	7.2	− 15.3	− 1.5	3.8
knitwear	59.9	2.2	− 16.1	− 0.5	3.1
Leather					
leather	36.7	5.2	+ 52.7	− 0.1	0.7
leather goods	69.9	8.5	− 45.1	+ 3.4	0.2
Footwear and Clothing					
footwear	57.1	3.3	− 21.9	+ 17.4	1.8
clothing (except knitwear)	44.2	2.1	− 7.1	0.0	6.7
household textiles	51.2	1.0	+ 2.1	+ 4.7	0.5
Wood Products					
sawed, processed wood, semi-finished products	67.8	15.8	− 57.1	− 15.8	1.0
cork products, brushes and brooms	54.7	1.7	− 14.1	+ 10.0	0.1

Continued

Annex 4.III continued

| Industry Group[2] | Gross Penetration[3] | | Net Penetration[4] | | % share[5] |
	Total	LDC	Total	LDC	in Emp.
Rubber and Plastic					
rubber products	69.0	1.0	+ 20.8	+ 21.1	1.5
Other Manufactures					
Toys and sports goods	186.1	15.7	+ 0.3	+ 9.4	0.3

Sources: Eurostat, microfiche trade data (SCE—2911) 1976-1978, *Irish Statistical Bulletin,* March, June, Sept. 1979.
1. Industry groups where LDC gross import penetration was at least 1%.   2. NACE Groups.
3. Imports as a percentage of apparent consumption, apparent consumption equals domestic production less
   exports plus imports.   4. Imports less exports as a percentage of domestic consumption.
5. Percentage share of the sector in total employment in manufacturing industry.

Annex 4.IV: Main Sources of Ireland's Imports of Textiles and Clothing from Less Developed Countries, 1978 (as percentage of all imports of these products from LDCs)

Countries[1]	Textiles[2] & Clothing	Textiles[2]	Clothing
Hong Kong	18.8	16.9	21.9
Brazil	11.5	18.5	0.9
Israel	11.5	4.6	22.0
India	10.8	13.2	7.2
South Korea	10.1	6.1	16.2
Pakistan	6.3	10.3	0.1
Taiwan	3.7	4.2	3.1
Malaysia	3.7	5.6	0.7
Mauritius	3.1	0.5	7.1
Philippines	2.9	0[3]	7.5
Singapore	2.9	1.2	5.4
Colombia	1.2	2.0	0[3]
Thailand	1.2	1.4	0.9
Tunisia	0.8	0[3]	2.0
Macao	0.6	0[3]	1.4
Total	89.1	84.5	96.4

Source: Central Statistics Office computer tabulations.
1. LDCs who supplied at least 1% of Irish imports of textiles or clothing from less
   developed countries in 1979   2. Excludes fibres   3. Less than 0.05%.

Annex 4.V: Data Used to Calculate the Market Shares in Table 4.10 (£m)

Cotton Yarn/Fabric (NACE 432)	1974	1980
Gross Output	22.7	53.5[1]
Consumption[2]	30.3	44.0
Exports[3]	10.9	39.0
Imports[3]	18.5	29.5
of which: UK	6.5	9.4
other EEC	1.1	3.5
other DCs[4]	4.4	7.2
state traders[5]	0.9	1.3
LDCs	5.5	8.0
Knitwear (NACE 436)		
Gross Output	41.0	54.9[6]
Consumption[2]	39.9	87.3
Exports[3]	16.3	36.2
Imports[3]	15.2	68.6
of which: UK	13.3	50.6
other EEC	0.4	6.7
other DCs[4]	1.1	4.9
state traders[5]	neg.	neg.
LDCs	0.4	6.4
Other Clothing (NACE 453/4)		
Gross Output	68.5	118.5[7]
Consumption	62.5	180.0
Exports[3]	23.9	60.5
Imports[3]	17.9	122.0
of which: UK	15.5	87.4
other EEC	1.1	17.0
other DCs[4]	1.0	9.6
state traders[5]	neg.	0.2
LDCs	0.3	7.8

Sources: Census of Industrial Production 1974, *Monthly Industrial Enquiry* Dec. 1980, *Wholesale Price Index* Dec. 1980 CSO Computer Tabulation.

1. Estimated using actual output in 1976 and net output and wholesale price indices for NACE 43.

Annex 4.V continued

2. Apparent consumption i.e. gross output plus imports less exports.

3. Export and import data taken from CSO Computer Tabulations of Trade by BTN, cross-classified to NACE as follows:

NACE Industrial Groups	*BTN*	*Tariff Headings*
432 Cotton Industry	5505	Cotton yarn, not for retail sale
	5506	Cotton yarn, for retail sale
	5507	Cotton gauze
	5508	Cotton terry towelling
	5509	Other woven cotton fabric
436 Knitting Industry	6002	Knitted gloves
	6003	Stockings, socks
	6004	Knitted under garments
	6005	Knitted outer garments
	6006	Knitted fabric
453/4 Clothing (except knitting)	61	Clothing and clothing accessories of textiles fabric, (excluding knitwear).

4. Includes Southern Europe.

5. Eastern Europe only.

6. Estimate using 1976 actual output, with NACE 436 net output and NACE 436 wholesale price indices for 1980.

7. Estimate using 1976 actual output, with NACE 453-6 net output and wholesale price indices for 1980.

166

5

Aspects of the Financial Behaviour of Multinational Companies in Ireland[1]

James Stewart

The real, as distinct from the financial, effects of multi-national companies (MNCs) located in Ireland have attracted a considerable amount of research interest. For example, much valuable research has been done in the area of employment, exports, and linkages. However, the financial behaviour of multinational companies has been largely ignored.[2] The financial behaviour and financial flows within the MNC may pose a number of problems for a country such as Ireland, with a large stock of foreign direct investment. One kind of problem which may arise relates to how government policy might best facilitate the financing of foreign investment in Ireland, without adversely affecting other parts of the economy. Another kind of problem may arise from the ease with which MNCs may move funds from one currency to another, and hence in aggregate their financial behaviour can have a considerable effect on exchange rates, and on foreign currency reserves. MNC financial behaviour may also pose problems for fiscal policy, because of their ability to artificially adjust profits and so alter tax payments in the various countries where they operate. Finally, the extent to which profits are reinvested, and the means by which MNCs finance investment, affects the balance of payments.

This chapter examines aspects of the financial behaviour of a number of MNCs operating in Ireland, and covers the period

1964 to 1980. The chapter is divided into three sections. The first section considers the extent to which companies in the study may have preferential access to bank credit, and examines the question of whether MNC investment tends to 'crowd out' indigenous investment by absorbing an increasing proportion of available funds. The possible use of transfer pricing by companies in the study is examined in the second section, while the third section considers some balance of payments effects of company financial behaviour. These three areas are, of course, interrelated.

The financing of MNCs affects the balance of payments, in that if the Irish subsidiary obtains finance from the parent company in the form of equity shares or long-term loans, this results in capital inflows, whereas local borrowing does not do so directly. Local borrowing may result in indirect capital inflows, depending on how lending agencies finance their operations. Similarly, the use of transfer pricing to switch profits to Ireland increases profits of MNCs in Ireland, and may increase retentions, and hence may reduce the need for additional finance from the parent company for investment purposes.

The study relates to all non-financial public companies which were foreign-owned subsidiaries operating in Ireland during the period 1964 to 1980. Public companies are the only companies for which published accounts are available. Most companies in Ireland, both foreign and indigenously owned, are private companies and publish virtually no financial information. Hence, there is little published information produced within Ireland relating to aggregate foreign direct investment. However, some data relating to US and UK direct investment in Ireland is published. The US data is available since 1973 and the UK data since 1965. US and UK direct investment in Ireland would account for the bulk of foreign direct investment. For the year 1973 after-tax profits of the study group amounted to about 10 per cent of post-tax profits of US and UK direct investment, and amounted to about 8.1

per cent for 1979. The total number employed by the study group amounted to approximately 9700 in 1980, of which 8500 were employed by manufacturing companies (88 per cent). In 1981, manufacturing companies in the study group employed approximately 8100, or 10 per cent of the total numbers employed in foreign-owned manufacturing companies. The year 1981 is the first year for which the Industrial Development Authority published employment for foreign manufacturing companies.

The largest single group of companies included in the study are wholly-owned subsidiaries of UK firms. Other companies included were subsidiaries of firms operating from the US, Canada, Netherlands, Switzerland, and Australia. Most of the firms included were involved in manufacturing activities. The main exceptions were two oil distribution companies (subsidiares of Shell and Exxon). During the period 1964 to 1980 the number of companies included varied between 18 and 26.

BANK BORROWING AS SOURCE OF FUNDS

For a number of reasons, local bank borrowing is likely to be an important source of finance to subsidiaries of multinational enterprises. One reason for this is to reduce exchange risk by borrowing in a local currency, rather than from the parent company, or from a fellow subsidiary in a foreign currency. In contrast, Hymer[4] argues that relative interest rates in host and source countries determines the extent of local borrowing. However, interest rates may differ between countries because of expectations that a currency is likely to be devalued or revalued, and hence under certain circumstances differences in interest rates may be due to borrowing or repayment of debt to reduce exchange risk.

Another reason for local borrowing is that restrictions have been placed on capital flows from the major capital exporting countries at various times. For this reason, host country borrowing may be used rather than source country borrowing. There may also be capital market imperfections in the host country resulting in preferential access to bank credit by MNC subsidiaries compared with domestic companies. Such pre-ferential access could arise, provided the parent company guarantees bank borrowing,[5] because of lower risk associated with size, or because of increased bargaining power associated with operations in several countries. If MNC subsidiaries have preferential access to bank credit, they may obtain an increasing share of this credit, at the expense of indigenously owned firms. Hence, domestically owned firms may be 'crowded out'.

Table 5.1, column 1, shows total bank lending, both long and short-term, to MNC subsidiaries included in the study for each year 1972 to 1980. This data was obtained from the annual report and accounts of each firm in the study. Table 5.1 also shows total bank lending to the manufacturing and services sector in Ireland (column 3) and total bank lending within Ireland (column 4). The year 1972 was the first year for which aggregate data on bank lending was published. Column 5 of the table shows bank lending to the study group as a percentage of bank lending to the manufacturing and services sector, and column 6 shows bank lending as a percentage of total advances. These ratios fluctuate considerably from year to year. For the period 1972 to 1974, the study group appeared to obtain an increasing proportion of total bank lending within Ireland, but the ratios at the end of the period examined are generally lower than those at the beginning of the period. This indicates that the study group obtained a lower proportion of total bank lending at the end than at the beginning of the period. Two factors may explain this result. First of all, a decline in the importance of the study group as a proportion of the total corporate sector, largely due to inflows of other foreign direct investment during this period. Secondly, the study group relied to a reduced extent on bank borrowing during the period 1975 to 1980 compared with 1972 to 1974, both as a proportion of external finance, and external finance plus gross internal cash flows.

Table 5.1: Bank Borrowing by Firms in the Study as Shown in the Balance Sheet, 1972 to 1980

Year	N[1]	Study firms total loans	Study firms total loans excluding oil companies	Total[3] advances to manu-facturing & services within State	Total[3] advances within State	⅓	¼	⅔	2/4
					IR£ million	%	%	%	%
		(1)	(2)	(3)	(4)	(5)	(6)	(7)	(8)
1972	24	14.274	8.516	376.2	854.4	3.79	1.67	2.23	1.0
1973	25	18.824	10.745	433.0	1016.8	4.35	1.85	2.48	1.57
1974	25	28.221	18.335	505.3	1130.6	5.58	2.50	3.63	1.62
1975	26	21.296	11.903	531.6	1237.0	4.01	1.72	2.24	0.96
1976	23	24.621	13.445	717.2	1650.2	3.43	1.49	1.87	0.81
1977	21	23.154	14.037	787.5	1935.5	2.94	1.20	1.78	0.73
1978	20	21.120	15.034	1108.7	2683.4	1.90	0.79	1.36	0.56
1979[2]	20	48.296	23.434	1503.0	3425.1	3.21	1.41	1.56	0.68
1980	18	53.911	22.211	2112.9	4306.0	2.55	1.25	1.05	0.51

1. N is the number of firms. 2. Includes borrowing by Irish Shell of £13 million in Irish Pounds and which is assumed to have been borrowed within Ireland. 3. The figures shown for each year relate to February of the following year.
Source: Quarterly Bulletin of the Central Bank of Ireland 1973-81. Annual Reports of Companies.

Because of the large amount of bank borrowing by the two oil distribution companies included, column 2 shows the total stock of bank borrowing if these two companies are omitted. Columns 7 and 8 show this figure as a percentage of lending to the manufacturing and services sector, and as a percentage of total bank lending. However, approximately the same results are obtained, that is a period of increasing share of bank credit from 1972 to 1974, followed by a decline, but with some fluctuations from year to year.

Although there are fluctuations in the relative share of bank lending to firms in the study, for most years bank lending was a positive source of funds. For the period 1964 to 1980, bank lending provided 19 per cent of gross funds, and bank lending as a percentage of external funds amounted to 55 per cent for the entire period, and 66 per cent for the period 1972 to 1980.[6]

Bank borrowing was, thus, an important source of finance for the MNC subsidiaries included in the study. Studies in other countries have also found local bank borrowing to be an important source of finance for MNCs. Brooke and Remmers found in a study of MNCs operating in the UK that local bank borrowing provided one-third of external finance, and Robbins and Stobagh in a study of US-based MNCs found that all subsidiaries borrowed locally. Brooke and Remmers, and Robbins and Stobagh did not examine the extent to which MNCs had preferential access to bank credit. However, in a study of MNCs operating in various Less Developed Countries, Lall and Streeten[8] did consider this question and concluded that there was no evidence that MNCs 'obtain greater access to commercial bank credit than domestic firms'.

Another form of 'crowding out', apart from that of gaining preferential access to bank credit, has also received some attention. That is the ability of MNCs to circumvent restrictions on credit, compared with indigenous firms, and so increase their share of total domestic investment.[9] During the period 1972 to 1980, 1974 and 1979 were years of general restrictions on bank credit. The year 1974 was also the year with the highest share of bank lending to firms in the study. In 1979 companies in the study also increased their share of bank borrowing compared with 1978 and 1980.

Ireland was part of the sterling area until December 1978 and experienced largely the same monetary conditions as the UK as there were no restrictions on capital flows. For example, Irish interest rates rose and fell in unison with those in the UK although with a lag of some months. Hence the hypothesis that MNCs are able to circumvent credit restrictions in Ireland by intracompany flows and higher retention rates needs to be examined in the context of the sterling area as a whole, and secondly within part of the sterling area, that is Ireland, during the period that the Irish pound and sterling were linked. This would involve information relating to currency flows, for example from US dollars to sterling, and also within the sterling area from the UK to Ireland. Whereas in this chapter flows into Ireland could not be disaggregated according to origin, as the data was obtained from the published accounts of companies incuded in the study.

Retention ratios, that is the proportion of company profits retained, were calculated using various definitions of internal flows for firms in the study group for the period 1964 to 1980.[10] Considerable fluctuations were found in retentions as a proportion of total financing, with 1968, 1971-72, and 1978-79 being years of above average retentions. However, as shown in the last section of this chapter, these years were also years of net capital outflows rather than inflows, which is contrary to the direction of the flows suggested by a desire to circumvent credit restrictions in order to finance domestic investment. Hawkins and Macaluso found no evidence of systematic adjustments to sources of funds in response to credit conditions in the UK for the period 1960 to 1975, despite the share of MNC investment increasing during periods of tight credit conditions. They suggest that this result may be because credit restrictions in the UK were often associated with exchange-rate pressures, resulting in a negative relationship between flows of funds into and out of sterling and restrictions on credit.

In summary, bank lending was found to be an important source of finance to firms in the study, although there was no evidence that the study group obtained an increasing proportion of bank credit, thus 'crowding out' domestic firms. There was also no evidence that firms in the study increased internal financing in order to circumvent credit restrictions to finance additional domestic investment, as periods of credit restrictions and increased retentions tended to be associated with net outflows of funds. These conclusions must be interpreted with caution as, firstly, a certain proportion of bank borrowing shown in company accounts may be from outside the state, although there is almost no evidence of this from the published accounts of companies. Secondly, there may be an element of 'window dressing' in figures for bank borrowing, for example repayment of loans prior to the preparation of audited accounts.

'PROFIT SWITCHING' TRANSFER PRICING

Transfer pricing generally refers to the prices set on intra-firm trade.[11] Intra-firm trade refers to trade within a firm, and includes trade between separate divisions or branches as well as between subsidiaries operating in different countries, although it is the latter form of intra-firm trade which arouses most interest. In many cases, there is no market price for goods traded within a firm, hence prices set on intra-firm trade may be quite arbitrary. Even if there is a market price, the firm may not wish to use such prices on its internal trade, so that prices set on internal trade may include an element of artificial profit or loss. Such transfer prices are referred to in this chapter as 'profit switching' transfer prices. 'Profit switching' transfer pricing may be used by an MNC in a variety of situations to transfer profits within the firm from one subsidiary to another. This could be done for many reasons, for example, in anticipation of a currency realignment. 'Profit switching' transfer pricing may also be used in conjunction with a variety of other techniques for intra-group movement of funds.[12] However, more generally 'profit switching' is likely to be used to reduce tax payments as described in the following example.

Consider company A in one country, with two subsidiaries B and C in other countries. Tax rates where A and B operate will be assumed to be 50 per cent, and those where C operates 10 per cent. If prices on goods sold from C to B are raised and prices on goods sold from A to C reduced, profits in A and B will be reduced, and will result in lower tax payments. Subsidiary C will make larger profits and pay tax on those profits at a rate of 10 per cent. It is important to note that as a result of these manipulations overall group pre-tax profits will remain the same, but net of tax profits will have increased.

The extent to which funds are moved or tax payments reduced by 'profit switching' will be a function of the volume of inter-subsidiary trade, and the proportion of artificial profit on the prices set. Other techniques for switching funds depend on the volume of intra-firm financial flows; however, internal transactions on goods are likely to be the most important component of these flows.[13] The use of 'profit switching' has implications for the balance of trade, and for the balance of payments, and as indicated in the above example, tax payments. While total tax payments can be reduced by 'profit switching' they may also be reduced in one country and increased in another, leaving tax payments for the firm as a whole unchanged. The use of 'profit switching' transfer pricing also distorts national statistics, in particular those relating to the value of trade flows, corporate profitability, and value added.

Empirical evidence relating to the use of 'profit switching' transfer pricing is notoriously difficult to obtain. The most comprehensive country study is that by Vaitsos for Colombia.[14] There appears to be no published study relating to the use of 'profit switching' transfer pricing in Ireland. However, if transfer pricing is used to switch profits to a subsidiary, this increases profits in the subsidiary and hence value added. Hence, an examination of profit rates or of value added as a percentage of sales could indicate the use of 'profit switching'.[15]

The following paragraphs summarise the evidence for 'profit switching' transfer pricing in Ireland. First of all, evidence is presented which shows that foreign firms in Ireland have higher than average value added when compared with indigenous firms. Secondly, it is shown that profits of US firms in Ireland are higher than in other countries. Thirdly, evidence is given which indicates that MNC subsidiaries in Ireland have the opportunity to use 'profit switching' transfer pricing because of the volume of inter-subsidiary trade. Finally, profit margins of firms in the study group are compared with those of the firm as a whole in order to indicate the possible use of 'profit switching'.

A study by McAleese shows that new industry in Ireland, most of which consists of subsidiaries of MNCs, does have higher value added as a proportion of gross output when compared with the national average.[16] This is particularly true of those sectors where foreign direct investment predominates, such as the chemical sector. O'Farrell and O'Loughlin,[17] using a different definition of value added (payments for royalties, licences, and interest were excluded), found similar ratios for 'New Industry' and the 'Rest of Industry' for the year 1976. However, in 'New Industry' wages and salaries accounted for 14.2 per cent of gross output compared with 23.5 per cent in the 'Rest of Industry'. This indicates higher profits gross of depreciation for 'New Industry'. The differences in value added shown in these studies, while consistent with the use of 'profit switching', could be explained by firms operating in different product areas, or by firms using different technology. However, it is likely that 'profit switching' transfer pricing is an important factor in accounting for these differences in value added.

Table 5.2: Value Added as a Percentage of Gross Output for 'New Industry' Operating in Ireland for the Year 1973

Sector	New Industry	New and Old Industry
Chemicals	62	49
Metals and Engineering	45	41
Other Manufacturing	53	39
National Average	38	36

Source: McAleese, D., *A Profile of Grant-Aided Industry in Ireland* (Dublin: The Industrial Development Authority), p. 41.

Surveys by the US Department of Commerce of US firms operating in Ireland show profit margins greater than those in other countries, particularly for firms in the Chemicals and

Allied Product sector. This sector accounts for between 62 per cent and 76 per cent of net earnings of US firms operating in Ireland, for the period 1973 to 1980.

Apart from the evidence on value added in relation to 'profit switching', MNC subsidiaries in Ireland also have considerable opportunity to use 'profit switching' transfer pricing, because of the volume of intra-firm trade. McAleese found that 95 per cent of US firms output was exported in 1974, 77 per cent of which consisted of exports to affiliates.[18] Imports amounted to 33 per cent of sales by value, of which imports from affiliates amounted to almost half (46 per cent) of total imports. Lower ratios were found for subsidiaries of other nationality. Subsidiaries of UK firms exported 82 per cent of output in 1974, 39 per cent of which was to affiliates. Imports amounted to 16 per cent of output by value, and imports from affiliates amounted to 38 per cent of total imports. O'Farrell and O'Loughlin reported that 29 per cent of subsidiaries in their study imported more than half of their raw materials. Excluding the food sector, which is predominantly Irish-owned, imports amounted to 62 per cent of sales by value.[19]

Finally, in examining the evidence for 'profit switching' transfer pricing in Ireland, profit margins of the subsidiaries in the study group are compared with those of the firm as a whole. A ratio of profits to sales greater than that of the firm as a whole may indicate the shifting of profits to the Irish subsidiary. This might happen because of lower tax rates in Ireland due to fiscal incentives, in particular export tax relief and, since 1980, a 10 per cent corporate tax rate. A ratio of profits to sales less than that of the firm as a whole may indicate the switching of profits away from the Irish subsidiary, for example to a tax haven. This might happen in the case of a non-exporting manufacturing company prior to 1980 (pre 10 per cent tax rate), or in the case of a non-manufacturing company which cannot benefit from the main tax reliefs.

Profit margins were estimated by calculating the ratio of pre-tax profits to sales. Where an estimate of pre-tax profits

PERSPECTIVES ON IRISH INDUSTRY

was not available net profits were used. Net profits were
defined as profits, less the tax charge for the current
accounting period as it appears in the Profit and Loss Account.
Extel and Moodies share information service was used to obtain
figures of profits before tax and sales of UK-based companies.
The annual *Fortune* magazine listing of the largest US and
non-US companies was used to obtain data on net income and
sales for four companies (Nestle, Westinghouse, Exxon and
Shell). While it was possible to obtain profit and sales figures
for all parent companies, some of the subsidiaries included in
the study do not disclose sales figures.

The periodic use of transfer pricing to switch profits may be
difficult to identify by comparing profit margins calculated on
yearly accounting data, because differences in profit margins
may arise for reasons other than 'profit switching'. The Irish
subsidiary may appear more or less profitable for reasons
which may be unique to the Irish economy, for example,
because of price controls, or higher or lower rates of inflation
in Ireland coupled with historic cost accounting. Profit
margins may also differ because of various intra-firm
payments, such as management charges for services performed
by the parent company, royalties, and interest payments.
However, differences in profit margins which persist over long
periods are consistent with the use of 'profit switching' transfer
pricing.

A number of subsidiaries in the study periodically reported
lower profit margins in Ireland compared with the group as a
whole, for example Rank Organisation (1973-75), Irish Dunlop
(1966-69) and Batchelors (1973-78). Some subsidiaries also
reported higher profit margins in Ireland compared with the
firm as a whole, for example, Lyons Irish Holdings (1970-75),
Gypsum Industries (1973-75 and 1977-78), and ACEC
(1973-78). Table 5.3 shows the results for four subsidiaries in
the study which had persistent differences in profit margins
compared with the firm as a whole over a number of years.
Only one firm consistently reported higher profit margins in

Ireland compared with the group as a whole, that is Readymix. Three companies consistently reported lower profit margins in Ireland compared with overall profit margins, that is Bovril, Irish Shell, and Esso Teoranta. It is interesting to note that all three companies are non-manufacturing and would be unable to benefit from the same level of tax reliefs as manufacturing companies. Hence, to the extent that these companies earn profits and pay taxes, they have an incentive to switch profits away from Ireland. This is in contrast to manufacturing companies, which may avail of numerous tax reliefs, and as a result, have an incentive to switch profits to Ireland.

Table 5.3: The Ratio of Profits to Sales Calculated for Various Irish Subsidiaries and for the Group as a Whole

Year	Irish Shell	Shell[1] Group	Esso Ireland	Exxon[1]	Bovril	Beecham Cavanham[2] Foods	Readymix Ireland	Readymix[3] Group
1970	n.a.		.0375	.0791	n.a.	.0714	.0658	.0424
1971	n.a.		.0164	.0781	n.a.	.0570	.1247	.0525
1972	n.a.	.0501	.0245	.0754	.0208	.0543	.1792	.0590
1973	n.a.	.0958	− 0.0344	.0950	.0141	.0533	.1799	.0498
1974	n.a.	.0822	.0103	.0747	.0151	.0337	.0916	.0256
1975	n.a.	.0657	.0112	.0558	.0048	.0321	.0123	.0307
1976	.0057	.0650	− 0.0048	.0543	.0011	.0310	.0966	.0445
1977	.0250	.0589	.0233	.0447	.0019	.0302	.0966	.0518
1978	.0268	.0473	.0205	.0458	.0036	.0269	.1269	.0578
1979	.0220	.1089	.0266	.0543	.0042	.1480	.0996	.065
1980	.0055	.0671	.0239	.0548	.0033	.146	.0221	.063

1. Defined as profits minus tax as in the Profit and Loss account over sales revenue minus excise taxes, and Net Income over sales revenue minus excise taxes as shown in various issues of *Fortune* (Chicago: Time Inc).

2. Defined as pre-tax profits over sales as shown in the Profit and Loss account and pre-tax profits plus interest over sales in various issues of the *Times 1000*, London: Times Newspapers and *Extel Handbook of Market Leaders*, (London: Extel Statistical Services).

3. Defined as pre-tax profits over sales as shown in the Profit and Loss account and pre-tax profits over sales as shown in *Extel Handbook of Market Leaders* (London: Extel Statistical Services).

Some of the differences in profit margins may be due to the Irish subsidiary operating in a different product market than the firm as a whole. However, this is certainly not true of the two oil companies, the bulk of whose world-wide revenues comes from the sale and distribution of oil products. The average profit margin of the Irish subsidiary of Exxon was 6.3 per cent of the profit margin of the firm as a whole for the period 1964 to 1976. For the period 1977 to 1978 profit margins were higher at approximately 40 per cent of those for the corporation as a whole. Sales figures for Irish Shell are only available for the period 1976 to 1980. The profit margin for 1976 was about 5 per cent of that for the group as a whole, increased to about 30 per cent in 1977, and fell to about 8 per cent in 1980.

In the case of the two oil companies, the change in profit margins had a dramatic effect on tax payments on profits declared in Ireland. The subsidiary of Exxon paid IR£1.8 million in corporate tax in 1980, and IR£3.0 million in corporate tax in 1979, compared with an estimated IR£2.13 million in the period 1964 to 1978. Irish Shell paid IR£1.85 million in corporate tax in 1980 and IR£3.36 million in 1979, compared with an estimated IR£0.24 million for the period 1964 to 1978.

One possible explanation of why the oil companies increased their profit margins in Ireland is a combination of historical cost accounting and increased value of oil stocks due to inflation. Stock profits arising from inflation are not totally exempt from corporate tax in Ireland. For the year 1981, Irish Shell declared a pre-tax loss of IR£15.3 million. Hence, Irish Shell will pay no corporate tax in future years until this loss has been exceeded by future taxable profits.

In summary, this section has presented evidence consistent with the use of 'profit switching' transfer pricing, particularly for US-based firms. In addition, some evidence in terms of differences in profit/sales ratios was presented for firms in the study group. The best examples, however, were for non-manufacturing firms. The implications for industrial policy relate firstly to the difficulty of interpreting data, relating for example to the value of MNC exports from Ireland, or profitability. Secondly, while 'profit switching' by exporting firms, or by manufacturing firms post 1980 does not affect tax payments in Ireland, it may have considerable implications for tax payments in other countries. This partly explains the occasional hostility of capital-exporting countries such as the US to tax concessions in Ireland and other countries. Excessive use of 'profit switching' by MNCs operating in Ireland could result in capital exporting countries effectively ignoring these tax concessions and taxing MNC profits directly in Ireland. Lastly, 'profit switching' in the case of the non-manufacturing and distribution sectors may have a considerable effect on corporate tax payments in Ireland.

BALANCE OF PAYMENTS FLOWS

This section examines the effect on the balance of payments of MNCs. The emphasis is on financial flows, rather than trade flows. Previous sections have discussed bank borrowing and 'profit switching' transfer pricing, and both these aspects of MNC financial behaviour have implications for the balance of payments. 'Profit switching' transfer pricing through the pricing of imports and exports affects the balance of trade. It also affects the absolute size of MNC subsidiary profits and hence funds available for investment, and is thus a direct substitute for capital inflows or outflows. Domestic bank borrowing affects the balance of payments to the extent that it is a substitute for capital inflows, or to the extent that it frees MNC subsidiary funds which may then be repatriated. Other aspects of MNC financial behaviour which directly affect the balance of payments are the proportion of corporate profits remitted as dividends, intra-firm short-term borrowing, and capital flows. These latter flows are the components of the overall balance of payments examined in this section. Secondly, aggregate Irish as well as US and UK data relating to direct investment inflows is also considered.

Ideally, in estimating balance of payments effects of MNCs, it would be necessary to obtain information relating to all financial flows and also real flows between the host country and other countries.[20] Table 5.4 shows information on just three of the potential flows that may take place, that is dividends paid, intra-group short-term flows, and capital flows. These flows are, however, likely to be among the more important potential or actual flows. In addition, for some years interest payments and management charges are included (Table 5.4, column 4) where these were disclosed as being paid to or received from the parent company or fellow subsidiary.

Payments of royalties, interest charges, and management fees may be large. Annex 5.I shows that for US affiliates operating in Ireland, fees and royalties amounted to 64 per cent of dividend payments for the period 1976 to 1979, but

Table 5.4: Some Balance of Payments Flows

Year	N[1]	Dividends	Dividends[2] paid within State	Intra-group flows (−outflow)	Other[3] flows	Capital flows	Capital[4] raised within State	Net flows (−1+2+3 −4+5−6)
		(1)	(2)	(3)	(4)	(5)	(6)	(7)
1964	21	1187	85	885	−5	250	25	13
1965	21	1367	132	1460	3	1347	−2	1631
1966	23	1398	140	1702	−3	578	24	1001
1967	22	1206	146	525	−5	−67	2	−599
1968	24	1322	138	−286	−10	−101	4	−1565
1966	22	1212	160	1929	−22	−24	0	875
1970	24	959	126	9648	−27	891	0	9733
1971	25	854	79	−3321	−13	279	0	−3804
1972	24	2094	133	−6717	22	1336	162	−7526
1973	25	1524	185	2983	11	1237	316	2554
1974	25	2895	315	2237	98	533	67	25
1975	26	2774	291	6052	72	1924	12	5409
1976	23	2400	349	−6323	−21	4255	0	−4098
1977	21	1929	399	2896	20	1070	271	2145
1978	20	3244	477	2042	18	48	27	−712
1979	20	3234	584	−600	15	38	12	−3239
1980	18	4150	666	3349	0	5169	7	5027

IR£000

1. N is the number of companies.
2. Obtained by multiplying dividends of majority-owned subsidiaries by .25, as local shareholdings in majority-owned subsidiaries tended to cluster (with five companies) in the range from 22% to 28%.
3. Consisting of interest payments and payments for managerial services which are shown in company accounts as payments to other firms within the group.
4. Obtained by multiplying share issues raised for cash for majority-owned subsidiaries by .25 to allow for local shareholdings.
Source: Annual Reports and Accounts of companies.

amounted to only 3 per cent of dividend payments for UK firms (Annex 5.II). In a study of American investment in Australia, Brash reported that total remittances of interest and fees were only slightly below those of dividends and profits.[21] In contrast, Lall and Streeten report that for Colombia there was no evidence that foreign firms remit profits via interest payments.[22] However, the data used consisted of published information by companies, similar to that used in this study, and inter-affiliate interest payments may not have been disclosed.[23]

Subsidiaries may also borrow abroad, or repay loans borrowed abroad. The published accounts of subsidiaries in the study do not separately identify foreign borrowing.[24] Although a number of parent companies have several sub-sidiaries operating in Ireland, it is assumed in this study that intra-group flows all take place outside the host country.

Table 5.4, column 7, shows that the net flow of items included varies considerably from year to year. For seven years, the net flow is negative (1967 to 68, 1971 to 72, 1976, and 1978 to 1979).[25] With one exception, the year 1971, these negative flows are all associated with periods of rising interest rates and tight money policies in the UK. These years were also charac-terised by large speculative outflows from sterling. The large negative flow for 1971 may be almost all accounted for by a reduction of IR£6.4 million in intra-group borrowing by one of the oil companies, which was matched by almost an equivalent sum in short term borrowing. If account is taken of borrowings of £15 million by one of the oil companies, which was denomi-nated in sterling, and hence likely to have originated outside the State, there is a positive flow of IR£10.9 million for 1976. However, the negative flow for 1978 is increased to IR£7.712 million, and for 1979 to IR£11.239 million due to repayment of this loan.[26] Hence, the break in the link between sterling and the Irish pound was preceded by a net outflow of funds, and a subsequent net inflow of funds in 1980.

The devaluation of sterling in 1967 was associated with a rise in interest rates and restrictions on credit in the UK. These policies were continued in 1968 due to continuing pressure on sterling.[27] The year 1976 was the most recent year of this study, in which there was large-scale speculation against sterling, resulting in a $:£ exchange rate of 1.57 for a time.[28] It is likely that rising interest rates, credit controls and devaluation pressures will be associated with an outflow of funds from the foreign-owned corporate sector, due to repayment of intra-group loans, payment of dividends, and other payments abroad. This outflow of funds, in turn, is likely to give rise to further credit restrictions. As indicated in the first section of this chapter, Ireland experienced largely the same monetary and credit conditions as the UK until the break in parity with sterling in 1979. However, this does not explain the net outflows for the period 1978 to 1979. It is likely that these outflows were the result of anticipations of a split between sterling and the Irish pound, and an expected devaluation of the Irish pound compared with sterling.[29]

A key aspect of the overall balance of payments flows examined is the movement in intra-group short-term borrowing. The amount and changes in intra-group short-term borrowing partly arises from leading and lagging operations which one author states to be 'by far the most widespread technique used by multinationals and other operators in avoiding currency risks'.[30] Leading and lagging refers to the pattern of payments or receipts of foreign currency. For example, delayed receipt of payment for exports, is referred to a lagging, or alternatively advance payment for imports is referred to as leading.[31] An accurate estimate of leading and lagging operations would require data relating to all currency transactions, and also for a shorter period than one year.

Trade credit received and extended is likely to be an important part of leading and lagging operations, but in the case of MNCs leading and lagging could also arise from other intra-group transactions. Mottiar and O'Reilly have examined trade credit received and extended for Ireland, and the distribution of currencies used in importing and exporting for 1980-81. They report that import credit exceeded export credit for both years, but that there was a marked fall in export credit for 1981, to the benefit of the balance of payments. It is interesting to note that while the aggregate flows were dominated by firms operating in the food, drink, and tobacco sectors, which are predominantly Irish owned, other sectors, such as the mechanical and electrical industries sector, which are predominantly foreign owned, had different trade-credit patterns, which are less favourable to the balance of payments.

For most years long-term capital flows were not very important for the study group compared with intra-group flows. The years 1976 and 1980 had the largest capital inflows due to increases in the share capital of one of the oil companies.

The overall sum of the flows considered amounted to an inflow of IR£6.87 million, which though positive, is not a very large amount. It is also of interest to note that it is possible for firms to retain all or nearly all their profits and still transfer an equivalent or greater amount of funds to the parent company or fellow subsidiaries. For example, in the year 1972 dividends for the study group amounted to IR£2.09 million and retentions IR£4.1 million, but there was a net outflow to the parent or fellow subsidiaries of IR£7.5 million. This was largely due to an outflow of intra-group short-term borrowing.

Published Irish estimates of aggregate net direct investment (which include both long-established and new firms) show positive capital flows for each year 1964 to 1980, with the exception of the year 1969.[33] These figures exclude unremitted profits,[34] and they also exclude dividends paid abroad. For the period 1961 to 1970 net direct investment flows into Ireland have been estimated by McAleese[35] to have amounted to IR£113.2 million, or 33 per cent of net capital flows, and gross direct investment flows into Ireland, for the same period, are estimated to have been IR£127 million.[36] This latter sum was broken down into IR£31 million in mining, IR£84 million in manufacturing, and IR£12 million in land purchases.

McAleese[37] has also estimated net foreign exchange earnings of 'new industry' operating in Ireland for 1974. 'New industry' would mostly be foreign owned. The study concludes that 'any reasonable set of calculations would show new industry as a major earner of foreign exchange'. For the year 1974 exports of 'new industry' were estimated at IR£579.9 million, and imports at IR£222.2 million, resulting in a trade surplus of IR£257.7 million. From this surplus repatriated profits are deducted, and other payments abroad which are estimated at IR£83.2 million, resulting in a net surplus of IR£174.7 million. This calculation does not include capital flows (loans, equity shares, etc) nor intra-group current account flows. Table 5.4, column 3, shows intra-group current account flows may be quite large and vary from positive to negative from year to year. This is also borne out for UK firms in Annex 5.II, column 5. In conclusion, an estimate of current account foreign exchange earnings may be be quite different from current account foreign exchange flows, or overall balance of payments flows.

Estimates published by the US and UK governments of foreign direct investment capital inflows, plus dividend pay-ments and payments for licences and royalties, show alternating positive and negative flows from year to year. Annex 5.I shows some balance of payments flows for US firms in Ireland for the period 1973 to 1980. Excluding payments for Research and Development, flows are positive for every year except 1973. If Research and Development payments are included for the years for which they are disclosed, 1973 to 1979 (inclusive), flows are also negative for the years 1977 and 1979. The pattern thus appears to be one of alternating positive and negative flows. The year 1979 was the only year of coincident negative flows with firms in the study group, and the years 1974 and 1975 were years of coincident positive flows.

Annex 5.II shows some balance of payments flows for UK direct investment in Ireland for the years 1965 to 1979. These flows include dividend payments abroad as well as payments for licences and royalties. Negative flows occurred in the years

1968, 1970, 1972, 1975-77, and 1979. As for US direct investment, the pattern is one of alternating positive and negative
flows. Overall for the period 1965 to 1979 for UK firms, flows
for nine of the fifteen years are of the same sign as those in the
study group, of which the years 1968, 1972, 1976 and 1979
were years of coincident negative flows with the study group.

For the entire period aggregate flows for UK firms are
positive, but if 1978 is omitted aggregate flows are negative.
This is because of a large positive flow on intra-company
account of £87.2 million for 1978. For the period 1973 to 1980
aggregate flows for US firms are positive. However, this
aggregate data may not be comparable to that used in the rest
of this study. Distributions by US firms in US government
statistics refer to payments to the US only. Dividends and
interest paid to fellow subsidiaries are treated in US data as
reinvestments. Hence it is possible that US Government data
overestimates retentions within Ireland, as a US owned firm
could pay dividends outside Ireland to a fellow subsidiary
within the group.[38]

To conclude the examination of aggregate US and UK data,
for three of eight years 1973 to 1980, estimated aggregate net
US flows of foreign direct investment into Ireland are negative,
and flows are negative for seven of the fifteen years 1965 to
1979 for UK firms. In both cases unremitted profits are
excluded, but dividends paid abroad are included, as well as
payments for licences and royalties. The years 1977 and 1979
were the only years in which both US and UK flows were
negative. There is a considerable difference between this data
and estimates of direct investment capital inflows into Ireland.
For the period 1973 to 1979 official Irish estimates of direct
investment capital inflows amount to IR£649.4 million,
whereas estimated inflows of UK and US direct investment,
which would account for the bulk of foreign investment,
amounted to only IR£75.3 million for the same period. The
bulk of this difference is accounted for by the inclusion of
dividends paid abroad, and payments for licences and

royalties, in the data for US and UK direct investment. In addition there may also be: (1) positive flows into Ireland from other countries, such as Germany, Japan, etc.; (2) differing response rates to information collected by questionnaire; (3) omission of flows from or to other countries, for example to tax havens, by subsidiaries of US and UK firms in US and UK government statistics.

Recent revisions to balance of payments data for the years 1979 to 1981 have underlined the need to consider current and capital flows when examining balance of payments effects of MNCs[39]. These revisions were largely made possible by improved data resulting from exchange control regulations. The main effect of these revisions was to increase current outflows "in respect of dividends, profits, and royalties". The bulk of these revisions are due to the operation of MNCs. In addition outflows for various services, such as technical services, were also increased and this may also reflect intra-firm payments. As inflows of direct investment were not adjusted, the net effect of these changes is to reduce the net flow of funds attributable to foreign direct investment, or indeed to increase the magnitude of the net outflow.

In summary, this section has examined financial flows into and out of Ireland by firms in this study group. There was some evidence that financial flows are sensitive to exchange-rate pressures and risk of devaluation. Intra-group short-term flows were also found to be large and to be quite variable from year to year. An examination of US and UK data relating to foreign exchange flows revealed alternating positive and negative flows, and this was contrasted with data on capital flows, which show positive inflows into Ireland for every year 1964 to 1979, with the exception of 1969.

There are two main implications for industrial strategy. Firstly, that MNCs operating in Ireland are likely to be sensitive to exchange-rate risks, and may react to this risk by domestic borrowing and repatriation of funds, which may exacerbate any currency crisis. Secondly, concentrating on data relating to capital flows, and ignoring current account flows, may exaggerate net flows of foreign direct investment into Ireland.

CONCLUSION

The first section of this chapter found some evidence that companies in the study obtained an increasing proportion of bank credit in the years 1972 to 1974, but not in later years. Hence firms in this study do not appear to have taken an increasing proportion of bank credit, thus 'crowding out' other firms. However, a comprehensive study of foreign direct investment in Ireland may show different results, due to the growth in the stock of foreign investment in Ireland in recent years, coupled with likely capital market biases which favour MNCs at the expense of domestic firms.

The possible use of 'profit switching' transfer pricing by MNCs generally in Ireland as well as companies in the study was also examined. Aggregate data relating to foreign investment in Ireland was found to be consistent with the use of 'profit switching' transfer pricing, in terms of higher value added, and the extent of inter-subsidiary trade, which provides a means to undertake 'profit switching'. Evidence consistent with the use of transfer pricing in terms of higher value added as a proportion of sales was also found for some companies in this study, particularly for non-manufacturing companies. 'Profit switching' which results in profits being switched into Ireland may occur if a subsidiary exports its output and is thus exempt from profits tax, or if a subsidiary for some other reasons has a lower marginal rate of tax in Ireland than in other countries where the MNC operates. Such use of transfer pricing has little or no effect on Irish tax revenues, but may cause difficulties for other countries. 'Profit switching' transfer pricing which switches profits out of Ireland, where those profits would otherwise be subject to profits tax in Ireland may result in a substantial loss of revenue to the Irish Exchequer.

On the basis of the financial flows examined, companies in the study appear to have had a small positive balance of payments effect. No consistent relationship between the retention of profits in Ireland and corresponding balance of payments flows was found. The variability and size of short-term intra-firm flows was also highlighted.

While overall the firms in this study had a small positive balance of payments effect, the small size of the inflow should not be surprising. Studies of foreign direct investment in other host countries have found negative financial flows. For example, Brooke and Remmers found in a study of MNCs operating in the UK that the outflow of capital for all firms in the study was 1½ times the inflow, and for US-owned firms the ratio was 3½ to 1.[40] Lall and Streeten in their study of foreign direct investment in various Less Developed Countries conclude that while all manufacturing investment had negative balance of payments effects, subsidiaries of MNCs had worse than average effects.[41]

Because of the relatively larger stock of foreign investment in Ireland compared with other countries, the aggregate effects of various financial actions, such as leading and lagging payments, is to tie the Irish economy much closer to events in the international economy. Changes in the Irish economy relative to other economies also have a greater effect than would otherwise be the case. Exchange controls, and restrictions on the movement of capital into and out of Ireland, which originated from the period when the Irish pound was part of the sterling area, are thus unlikely to be removed.[42] Perversely, perhaps, one effect of such barriers on domestic firms, as Lessard remarks,[43] is likely to be a stimulus to the 'growth of MNCs which can bypass the affected markets'.

It would be presumptuous to suggest policy options on the basis of such a small study group. Nevertheless this study does suggest two main areas worth further enquiry. First of all, the question of how MNCs finance themselves needs to be comprehensively examined. This examination would also throw some light on the question of the size of both capital and current inflows associated with foreign direct investment. Secondly, there is the question of how MNCs react to exchange risk, and the possibility of devaluation. There is a need for much greater information relating to both MNCs' financing and exchange rate flows. This is particularly true of certain sectors and firms (electronics, aluminium) which account for large values of imports and exports. The policies of such companies in relation to foreign exchange flows and exchange risk, should be an important variable in managing exchange rates and currency reserves.

In addition, to a certain extent there is a trade off between monitoring and control. Greater information about MNC foreign exchange flows may obviate the need for exchange controls in response to a future currency crisis. A considerable volume of data relating to foreign exchange flows is already collected, and this information should be used in formulating options for industrial policy. For example, to the extent that exchange-rate risk is seen as an obstacle to financing investment, or results in destabilising flows across the exchange rate, with resulting fluctuations in interest rates, there may be a case for reallocating fiscal incentives from a package of grants and tax relief to one of exchange-rate guarantees and interest-rate subsidies for certain sectors or products. Such a policy option would be given added weight if export tax relief and a 10 per cent corporate tax rate is effectively neutralised because capital exporting countries (such as the US) perceive these fiscal incentives as helping US based companies to avoid US corporate taxes through the use of 'profit switching' transfer pricing.

FOOTNOTES AND REFERENCES

1. The author would like to thank the editors of this book for helpful comments, as well as Robin Murray and Rafique Mottiar. Remaining errors, omissions and inaccuracies are solely the responsibility of the author.

2. This may be partly explained by the difficulty in obtaining relevant data. See Stewart, J.C. 'A Study of the Financing of Multinational Companies in Ireland 1964-'80', *Journal of Irish Business and Administrative Research*, Vol. 4, No. 2, (1982), p. 85.
3. A more detailed description of the firms included in the study is contained in Stewart, *ibid.*, pp. 72-4.
4. Hymer, S. H., *The International Operation of National Firms*, (Cambridge, Mass.: M.I.T. Press, 1976), p. 179.
5. See Lessard, D. R., 'Transfer Prices, Taxes, and Financial Transfers Within the Multinational Corporation', in Hawkins, R.G. (ed.), *The Economic Effects of Multinational Corporations* (Greenwich, Connecticut: JAI Press, 1979), p. 104.
6. Stewart, J. C., *op. cit.*, Table (3), p. 77.
7. Brooke, M. Z. and Remmers, H. L., *The Strategy of Multinational Enterprise* (London: Longman, 1970), p. 188, and Robbins, S. M. and Stobagh, R. M., *Money in the Multinational Enterprise* (London: Longman, 1974), p. 188.
8. Lall, S. and Streeten, P., *Foreign Investment, Transnationals and Developing Countries* (London: MacMillan, 1977), p. 118.
9. Hawkins, R. G. and Macaluso, D., 'The Avoidance of Restrictive Monetary Policies in Host Countries by Multinational Firms', *Journal of Money, Credit and Banking*, Vol. IX, No. 4 (1977), pp. 562-71.
10. Stewart, J. C., *op. cit.* Table (4), p. 79.
11. For a more detailed description of transfer pricing and its use in shifting liquid assets see Lall, S., 'Transfer — Pricing by Multinational Firms', *Oxford Bulletin of Economics and Statistics*, Vol. 4, No. 3 (1977), pp. 353-71; and Murray, R. (ed.), *Multinationals Beyond the Market* (Brighton, Sussex: Harvester Press, 1981). Murray, R. (ed.) chapters 3-7 has interesting descriptions of transfer pricing in relation to banana exports from Central America, copper exports from Zambia, aluminium exports from Greece, and the use of transfer pricing in various service industries. Penrose, E. T., *The Large International Firm in Developing Countries* (London: Allen and Unwin, 1968), chapter 6, describes the use of transfer pricing by the multinational oil companies.
12. See Lessard, D. R., *op. cit.*, p. 104; or Plasschaert, S. R. F., *Transfer Pricing and Multinational Corporations. An Overview of Concepts, Mechanisms and Regulations* (Farnborough: Saxon House, 1979), pp. 42-5.
13. See Lodin, S., 'International Enterprises and Taxation' in Eliasson, G. and Sodersten, J. (eds.), *Business Taxation, Finance, and Firm Behaviour* (Stockholm: IUI, The Industrial Institute for Economic and Social Research, 1981), p. 115.
14. Vaitos, C., *Intercountry Income Distribution and Transnational Enterprise* (Oxford: Clarendon Press, 1974). Various other empirical evidence is summarised in U.N.C.T.A.D. *Dominant Positions of Market Power of Transnational Corporations — Use of the Transfer Pricing*

Mechanism (New York: United Nations); Stewart, J. C., 'Multinational Companies and Transfer Pricing', *Journal of Business Finance and Accounting*, Vol. 4, No. 3 (1977), pp. 353-71; Murray, R., *op. cit.*

15. There was some published evidence of profit switching by non-charging of interest for one subsidiary in the study. A document published by Readymix Ltd in 1972, relating to the issue of shares, states that the 'company had the use of substantial interest free funds from Ready Mixed Concrete (U.K.) and its subsidiaries during the period 7th December 1966 until 17th February 1971'.

16. McAleese, D., *A Profile of Grant Aided Industry in Ireland* (Dublin: Industrial Development Authority, 1978), p. 41.

17. O'Farrell, P. N. and O'Loughlin, B., *An Analysis of New Industry Linkages in Ireland* (Dublin: Industrial Development Authority, 1980), p. 13. J. O'Leary illustrates the same point using data for 1980 published in 1984. This data shows large variations in net output per employee for various sectors of Irish industry for 1980. For example, the pharmaceutical sector had net output per employee of £75,730, and the chemical sector £30,500, compared with an average of £12,190 for all manufacturing sectors. See J. O'Leary, "Some Implications of the Revision to the Balance of Payments and the National Accounts", *The Irish Banking Review* (Sept. 1984), pp. 13-34.

18. McAleese, D., *op. cit.*, p. 37.

19. O'Farrell, P. N. and O'Loughlin, B., *op. cit.* pp. 8-9 and p. 18.

20. Lall, S. and Streeten, P., *op. cit.*, chapters 7-9, emphasise the need to consider indirect effects, such as the effect of foreign direct investment on local wage rates, and alternative situations without any foreign investment in evaluating the total balance of payments effect.

21. Brash, D. T., *American Investment in Australian Industry* (Canberra: Australian National University Press, 1966), p. 256.

22. Lall, S. and Streeten, P., *op. cit.* p. 118.

23. Profits may also be transformed either by undercharging interest, or by charging no interest. An example of this for one firm in the study is given in footnote 15.

24. The Irish Shell Annual Report for 1976 is an exception.

25. An outflow of funds might also be expected to lead to a run down in cash balances, as well as an incrase in short term borrowing. Cash balances fell in 1966-68, 1970-71, 1975-76 and 1977-78, while bank borrowing increased in 1966, 1968, 1972, and 1976. Although the years are not entirely the same, there is sufficient overlap to support the hypothesis. In addition, a simple Pearson correlation coefficient was calculated between short term bank borrowing and cash balances for the deficit years grouped together. A small negative correlation coefficient was obtained of -0.03. For particular years, a larger negative coefficient was obtained, for example, -0.201 for 1968, and -0.101 for 1979.

26. Irish Shell converted an £8 million sterling loan to Irish pounds in 1979, and it is assumed that these funds were borrowed domestically, rather than from outside the State.

27. Blackaby, F. T., *British Economic Policy, 1960-74* (Cambridge: Cambridge University Press, 1978), pp. 66-7.
28. Bacon, R. and Eltis, W., *Britain's Economic Problem: Too Few Producers* (London: MacMillan, 1980), pp. 131-2.
29. In some cases, accounting periods in the year ending up to June 30 are attributed to the preceding calendar year. Hence, the year 1978 in Table 4 partly reflects the post-February 1979 Balance Sheet positions of some companies when the Irish pound and sterling diverged from parity.
30. Plasschaert, S. R. F., *op. cit.*, p. 62.
31. See O'Connell, T., 'Aspects of Forward Exchange Markets', *Central Bank Annual Report*, No. 1 (1980), pp. 118-40, especially pp. 124-8, for a comprehensive discussion of the technical aspects of leading and lagging.
32. Mottiar, R. and O'Reilly, L., 'Trade Credit and the Distribution of Currencies in Irish External Trade', *Quarterly Bulletin of the Central Bank of Ireland,* summer, 1981, pp. 54-69.
33. Source: McAleese, D., 'Capital Inflows and Direct Foreign Investment in Ireland, 1950-1970', *Journal of the Statistical and Social Inquiry Society of Ireland,* Vol. XII (1971-72), p. 72, and various issues of the *Irish Statistical Bulletin.*
34. Eurostat, *The Methodology of Ireland's Balance of Payments* (Luxembourg: Statistical Office of the European Communities), p. 12. See also Kirwan, F. and McGilvray, J., *Irish Economic Statistics* (Dublin: IPA, 1983), pp. 104-12, for a general description of balance of payments data in Ireland.
35. McAleese, D., *op. cit.*, Table 4, p. 72.
36. *Ibid.*
37. *Ibid.*
38. McAleese, D., *A Profile of Grant-Aided Industry in Ireland,* p. 51.
39. Central Statistics Office, *Revisions to the Balance of International Payments and the National Accounts,* (Dublin: Stationery Office, 1984.)
40. Brooke, M. Z. and Remmers, H. L., *op. cit.,* p. 54.
41. Lall, S. and Streeten, P., *op. cit.,* p. 132.
42. Central Bank of Ireland, 'Exchange Control', *Quarterly Bulletin* (Summer 1979), pp. 33-6.
43. Lessard, D. R., *op. cit.,* p. 122.

Annex 5.I: Some Financial Flows Relating to Aggregate United States Investment in Ireland, 1973-1980

Year	Income[1] (1)	Distri- butions[2] (2)	Equity plus current account flows (3)	Fees and royalties (4)	Capital[3] expenditure (5)	Net flows (6) = (3-2-4)
			$ Million			
1973	78	2	−3	—	48	−5
1974	99	24	51	—	92	27
1975	144	28	58	—	96	30
1976	182	49	106	17	185	40
1977	302	78	100	25	364	−3
1978	295	7	72	33	215	32
1979	410	59	94	48	376	−13
1980	399	26	68	n.a.	261	—

1. Income is defined as the US parent's equity in the net income (after foreign income tax) of their foreign affiliates plus net interest received on intercompany accounts, less withholding taxes on dividends and interest. Affiliates are defined as any company in which a US company has a 10% or greater equity interest.   2. Distributions are defined as payments of interest and dividends to the US parent, US statistics may overstate retentions and hence understate distributions, as no account is taken of financial flows from subsidiary to subsidiary outside the US.   3. This data relates to majority owned affiliates. For 1980, the figure refers to planned expenditure.
Source: Survey of Current Business 1974-81, published by the Department of Commerce of the United States.

Annex 5.II: Some Financial Flows Relating to Aggregate United Kingdom Investment in Ireland, 1965-1979 (excluding oil companies)

Year	Net[1] earnings	Distribu- tions[2]	Deprecia- tion	Net acquisition of share & loan capital	Inter-[3] company account	Credit extended credit received	Royal- ties	Balance of payments effect
				£ Sterling million				(8) (4 + 5 − 2 − 7)
	(1)	(2)	(3)	(4)	(5)	(6)	(7)	
1965	10.3	4.0	4.0	4.6	−5.1	0.2	—	3.5
1966	9.1	6.1	4.4	−10.9	6.5	1.3	—	1.7
1967	10.4	6.3	5.1	0.7	5.3	1.1	—	12.3
1968	12.9	6.9	5.8	1.5	−5.1	−1.1	—	−10.5
1969	15.2	8.4	6.8	6.9	4.8	1.7	—	3.3
1970	14.0	11.2	5.2	1.0	5.3	—	—	−4.9
1971	19.7	8.1	7.9	8.5	0.3	−5.7	—	6.4
1972	21.6	10.5	9.3	4.7	−5.5	−0.7	—	−11.3
1973	34.1	18.1	11.4	12.7	17.1	2.6	0.55	11.15
1974	33.7	13.5	12.6	−0.6	29.7	7.1	0.77	14.83
1975	48.7	14.5	20.6	2.0	−12.0	−3.6	0.64	−25.14
1976	59.0	28.0	21.2	3.2	5.8	13.2	0.70	−19.7
1977	64.6	16.1	25.3	—	9.2	11.6	1.08	−7.98
1978	86.0	20.8	n.a.	16.7	87.2	n.a.	1.11	81.99
1979	96.5	27.5	n.a.	6.2	−12.0	n.a.	0.08	−33.38

1. Net earnings are defined as UK companies share of overseas subsidiaries and associates net profits + interest received + net profits of branches overseas, and after deducting depreciation and overseas tax on dividends.
2. Distributions are defined as dividends received by UK companies + interest received + branch profits. To the extent that branch profits are retained in the branch, distributions are over-estimated. Distributions may also be understated as no account is taken of inter-subsidiary financial flows. 3. This includes credit extended — credit received and subsidiaries, which are separately identified in the published statistics. For some years, loans to branches were not disclosed, and so column (5) relates to loans to subsidiaries only.
Sources: Business Monitor M4 and MA4, 1970 to 1979. *Board of Trade Journal*, May 9, 1969, July 19. 1968, and June 30, 1967, London: H.M.S.O.

6

Technology and Industrial Development: The Irish Electronics Industry in an International Context[1]

Ronan O'Brien

Irish indigenous industry, which accounts for two-thirds of manufacturing employment, bears a strong resemblance to that of Third World countries in terms of its structure. It is concentrated in the same mature industries which are easy to enter and which have low or stagnant long-term rates of growth internationally, notably clothing, textiles, footwear, furniture, food and drink, simple metal products, and building materials.[2] The longer-term outlook in Ireland for many of these industries is poor where they are open to international competition.[3] A shift in indigenous industry structure towards industries with long-term international growth prospects, notably electronics, certain engineering products, software, and perhaps speciality chemicals, is long overdue, but remarkably little progress has been made in this direction over many years.[4] In Ireland, as elsewhere, access to technology has been one of the most important barriers for firms trying to enter the latter group of industries. The problem of technological barriers and how they might be overcome is the general subject of this chapter. Throughout, technology is placed in the context of the other factors in competition.

The other part of the industry in Ireland, subsidiaries of foreign multinational firms, already has the technology, marketing, and managerial expertise as part of their international organisations. Providing financial incentives to get them to set up production units in Ireland seemed an easy way to overcome the barriers to entering international markets. In Ireland, these firms now almost totally dominate the second group of industries mentioned above. One of the issues considered in this chapter is the extent to which these firms can, over the longer term, adequately substitute for building an indigenous capability in the growth industries. This question is given added urgency by the slowdown in new overseas investment to Ireland and the likelihood of it being harder to attract in the future.

The central issue which the chapter addresses is how a country like Ireland which is industrialising relatively late can build up a capability in the group of growing industries, which can provide the base for further expansion over the longer run. Within this general issue, the focus here is on the role of technology in the process, and as a background to this, the first section examines the role of technology in competition. Since the competitive role of technology changes markedly over the life cycle of an industry, this changing role is also analysed in the context of the evolution of industries, and the implications for different types of countries are outlined. In addition to being late industrialising, a second characteristic of Ireland is that it is located on the periphery of Europe, at some distance from the main centres of industry and major markets. This has important implications for its attempts to build up a technological capability in particular, and so the second section examines the effect of location on technological capability. The first two sections then form the background for the rest of the chapter which discusses Ireland's and other comparable countries' attempts to build an electronics industry. By focusing on a single industry we can investigate the development process involved in greater detail; generalisations to other industries can be made where there are sufficient similarities.

A standard prescription for a late industrialising country is to protect its domestic market on a temporary basis while an industry goes through a process of learning the skills and organisational techniques necessary to compete internationally.[5] This is of limited applicability to Ireland because of its third salient characteristic, the small home market, which is too small to allow a build-up of output that would support the necessary learning processes on a sufficient scale. It is argued here, that this combination of circumstances under which Ireland is attempting to industrialise, makes it necessary to adopt measures which lie outside most of the standard prescriptions. Certain foreign countries have faced some or all of these conditions, i.e. late industrialising, peripheral location, and small home market. The third section draws some important lessons for Ireland from their approaches to competing in electronics.

The experience of the electronics industry in Ireland is then examined in the fourth section, in the context of the three factors conditioning its development, listed above. This is followed by a discussion of how the barriers to building a successful and soundly-based electronics industry in Ireland might be overcome. Some implications of the analysis for other industries are mentioned.

The emphasis throughout is on examining the actual *process* by which countries' competitive capabilities can be built-up, with special attention to the technological area. Three vehicles for building these capabilities are considered: (i) foreign multinational firms, (ii) small indigenous firms (in particular trying to repeat the experience of Silicon Valley), and (iii) large indigenous firms. The relative effectiveness of each of these for the purpose is a constant theme for investigation throughout the chapter.

TECHNOLOGY AND COMPETITION

The role of technology in competition varies considerably between industries. In cases where the important technology in an industry is restricted to one or a few firms, it provides a source of monopolistic advantage for these, resulting in super-normal profits and often high growth. Many firms therefore engage in research and development activities (R & D) in order to develop new technologies or improve existing ones. Their results can be protected to a greater or lesser degree from imitators by patenting, copyright of designs, or secrecy, even though these rarely afford sustained protection over a long period of time.[6] Industries, then, differ in the extent to which any commercial benefit from the technological developments made by a firm can be *privately appropriated* by that firm. They also differ in the degree of *technological opportunity* available, i.e the relative ease of achieving new developments for a given expenditure on R & D.[6a]

Differences in appropriability and technological opportunity have a major impact on the level of effort which firms devote to R & D. For example, in industries where patent protection is very strong and therefore appropriability is high, high rates of R & D are prevalent. An example is the pharmaceutical industry where R & D expenditure is 6.3 per cent of value added (US data is used here and in the examples below).[7] In other industries, where the technological opportunity is low, for example in mature technologies, or where appropriability is low — perhaps because the technology is developed mainly by the machinery suppliers to the industry and, therefore, is made available to all competitors — R & D within the industry is low. In textiles and clothing where both of these conditions hold, R & D is 0.4 per cent of value added and technology is relatively unimportant in competition. In the electronics industry, technological opportunity is high in most segments and R & D levels are correspondingly high. Of the five major product groups in the industry, R & D is highest at 11.7 per cent in computers and office equipment. Consumer electronics is the only mature sector, and the corresponding R & D figure is only 1.1 per cent.

There are also differences in appropriability between different firms in a single industry. Large firms with established marketing and production networks can quickly take advantage of successful developments over a large sales volume, and in the course of doing so may also pre-empt the market from later imitators. Smaller firms are often unable to generate a similar volume of sales as quickly, and so reap a smaller benefit, while also allowing imitators the opportunity to enter and establish strong market positions. The length of the *response time* — the period that an imitator takes to copy and come to the market with a competitive product or process — is an important determinant of the degree to which the innovator can exploit its monopoly position. In industries where the technology is developing rapidly, as in most electronics products, the response time is particularly important since products tend to have short life cycles. Firms whose technological capability is close to the 'technological frontier' are in the best position to imitate quickly, and thereby remain competitive in these industries.

In addition to the differences in technological opportunity and appropriability, some technologies display a *cumulative* process of development. In these cases, the outcome of past R & D determines the starting point for future developments, and where the lessons from that R & D can be kept within a firm, those with a strong background of previous R & D are in the best position to make the new developments. Technology followers may then find themselves falling further and further behind. This is the case with the European semiconductor industry, for example. In contrast, where there are *technological disjunctions,* i.e. where new technologies do not come from the old and, therefore, the latter are suddenly and sharply devalued — new entrants may gain dominance if they master the new technologies. These disjunctions occur rarely, however. In electronics, two major developments along these lines took place when semiconductor components replaced valve components in the 1950s and early 1960s, and when microprocessors replaced earlier circuit technologies in the 1970s.

The electronics industry can thus be characterised broadly as follows. Technological opportunity is high due to the rapid succession every three or four years of new generations of semi-conductor components with sharply declining price/performance ratios. When these components are incorporated into the design of products, sharp price reductions and/or major improvements in functional capability are achieved. Firms which get to the market quickly with the new products obviously have an advantage. Consequently, high levels of R & D are prevalent. The economic benefits are appropriated mainly through secrecy and copyright of designs; patents rarely afford much protection in this industry. Appropriability is strongly enhanced by a firm's ability to penetrate the market quickly and pre-empt followers. Rapid imitation requires a high level of ongoing R & D, and usually involves a different design, often with enhanced functionality of the product. Response times are very important in the industry, as the innovating firms may have developed new products by the time the imitator has responded to the first. In general, electronics technology has considerable cumulative features.[8] However, the effect of this is partly tempered by diffusion of the technology out of the firms making the major developments, especially to firms located nearby. This cumulativeness causes considerable difficulties for late entrants in electronics. Because of the importance of product innovation in reducing product cost and enhancing its functionality, relative manufacturing costs *per se* do not play a major role in competition until the technology begins to mature and become standardised in a particular segment. The electronics industry contains many segments and the generalisation above involves considerable simplification; some of the complexities will emerge later.

The role of technology in competition also changes considerably over *the life cycle* of an industry. This has important implications for the stages at which different countries can best compete. As an industry evolves through its various phases of emergence, growth, maturity, and decline, technology becomes less important as a differentiating factor in competition between firms, and other factors become more important. Certain generalisations can be made about the relative importance of the various factors.[9]

New industries generally emerge on the basis of new technologies, and during the *emergent* or *introductory phase,* technology is the critical barrier facing firms trying to enter an industry. If a firm possesses the necessary technological capability, entry to the industry is relatively easy; however, access to the technology is very restricted. At this stage, competition is generally based on the performance qualities of products, and these are sold at a high price to customers who are relatively insensitive to price. There is little opportunity to achieve economies of scale since demand is low as yet, and the industry contains a relatively large proportion of small innovative firms. The pioneering firms have a monopolistic advantage due to their control over the new technology. If this advantage can be maintained at least to some degree until later stages as sales expand, then high rates of return and rates of growth are possible for them.

In the *growth phase* sales are growing rapidly. This makes entry very attractive commercially. The technologies become more widely known or 'diffused', and so, entry is easier. As sales grow, opportunities for scale economies usually arise in production, R & D, marketing, distribution or servicing. Large firms often enter at this stage. Emerging barriers to entry include economies of scale, capital resource requirements, and access to distribution channels.

During the *transition to maturity* the growth in sales slows and overcapacity develops; this leads to sharp competition, with severe price cutting. Many smaller firms with limited financial resources are driven out of the mainstream markets. Some of the smaller firms retire to specialised niches, others leave the industry, and others are taken over or liquidated.

In the *mature phase* there is frequently a fairly stable oligopoly with a small number of dominant firms, although there is considerable variation between industries in this phase. Sizeable economies of scale often exist and competition is largely on price or minor product differentiation accentuated by advertising. At this stage, the technology is fairy easily obtainable and firms from the less developed countries enter, using their extremely low labour costs as a competitive advantage in price competition.

This general picture of the industry life cycle implies that different types of firms have a competitive advantage at different stages of the cycle. Three of these are especially relevant to this chapter. Firstly, *new, technology-based, firms* have their best chance of entering and subsequently growing to a large size if they enter at the introductory stage, or, to a lesser extent, at the early growth stage. Some examples of electronics industry segments which were pioneered by such firms are minicomputers (Digital Equipment Corporation), micro-computers (Apple), 'fail-safe' computers (Tandem) and video games (Atari). This normally happens only in the most advanced large industrial countries, particularly the United States. These have both the necessary technology base and the type of customers who will purchase the initially expensive new products.

Secondly, *small and medium-sized firms in less advanced countries* which do not have extremely low labour costs have their best opportunity of entering during the growth phase. These firms do not have the technology base within their country to enter during the emergent phase, nor the scale to enable them to compete in the volume markets which arise in subsequent phases. The technology is more widely available during the growth phase, and they can avoid volume markets by competing in specialised or 'niche' markets which typically begin to develop during this phase. These firms can take the technology and apply it to specialised tasks. Their competitive strength lies in their capability to do this more effectively and/or more cheaply than other firms which may be larger but less specialised. This optimal strategy would apply to nearly all firms in small developed countries such as Denmark or semi-developed ones such as Ireland.[10]

Thirdly, *firms in very late industrialising countries* such as the NICs or 'newly industrialising countries' (South Korea, Taiwan, Hong Kong, etc.) have their greatest opportunity of entering an industry at a late stage of the life cycle, since they initially have a low technical capability, a relatively unskilled labour force, and cheap labour.[11]

TECHNOLOGY AND LOCATION

There is a strong tendency for technical capabilities to concentrate in certain advanced locations. These locational tendencies affect the stages of the industry life cycle at which firms in a particular country or region can compete, and has major implications for peripheral areas in particular.

New technologies tend to emerge in the large developed countries, especially the United States.[12] Most of the underlying applied R & D work is carried out by large corporations, much of it for military and space purposes. Within those countries R & D facilities are strongly concentrated in a small number of large urban locations.[13] Within each industry, the concentration is even greater. In the United States, for example, Boston and San Francisco (Silicon Valley) are the key centres for electronics R & D, Los Angeles for aerospace, Philadelphia for chemicals, San Diego for biological and related research, and Boston for medical instruments.

New industrial laboratories and new technology-based spin-off firms also tend to be located in those same areas. The attractions are: access to skilled research labour (the single most important factor), to information on other R & D activities in the same field and to information from potential customers, to specialist services and special materials, and proximity to advanced customers who will be the first adopters of new products.[14] These concentrations of R & D facilities mean that not only new technologies but also subsequent major improvements to the technologies originate largely in these locations.

The location of advanced customers who tend to be the first adopters of new products also has an important influence on where the first commercial application or innovation takes place. The early versions of a new technology are very expensive to produce, and military and space customers in particular have been prepared to pay the necessary prices. US firms have had a major advantage in electronics due to the nature and timing of this large demand from the state (see Table 6.1). Firms with a presence in the most advanced countries and regions have an important starting advantage over others, one which may never be overcome. The advanced technology base and the presence of advanced or high income customers for the associated products enables firms in the large developed countries to enter industries at an early stage.

Although there are strong tendencies for industrial technologies to originate in existing advanced locations, they diffuse outwards to other areas over time. The diffusion occurs in several ways: through other firms imitating the technology, through other firms licensing the technology from the technology leaders, skilled personnel leaving for other firms, through the location of production elsewhere by the leaders, and through channels such as specialist consulting firms and equipment suppliers. The diffusion process does not benefit all the less advanced areas equally. Imitation and licensing are usually undertaken first by firms with an advanced technical capability in the same general area of technology, and these early followers generally have a competitive advantage over late followers as a result.

The diffusion of production activities to lower-cost locations does not bring about a diffusion of technical capabilities in equal degree. Being able to manufacture and assemble a

Table 6.1: Military/Space Share of US Production of Computers and Integrated Circuits

Computers		Integrated Circuits	
1954	100%	1962	100%
1955	79%	1963	94%
1956	62%	1964	85%
1957	60%	1965	72%
1958	71%	1966	53%
1959	72%	1967	43%
1960	60%		
1961	55%		
1962	48%		

Source: Schnee, J., 'Government programs and the growth of high-technology industries', *Research Policy,* vol. 7, no. 1 (1978), pp. 8-9.

product does not necessarily require the capability to design and develop the product or process involved. Technical capabilities remain much more concentrated spatially, although a certain amount of diffusion of lower-level technological activities does take place in tandem with production. Furthermore, the less advanced areas to which technology is being diffused are vulnerable to new developments in the advanced areas which make the previously diffused technology obsolete. This limits the diffusion process, which may have to start all over again. This is a problem especially in industries where technology is changing rapidly, such as electronics.

For countries such as Ireland, which are technology followers (rather than leaders), strategies to promote the diffusion or transfer of technologies to their firms are extremely important. Much of the rest of the chapter is concerned with the processes by which this can be achieved.

The discussion so far has largely concerned independent firms. But, as multinational firms (MNCs) operate in more than one country, their institutional practices on where they locate their technical capabilities have to be considered also. This issue is particularly important for those countries which, like Ireland, have based much of their development on MNCs. The host countries want the multinationals to undertake R & D for two main reasons: firstly, so that they will be more rooted in the country and have greater growth potential; secondly, so that they will have greater potential for transferring technology to the rest of the country, for example, through the movement of highly-skilled personnel out of the MNCs.

Essentially, the MNCs follow the general locational tendencies outlined above, with their R & D concentrated in the advanced locations, but with an additional tendency to locate most of it in their own home country. Data for United States multinational manufacturing firms as a whole show that only 8.6 per cent of their R & D expenditures were incurred abroad in 1977, even though a much greater proportion of their employment was located outside the US (Table 6.2). The figures for electronics show an even greater difference.

Table 6.2: Research and Development Activities Located Abroad by US Multinational Firms

	Proportion of R & D expenditures incurred outside U.S.A.	Proportion of employment outside U.S.A.
All manufacturing	8.6%	26.6%
Electronics industry	5.9%	32.2%

Note: Electronics industry data obtained by aggregating US Standard Industrial Classification categories 357, 365, 366, 367, 381 and 382.
Source: US Department of Commerce, *US Direct Investment Abroad, 1977* (Springfield, Va., US Government Printing Office, 1981).

When MNCs do locate R & D abroad it is usually in the larger developed countries, again because these countries provide the experienced R & D personnel and sophisticated support infrastructure necessary.[15] This is further supported by aggregate data on US MNCs (Table 6.3), which shows almost two-thirds of R & D expenditures abroad are incurred in France, Germany, and the UK, even though only about one-third of employment abroad is in these countries.

Table 6.3: Proportion of R & D Activities Abroad Located in the Large Developed Countries (France, Germany, UK)

	Proportion of all R & D expenditures abroad incurred in the three countries	Proportion of employment abroad in the three countries
All manufacturing	58.3%	37.7%
'Electric and electronic equipment'	62.0%	29.0%

Note: 'Electronic and electronic equipment' is SIC category 36. No separate data is published for electronics alone.
Source: US Department of Commerce, *op. cit.*

Within the low proportions of R & D performed abroad on average, certain types of MNC tend to do more than others. Research evidence given below indicates a strong positive relationship between the degree to which a subsidiary has responsibility within the corporation over particular products and their performance of R & D. However, only a minority of MNCs have this form of organisation.

Some less advanced countries which have a low technological capability, notably Ireland, Singapore and Puerto Rico, have adopted a policy of attracting MNCs as the main means of industrialising. The discussion here illustrates the problems with such an approach. Because of the attractions of the more advanced central locations for R & D activities, the multi-nationals tend to carry out little R & D in those less advanced peripheral countries, and therefore this approach does not appear to be a viable one for effecting major improvements in these countries' capabilities for developing technologies. Unless these capabilities are built up, countries remain dependent on branch plant manufacture and low labour costs, and find it virtually impossible to sustain long-term industrial development and improvement of incomes. The next section outlines other, more successful, approaches that have been used in the electronics industry. Some of the approaches have also been applied to other industries in similar circumstances.

THE DEVELOPMENT OF THE ELECTRONICS INDUSTRY IN SELECTED COUNTRIES

Both the requirements for competing at each stage of the industry life cycle, outlined in the first section, and the effect of location on technical capabilities, discussed in the second, have had a major influence on different countries' ability to compete in electronics. These influences are traced out in the remainder of the chapter. The precise effects in each country have depended on the particular conditions facing the firms there, on the starting abilities of the firms, and on the strategies adopted by each government. Three types of country in particular have faced some or all of the three main conditions that we have identified in Ireland: the newly industrialising countries (NICs) such as South Korea, the small developed countries such as Denmark, and the peripheral European countries such as Scotland. The first two are considered here and Scotland is referred to in the next section with the Irish electronics industry. The experience of the countries looked at here contains some interesting lessons for Ireland. In examining in some detail the processes by which the obstacles were overcome and a competence was built up in the various countries, particular attention is given to the types of firms most involved and to the role of technology.

Before discussing the various countries, it is useful to see the share of foreign multinational firms in each (Table 6.4). (Precise figures could not be located for Finland, Norway, and

Sweden; another small developed country, the Netherlands, is included instead.) The table shows that the MNCs have a much greater involvement in the industry in Ireland than in most of the other countries.

Table 6.4: Employment Share of Foreign Multinational Firms in the Electronics Industry: Ireland and Selected Other Countries

Ireland (1983)	90%
Scotland (1978)	90%
Singapore (1976)	84%
South Korea (1979)	45%
Hong Kong (1978)	41%
Taiwan (1981)	40%
Denmark (1978)	37%
Netherlands (1981)	13%

Note: In S.Korea, Hong Kong, Taiwan and Denmark, there is significant involvement of foreign firms with indigenous ones, for example through joint ventures; these activities are included in the figures in the table. If these were excluded, the figures for the MNC employment share would be lower for those countries than shown above.
Sources: Ireland: data from the National Board for Science and Technology; see note to Table 6.5.
Scotland: Booz, Allen and Hamilton, *The Electronics Industry in Scotland* (Glasgow, Scottish Development Agency, 1979).
Singapore: Lim, L., *Multinational Firms and Manufacturing for Export in Less-Developed Countries: The case of the Electronics Industry in Malaysia and Singapore*, Ph. D.Dissertation, Univ. of Michigan, 1978.
South Korea: Kim, W., 'Challenge to US Domination — The Promises of Technology for Newly Industrialising Countries', paper to Financial Times World Electronics Conference, Monte Carlo, 5-7 May 1980.
Hong Kong: *Report of the Advisory Committee on Diversification, 1979* (Hong Kong, 1979), p. 63.
Taiwan: 'Taiwan's spur to technology', *Electronic Business*, Jan. 1982, p. 114.
Denmark: SRI International, *The Electronics Industry in Denmark* (Menlo Park, Cal., SRI International, 1978).
Netherlands: *Financial Times*, Survey on Netherlands, 23 Nov. 1981.

The experience of *the newly industrialising countries* is considered first. Mention is also made of Japan since it has some similarities with the NICs and was used as a model by some of them, although its very large domestic market makes it less relevant for Ireland. The four countries chosen for examination here, South Korea, Taiwan, Hong Kong and Singapore, account for 80 per cent of all electronics exports from the less developed countries.[16] When they began developing their electronics industries within the last 20 to 25 years, they were faced with the problems of starting from a very low base of technology, skills, and international marketing capability, a lack of organisational strength in existing indigenous electronics firms, and poor infrastructure for the industry in terms of suppliers of parts and services. They are also located at a considerable distance from the most advanced countries in North America and Europe. They have had differing degrees of success in overcoming the obstacles facing late industrialising countries; these differences contain interesting lessons in themselves.

Foreign *multinational firms* account for a minority of employment in the industry in these countries, with the exception of Singapore (Table 6.4). The MNC subsidiaries have largely been 'offshore manufacturing platforms' for US and Japanese firms. They have performed the low-skill labour-intensive stages of production, returning the products to the parent companies for the higher-skill stages of final assembly and testing. There has been a slow upgrading of the production facilities as production competence grew and as wages increased, so that some of the plants now incorporate a degree of higher-skill production activities also.

The MNCs have performed virtually no R & D in any of the countries, and have had little impact on the technical capability of indigenous firms. There has been some transfer of production-related skills to indigenous firms, but overall there has been little movement of skilled personnel to those firms. While the MNCs have provided considerable employment, they have contributed little to the longer-term technological development of the industry in these countries.[17]

The *indigenous firms,* on the other hand, have had quite a different pattern of development. Initially, they entered the industry by producing the simple products at the mature stage of the industry life cycle, especially the simpler consumer products such as radios, black and white TV sets, and audio equipment.[18] The technology for these products was easily obtainable and changing slowly, so that there were low technological barriers to entry. The firms competed on price, using their extremely low labour costs as a competitive advantage. The technology was imported in a 'packaged' form, with the licence deals involving product designs, production specifications, supply of parts, and import of foreign technical personnel to oversee production start-up. The products were usually marketed abroad by the technology suppliers under the suppliers' own brand labels.

Later, as the firms' technical capabilities improved through learning the simpler technologies, they developed the capability of imitating foreign technologies and of modifying the technologies imported through licensing. They were gradually able to move to more complex consumer products such as cassette players and colour TVs. The larger firms began to develop their own international marketing capabilities, which helped to overcome some of the biggest problems of peripheral location by feeding back information on market and technology developments to the home country. The industry has grown dramatically in the most successful countries; in Korea, for example, total employment in electronics grew from 30,000 in 1970 to 214,000, or 11 per cent of the workforce in the manufacturing, in 1979.[19]

The success of these countries' industrialising efforts has resulted in higher labour costs, so that other developing countries such as the Philippines and Malaysia began to pose a competitive threat in the products with low barriers to entry. This has forced the firms in the NICs to move to products which are at an earlier stage of the industry life cycle where the technological barriers to entry in particular are higher. Examples are video recorders, instruments, telecommunications products and computer-related products. However, the companies have now run into a major problem. Foreign firms are refusing to license the relevant technology since they do not want to encourage direct competition in products which they are still producing themselves, especially from the more threatening Korean and Taiwanese firms. This has forced the NIC firms to do their own R & D work but this is difficult since the technologies concerned are changing rapidly. The products which they develop are quickly made obsolete by advances in the developed countries.

The larger firms have adopted a number of strategies to overcome the obstacles. They have mounted substantial R & D efforts at home, have bought into small high technology firms in the US in order to transfer the technology back home, and have set up R & D facilities in the most advanced locations such as Silicon Valley, employing highly skilled researchers at very high salaries. However, only the very large South Korean and Taiwanese firms have been able to afford these strategies; the smaller firms such as those in Hong Kong have run into major obstacles.

The state has played a major direct role in the development of the industry in the more interventionist countries: South Korea, Taiwan and Singapore. These countries were very much influenced by the success of the Japanese government measures in the past. By protecting the home market against imports and controlling foreign direct investment aimed at that market, the state provided a protected environment in which the 'infant industry' firms could learn the technology and build up their organisational strength and scale sufficiently to compete in international markets. This approach has proved most successful in the countries with the largest home markets, namely, Japan, Korea and Taiwan, in that order.

Taking some lessons from the Japanese experience, the state in Korea, particularly, identified priority sectors within electronics and intervened to get the large firms from other industries, especially the large industrial groups, to enter these. The aim was to build a small number of firms large enough to compete on export markets. The conferring of benefits on firms was strongly tied to targets, especially targets for exports, and these were enforced. In Korea, as in Japan, the state is now drawing back to some extent from intervening directly since the firms have accumulated sufficient organisational and financial strength to compete internationally with less government support.

Intervention in the structure of the indigenous industry to create large firms has been a powerful mechanism for overcoming rapidly the particular barriers to competing in electronics which firms in the NICs faced. The larger firms have proved to be the best organisational setting for overcoming problems of peripheral location, such as access to information on overseas markets and technologies in a rapidly changing industry. These firms have also proved to be superior at overcoming the technological barriers to development facing late entrants. They have had sufficient scale and organisational strength to negotiate technology licensing and joint venture agreements involving technology transfer from abroad, on reasonable terms. The smaller firms, on the other hand, such as those in Hong Kong and all but a few in Taiwan, have not been able to overcome these obstacles. In these countries the state is trying (in Taiwan) or studying (in Hong Kong) various measures to overcome the critical problems faced by the firms, such as providing state R & D laboratories at considerable cost.[20] These measures have had little impact so far, and the experience of other countries indicates that R & D by state laboratories is a poor substitute for R & D within firms.[21]

The larger firms in each country have played a particularly important role through providing the developmental thrust to the industry as a whole, especially in Korea and Japan. They actively sought out technologies from abroad and implemented them; the technologies were then diffused to other firms in the country concerned. They have also provided a good organisational setting for building up technological, marketing and strategic management skills in the country, and so providing the foundations on which further development could be built.

The *small developed countries* given most attention here — Denmark, Finland and Norway — have each faced broadly similar circumstances in developing their electronics industry. Firstly, they have a small home market. Secondly, they are technology followers relative to the most advanced countries in electronics. Thirdly, they do not have the sophisticated military and space customers to purchase the early versions of new technologies and to finance research into them. They do, however, have advanced customers for the subsequent application of these technologies to specialised tasks — in particular, some highly developed industries and services — and this is a significant advantage. Indigenous firms dominate the industry in each country. Some references are also made here to Sweden, which mainly differs from the other three in that a giant indigenous firm, Ericsson, dominates the industry there, having entered the industry at an early stage, many decades ago.

The three countries have not been very late entrants to the industry like the NICs, nor do they have the forefront technology to pioneer major segments such as computers by entering at the emergent phase. In the 1950s and early 1960s, especially, they used to compete mainly in consumer products such as radios and TVs when these were still in the growth phase. They have withdrawn from these areas as the products matured, and now compete largely in products which are in the growth phase, in very specialised niche markets, especially in the instruments and industrial control area. The three countries have a greater proportion of their output in this product group than any other country, and much greater than most;[23] also, their specialisation in this area is increasing. By pursuing this strategy their firms have been able to attain high international market shares in their very specialised areas, thereby partially overcoming the limitations of having a small domestic market. Exports are a very high proportion of their sales; in Denmark, for example, 85 per cent of the industry's output is exported to a broad spread of countries.[23]

The firms are small-to-medium by the standards of the industry internationally, but are much larger than Irish electronics firms: 73 per cent of employment in the Danish industry is in firms with over 200 employees, whereas in 1983 not a single Irish indigenous firm fell into that category. They compete in their niches on product features, performance and service rather than price, so that they sell at premium prices. Their very high labour costs — about two and a half times those in Ireland per hour[24] — are not considered to be a major competitive disadvantage by the firms, because price is not a key factor in competition for them.[25]

The technological strategy adopted in these countries has essentially been one of applying electronics technology to specialised tasks such as control of particular types of machinery, or measurement in specialised areas such as laboratories. This has involved buying in fairly standard components or modules and assembling them into products or systems, with large amounts of design and software involved. A base of advanced customers within the country in the applications areas has played a very important role, since developing applications-oriented products requires close interaction with the customer to meet the latter's precise needs. Meeting these requirements is the main competitive characteristic of the products when they are subsequently marketed. The following are some examples of specialised electronics products developed on the basis of sophisticated domestic industries and then successfully sold internationally:

Denmark: food processing and food processing machinery
— instruments and controls for the industry
Finland: wood processing and wood processing machinery
— plant automation systems for the industry
Sweden: banking — banking terminals

Norway: shipping — satellite communication for ships
shipbuilding — numerical controls for machine
tools to automate manufacture of ships.

The larger firms have provided the growth and
developmental thrust to the industry in each country, as in the
NICs discussed above. The growth has mainly come from those
firms penetrating export markets, especially in Europe. The
larger firms can spend a lot of money on R & D, supporting
new product developments which have a long payback period
and which usually take two to four years to develop. They can
also fund the large sales and service expenditures abroad that
the niche applications strategy involves. Entry by large industrial groups with considerable finance and organisational
strength has had a major impact. A partial exception to this is
Denmark, where many of the firms are independent entities; it
is interesting to note, therefore, that the growth of Danish
firms is often limited by lack of funds.[26]

The state has sometimes played a direct role in starting up
firms in key areas of opportunity through state-owned firms
and joint ventures with private firms. It is notable that this has
happened especially in Finland, which was the last of these
countries to industrialise and consequently had a much more
limited base of firms to start with than the others. It has had
mixed success in these efforts, ranging from an ill-conceived
initiative to manufacture a mature standardised product, TV
picture tubes, to highly successful paper-mill automation
systems exported to the US and Canada. In Sweden and
Norway there have been similar but less frequent initiatives by
the state in areas considered to be of strategic economic
importance to the country: minicomputers and computer
terminals (Sweden) and numerical controls for machine tools
(Norway). In both cases, the efforts have provided an important foundation of skills and organisational capabilities for the
subsequent development of the industry in the country.

Apart from these initiatives, the main direct role of the state has been the important one of early purchaser of new sophisticated products such as medical equipment and tele-communications products. The technology development work has been done almost exclusively by the firms themselves rather than by the higher education sector or by state research institutes. This is appropriate to an applications strategy where fulfilling the precise needs of the target customer group is vital.

In summary, then, the three small developed countries, Denmark, Norway and Finland, have quite successfully overcome the barriers which they faced in competing inter-nationally in electronics. Firms in these countries have avoided price competition in volume markets where there are consider-able economies of scale. Their larger firms, especially, have built a foundation for further development and growth in international markets by developing considerable expertise in applying technologies to specialised tasks and in marketing the products internationally.

There is a stark contrast between the experience of the countries examined in this section and the Irish case examined below, despite many similarities in the obstacles faced. The most successful of the NICs and the small industrialised coun-tries have built up a base of large indigenous firms which are a source of self-generating expansion and which have provided a means of overcoming the technological barriers to entering international markets in electronics.

THE ELECTRONICS INDUSTRY IN IRELAND

The obstacles facing the development of an electronics industry in Ireland have some important similarities with those faced by the NICs and the small industrialised countries. In Ireland's case there have been three central conditioning factors. Firstly, Irish firms are late entrants to the electronics industry, and so have to compete with existing sophisticated firms abroad. Related to this, since Ireland is a late industrialising country its firms do not have a local base of sophisticated cutomers, nor ready access to the range of components and services available to firms in more advanced countries. Secondly, being on an island located on the periphery of Europe at some distance from the largest and most sophisticated markets, firms in Ireland face problems of access to information on technology, markets, and competitors — a considerable problem in a rapidly-changing industry — and also higher transport and selling costs. Thirdly, Ireland has a small home market and this makes it difficult for an 'infant industry' to grow and learn in an environment which is unprotected from advanced competitors abroad. These factors have affected both the multinational and indigenous firms in Ireland, though in very different ways, as we see below.

In order to examine a number of key issues in the development process of the electronics industry, the Science Policy Research Centre (SPRC), University College Dublin, carried out an in-depth study for the National Board for Science of Technology at the end of 1980 and during 1981.[27] Much of the material on the Irish industry used below is based on the research for that study, which included a survey of the industry in 1981. Details of the gathering of data in the study are given in the appendix to the chapter. The data used in this section are from that study unless otherwise indicated.

Despite the three obstacles mentioned, the Irish electronics industry grew very rapidly in the 1970s, particularly in the latter half of the decade, and in the early 1980s. Many firms commenced production and employment doubled (Table 6.5).

The growth was largely due to new multinational firms entering the country. In 1981 multinational firms employed 87 per cent of the total (1983: 90 per cent); by 1981 new indigenous firms established from early 1973 employed only 500 people, 4 per cent of the total. The MNCs, which are mainly US firms (71 per cent of MNC employment in 1981), use Ireland essentially as a low cost production location within the EEC (including taxes in 'costs' here). The low costs are due

Table 6.5: Growth of the Electronics Industry in Ireland

	1973	1983
Employment	7757	16,000
— as % of total manufacturing	3.8%	8.0%
Number of firms	36	189
Gross output	£52.5m	£1,410m
Exports	£28m	£1,350m
— as % of total manufactures	6.1%	31.0%

Note: Export figures include an estimate for Shannon Freeport Zone, based on survey data. Gross output figures for 1983 calculated from exports, based on 1981 survey data on percentage of output exported.
Sources: 1983: data on employment and number of firms in electronics from a database developed by the author for the National Board for Science and Technology, compiled from a wide variety of sources; exports data from *Trade Statistics of Ireland.*

to low corporate taxation, high direct financial incentives, and relatively low labour costs; these more than offset the logistics cost penalties of serving the European market from Ireland's peripheral location. On the other hand, the three obstacles to competing from Ireland outlined above had a much greater impact on the indigenous sector's development, effectively offsetting the financial inducements available, as we indicate later.

We first examine the contribution of *the multinational firms* to the longer-term development of the industry. In doing this, we consider the type of production activities located in Ireland, the extent to which they locate the key competitive functions in the country, and the external effects of these firms on the rest of the industry (i.e. external economies).

The MNCs in Ireland have been engaged in more complex production activities than the offshore MNC plants in the NICs and Puerto Rico. The latter are largely engaged in the lower-skill stages of production, particularly the assembly of semiconductor components, consumer products, and computer sub-assemblies. Apart from some consumer products, these are then sent back to the parent company for the higher skill stages of final assembly and testing. The Irish plants tend to carry out both types of activity, sending the final products on to the European market. The most highly skilled production-related activities of these firms, plant engineering and wafer fabrication, however, still tend to be kept in the home country. Also, the MNCs in Ireland produce more complex products in addition to the simpler ones assembled in the NICs, including computers, instruments and telecommunications equipment. Table 6.6 shows the distribution of employment and firms by main product group.

Table 6.6: Employment and Number of Firms by Main Product Group

| | Employment | | | No. of Firms | |
	MNCs	Indig. firms	Total	MNCs	Indig. firms
Components	2946	167	3113	23	6
Computers, peripherals, office equipment	3847	34	3881	13	1
Consumer products	1760	536	2296	11	10
Instruments and industrial control	1492	89	1581	17	9
Telecommunications	1537	930	2467	9	8
Subcontract assembly	10	20	30	1	1
Total	11,592	1776	13,368	74	35

The multinational firms have provided considerable employment and exports for Ireland, as well as some opportunities for sub-supplier firms. However, they have not provided the developmental thrust to the industry as a whole which the leading indigenous firms have done in the more successful of the NICs and in the small developed countries. The main contribution which the MNCs could have made towards building a base for the industry's self-development would have been to locate the key competitive functions in most electronics segments, i.e. R & D and marketing, in Ireland. These activities can have an impact on the industry in two main ways: firstly, through increasing the potential for subsequent expansion of the subsidiaries themselves; secondly, through a number of external effects. Chief among the latter are the creation of spin-off firms through personnel with the key competitive skills leaving and setting up their own firms, the movement of similar personnel to existing firms, and encouraging the growth of a base of sophisticated services to the industry which would be of benefit to other firms.

Research and development was performed by 22 of the 74 MNCs, i.e. 30 per cent, in 1981. However, the amount carried out by most of those firms was very small; only four had more than ten people (full-time equivalent) engaged in R & D (Table 6.7, col. 2).

Table 6.7: Size of R & D Effort by Electronics Companies Performing R & D

Size of R & D Effort (No. of people engaged, full-time equivalent)	No. of Firms	
	MNCs	Irish
20 +	3	1
10 — 20	1	—
5 — 10	9	1
2 — 5	3	4
0 — 2	2	6
Total	18	12

Notes: (1) Full-time equivalent: e.g. two people engaged 50 per cent of their time = 1 person full-time equivalent.
(2) Precise data on R & D effort in terms of number of people engaged (full-time equivalent) could not be obtained for three Irish firms and four MNCs. However, other information indicates that those Irish firms have less than five people and the MNCs less than ten people engaged (full-time equivalent), and so would not affect the overall pattern as indicated by the table. All R & D-performing firms in the industry in 1981, apart from these seven, are included in the table.

Table 6.8: Research and Development in the Electronic Industry of Ireland and Selected Other Countries (R & D expenditure as % of sales)

UK (1981)	10.8%(1)
USA (1982)	8.1%(2)
Denmark (1979)	8%
Finland (1981)	7.1%
Japan (1982)	6.4%
S. Korea (1979)	1.3%
Ireland (1982)	0.9%
Taiwan (1981)	0.3%

Note: (1) Approximately 50 per cent of the UK figure is accounted for by R & D carried out by firms on military projects (Soete and Dosi, p.21). In the UK case, unlike the USA, this dependence has had some strong negative effects on the industry. See the references in note 51.

(2) The figure here is obtained by aggregating the sales and R & D figures for the categories 'Electronics', 'Computers', 'Office Equipment', 'Information Processing: peripherals, services', 'Instruments: measuring devices, controls', and 'Semi-conductors'; 'Telecommunications' firms were not included since the figures mix telecommunictions network services with manufacturing activities. Federally funded R & D performed by firms was then added to this figure; this amounted to 28 per cent of the total.

(3) The figures may not be totally compatible across countries since definitions of R & D may vary.

Sources: UK: L.Soete and G.Dosi, *Technology and Employment in the Electronics Industry* (London, Frances Pinter, 1983), Tables 7 and 15.

Denmark: Buhl C., 'Factors in Technological Decisions in the Danish Electronics Industry', in Kristensen, P., and Stankiewicz, R. (eds.), *Technology Policy and Industrial Development in Scandanavia* (Lund, Research Policy Institute, 1981).

USA: 'R & D Scoreboard 1982', *Business Week International*, June 20, 1983. Federally funded R & D in electronics computed from C. Freeman, *The Economics of Industrial Innovation,* (London, Frances Pinter, 1982, Table 1.3a).

Finland: R & D data from OECD, 'International Statistical Year 1981: Finland' (Paris, OECD, 1984, mimeo); output from *Mackintosh Electronics Year Book 1983* (Luton, Mackintosh Publications, 1983).

Japan: *Electronics Industries in Japan: 1983 Edition* (Tokyo, Electronic Industries Association of Japan, 1983).

S. Korea: Kim, W., op. cit.

Ireland: R & D data from National Board of Science and Technology, R & D survey 1982; sales estimated from exports data in *Trade Statistics of Ireland.*

Taiwan: 'Taiwan's Spur to Technology', *Electronic Business,* January 1982, p.114.

Given the dominance of multinational firms in the Irish industry, the result of their level of R & D has been that R & D in the industry as a whole is miniscule by international standards. Table 6.8 shows R & D expenditure as a percentage of sales for a variety of countries. The total quantity of R & D performed in the Irish industry is less than that by single firms of medium size in other countries (e.g. Dataproducts or Teradyne), and even some individual firms in the NICs, for example Samsung the South Korean firm.[28] Also, the proportion of R & D in total activity of the industry had not shown a noticeable increase over time, despite an increase in the absolute amount performed. Calculations from the earlier surveys in 1977 and 1979 both give the same figure as that for 1982 in Table 6.8, 0.9 per cent of sales.

Table 6.9: MNCs — Relationship between (a) Proportion of Firms' Output made only in Ireland and (b) their R & D Activity

(a)	(b)		
% of output made only in Ireland	R & D expenditure as % of sales (arithmetic average)	Proportion of firms not doing R & D (%)	(No. of the sample firms in each category)
90 — 100	7.4	0	(4)
50 — 90	—	—	(0)
10 — 50	2.9	0	(5)
0 — 10	0.8	33	(3)
0	0.4	63	(8)

Note: All the MNCs surveyed (i.e. all the firms in the table) were multi-product firms; the '% of output made only in Ireland' is the proportion of their output accounted for by those products which are made only in Ireland.

Because of the importance of the R & D issue, it was examined in considerable depth in the SPRC study. The electronics MNCs in Ireland were found to conform with the general pattern of R & D location outlined earlier. The R & D of strategic importance to the corporations tended to be centralised in one or two locations, normally in the home country. This usually involved some R & D with a relatively long time horizon, and its attraction to a country would contribute to the sort of advanced technology base necessary for spin-off firms to enter new industry segments during the emergent phase. However, when such facilities were located outside the home country it was always in the large developed countries. The R & D involving lesser developments tended to be dispersed more widely, normally at the production plants for the products.

Despite their low overall level of R & D, certain MNCs in Ireland do considerably more than others. In particular, those that are the sole manufacturers of particular products within the corporation tend to do much more R & D (Table 6.9).

The relationship in the table is a very strong one; very few firms surveyed deviated from the general trend. As a result, the rank correlation coefficient between the proportion of firms' output which is made only in Ireland and their R & D expenditure as a proportion of sales is 0.84, significant at the 0.05 per cent level. The firms' other products (i.e. those not included under (a) in the table) are already being made at other plants in the corporation, and the development work on them has usually been allocated already to those plants. The survey also indicated that the same firms which have a high proportion of output made only in Ireland have a much greater tendency to do the type of R & D that is aimed at *new products,* as opposed to R & D on product modifications or on processes. A parallel study in Canada came to similar conclusions, based on case studies of four firms, and used the term 'world product mandate' to describe the subsidiary's role.[29] Additional evidence is provided by US Department of Commerce data on US manufacturing firms as a whole: (a) firms in those product groups within electronics which are more fragmented and where the subsidiaries tend to have more product autonomy (e.g. instruments and control equipment), carry out more R &

D per employee abroad than (b) those which have a more centralised organisation (e.g. firms in computers and related products).[30] These findings could be of considerable importance to host countries which are trying to attract R & D and other development-aiding functions of multinational firms, and to future industrial policy in Ireland. It must be pointed out, however, that only a minority of MNCs are organised in this way.

A strong association was also found between the amount of R & D carried out and the degree of responsibility the Irish subsidiary has for *marketing,* particularly for the higher level marketing functions such as product planning. Given the importance of information flows from marketing to R & D, especially in a rapidly changing industry, this is not surprising. The information from marketing is necessary to give commercial direction to R & D, and this exchange is difficult to conduct at a distance. However, the marketing function appears to be even more subject to locational pulls than R & D, with the emphasis on being centrally located in the larger markets. This is particularly true of the higher level marketing functions: only one in seven of the surveyed firms had a significant role in product planning (the proportion is likely to be even lower for the population as a whole, because the sample was deliberately biased towards R & D-performing firms and these tend to have more marketing responsibility than other firms). The problem of location of the marketing function is accentuated by the tendency of US and Japanese firms to set up marketing subsidiaries in Europe when initially exporting from the home country, before setting up a manufacturing facility. These marketing subsidiaries are normally located in centres such as Brussels or Geneva, and are unlikely to be relocated to Ireland subsequently.

Because the MNCs rarely carry out the higher-level activities in Ireland, the level of *technical skills* in the industry as a whole is considerably lower than in the more advanced countries such as the USA and Denmark, but higher than the NICs (Table

6.10). The percentage of engineers, technicians, and non-craft production workers in the table are particularly important indicators in the context of this chapter. The skill profile is higher in Scotland largely because the MNCs are engaged in the production of more complex products in smaller volumes, especially mainframe computers and military equipment.[31] Within Ireland, the levels are very similar in the MNCs and the indigenous firms, because the latter also tend to have a low technical profile.

The *external effects* related to technology which the MNCs have are mainly indicated by (a) the extent to which new spin-off electronics firms are created, (b) the mobility of skilled personnel, and (c) technology service linkages. First, the level of spin-offs from the MNCs have been extremely low. Four of these spin-offs existed in 1981, with only 42 employees between them, and none had truly innovative products at the time of start-up.[32] The type of process which has occurred in Silicon Valley, where there has been a high rate of new innovative firms spinning off from existing ones, has not taken place in Ireland. Given the requirements necessary for this process to happen, including a base of sophisticated research and development work in the existing firms, this is to be expected. The same overall pattern is found in Scotland and in all of the other countries where MNCs predominate, and for the same reasons.

Second, there appears to have been little movement of skilled personnel to the indigenous electronics firms. An in-depth study tracing skilled personnel who had left two large electronics MNCs in Ireland found that when they had gone to other manufacturing firms, it was overwhelmingly to other MNCs.[33] The same mobility patterns have been found for multinational electronics companies in Singapore and Malaysia.[34]

Third, there has been a low level of usage of Irish technology services such as contract R & D work. All of the MNCs doing R & D used Irish technology services either from state institutes or

Table 6.10: Skill Profile of the Electronics Industry in Ireland and Selected Other Countries
(% of total employment in each skill category)

	Singapore(1)	Ireland	Scotland	UK	USA	Denmark
Managerial, Administrative, Clerical, Supervisors	N.A.	23	35*	34	24	} 29
Engineers/ Professional Technical	} 6	5	9	10	17	
Technicians		9	13	14	11	} 32
Craftworkers		3	8	8	10	
Non-craft production workers		57	35	31	32	} 39
Other workers	} 90-95	3	*	3	6	
Total	100	100	100	100	100	100

Notes: (1) Data on Hong Kong indicates a skill profile broadly similar to Singapore; the categories were not strictly compatible with those in the table so they have not been included here. *Report of the Advisory Committee on Diversification, 1979* (Hong Kong, 1979), p.62.
(2) For Scotland, 'Other workers' is included with 'Managerial, etc'.
(3) N.A. = not available.
Sources: Singapore: Lim, L., *op. cit.*
Ireland: Engineers and technicians from SPRC study; other categories from Murray, P., and Wickham, J., 'Technocratic Ideology and the Reproduction of Inequality: the Case of the Electronics Industry in the Republic of Ireland' in Day, G., and Robbins, D (eds.), *Diversity and Decomposition in the Labour Market* (London, Gower Press, 1982).
Scotland: Booz, Allen and Hamilton, *op. cit.*
UK: Brayshaw, P. and Lawson, G., *Manpower and Training in the Electronics Industry,* EITB Reference Paper RP/5/82 (Watford, Engineering Industry Training Board, 1982), p.11.
USA: Pacific Studies Center, *Global Electronics Information Newsletter,* Sept. 1982.
Denmark: SRI International, *op. cit.*

from the higher education sector, but in almost all cases these made up only a small part of the subsidiary's R & D efforts. There was a low level of usage of the higher education sector, particularly of the universities; this is partly due to the lack of basic or applied research being undertaken by the firms in

Ireland. The firms' R & D activities are very much at the development end of the spectrum which runs from basic research, through applied research, to product or process development. Universities rarely supply services to this kind of development work in other countries, and when companies look for such services, they tend not to go to universities.[35]

In summary, then, the electronics MNCs in Ireland are strongly affected by the particular circumstances of the country. They locate little of the key competitive function of R & D in Ireland, partly because MNCs tend to locate most of it at home in any case, but also because Ireland has a number of disadvantages for R & D for these firms. The corresponding advantages are available in relatively few locations in the world and cause it to be heavily concentrated in these few areas. Largely because of the limited scope of their activities in Ireland, they have relatively little external technological and other effects on the rest of the industry. They do not act as a driving force for the industry as a whole in the way large indigenous firms in other countries have done, especially in the field of technology development. In addition, the MNCs will be harder to attract in the future; other European countries have increased their incentives and promotional efforts sharply, in many cases copying the innovative efforts of Ireland's Industrial Development Authority in marketing their countries abroad as a location for industry.

The findings reported here on skill levels and research and development in the MNCs indicate a higher level of both than the Telesis Report claimed.[36] The conclusions drawn here on the longer-term outlook for significant improvements in the levels of skills and of the key competitive functions of R & D and marketing are similar to those of the Telesis Group, however. Both studies agree on the reasons for this — the locational attractions of the MNCs' home base and of the large developed countries for these functions, and the difficulty of overcoming these forces in Ireland.

It is interesting to compare the experience of Ireland with

that of Scotland, another peripheral country within Europe, where the firms have faced many of the same obstacles as those in Ireland. Even though Scotland is obviously not a late-developing country, its indigenous firms have entered the electronics industry at a late stage. It is similar to Ireland in that subsidiaries of multinational firms dominate the industry (Table 6.4). The MNCs there have broadly similar production activities to those in Ireland. The attraction of the vital functions of R & D and marketing towards the more central areas has hindered the industry's development there also. Even though Scotland has had a large MNC presence in electronics for a much longer period, from the 1940s and 1950s, a recent study concluded that 'the majority of non-Scottish operations were established as manufacturing satellites and few have progressed significantly beyond this role'.[37] Few firms have spun off from the MNCs and there has been very limited development of an indigenous electronics sector.

The indigenous firms in Ireland have had quite a different experience from the indigenous firms in the more successful NICs (South Korea and Taiwan) and the small developed countries discussed earlier. In facing the barriers outlined earlier, Irish firms have not had the competitive advantage of extremely low labour costs such as the firms in the NICs have had. Hence they could not successfully enter international competition in segments of the industry which were in the mature phase, when technology is usually widely available, as did the firms in the NICs. The remaining options were to enter in the emergent or growth phases, when technology is usually an important differentiating factor between firms' competitiveness. The extent to which they were successful in either of these is now examined.

The indigenous sector has failed to grow to a significant size; total employment amounted to 1776 in 1981, 13 per cent of the total industry, in 35 firms. The individual firms are very small; in 1981, only five had more than 50 employees (Table 6.11).

Even the five largest were very small compared with their international competitors and their international market share in the segments in which they were competing was minute.

Table 6.11: Size Distribution of Irish Indigenous Firms, 1981
(no. employed)

Size	No. of companies	Total employment
501 +	1	800
201 — 500	1	272
101 — 200	—	—
51 — 100	3	185
21 — 50	8	287
11 — 20	12	175
1 — 10	10	57
Total	35	1,776

The dynamic phenomena associated with places like Silicon Valley have not occurred in Ireland. Firstly, a high rate of new technology-based firms entering segments which are in the emergent or early growth phase and growing rapidly has not occurred. Table 6.12 compares the average rate of growth of indigenous Irish firms and firms in the US; dramatic differences between the two countries are apparent. Even though the US figures probably overstate the average size of their firms since it covers the members of the American Electronics Association, and is therefore likely to have a more complete coverage of the larger firms, *no* Irish firms has managed to grow at the average US rate as given in the table.

Secondly, only six of the thirty-five indigenous firms were founded through spin-off from electronics firms, four from MNCs and two from Irish firms, and only one of these was founded on the basis of even a moderately innovative product,

Table 6.12: Average Growth of Indigenous Irish Firms Compared with Firms in the USA
(Average employment size vs. length of time established)

		Length of time (yrs.)				
		0 — 5	6 — 10	10 — 15	16 — 20	20 +
Average	USA	91	363	690	1,879	13,099
Employment	Ireland	18	31	15	289	8
per Firm	Ratio of USA to Ireland	5:1	12:1	..(1)	7:1	..(1)

Note: (1) These categories contain two or less Irish firms; this is regarded as being too few for the comparison to have any meaning.
Source: USA: *Small Business and Innovation*, Joint Hearings before the Select Committee on Small Business, United States, Ninety-Fifth Congress (Washington, US Government Printing Office, 1978).

again contradicting US experience.[38] About six other firms have spun off between the SPRC study and the early part of 1984 (again, two from Irish firms and four from MNCs); all have started very small and do not appear to be displaying the dynamic characteristics associated with the US experience. Higher education institutions have also generated start-ups at a low rate — only three firms, with 32 employees between them by 1981. Despite this overall lack of dynamism, it is of some interest that the most technology-intensive indigenous firms are included in these two groups. The study found that the nine firms originating from these two sources contained 8 of the 14 Irish R & D-performing firms, including those with the highest ratios of R & D expenditure to sales. The other 26 firms, which made up the bulk of the indigenous sector, were mainly in low technology areas. The fact that nearly 80 per cent of these performed no R & D did not augur well for their survival in an industry such as electronics with very short product life cycles.

There has, in fact, been quite a high failure rate among indigenous firms. Seven of the largest indigenous firms in the industry and several smaller, ones, accounting for over 70 per cent of indigenous employment at the time, have either closed or got into major difficulties in the two years since the study was completed. The study indicated that most of the firms concerned had neither the technological resources nor the scale needed to compete internationally in the segments in which they were operating.

Most of the indigenous firms have started in a protected market, mainly in passive components, monitoring or control systems, and telecommunications. The first two product groups have a significant degree of natural protection because of the necessity for close interaction with the customer on customised products and/or transport costs, and telecommunications has been protected by preferential public purchasing. Most of these firms have remained largely within the protected local market. A minority of indigenous firms have exported two-thirds or more of their output, and some of these have had reasonably innovative products, but have been too small to mount sustained marketing and product development efforts on the scale necessary to grow in international markets. Most exports by indigenous firms have gone to the nearby UK market and there has been very little penetration of markets on a wider scale such as continental Europe.

The earlier discussion on technology and competition indicated that in an industry as dynamic as electronics, where technological change continually threatens to undermine firms' market position, firms are required to devote considerable resources to technological improvement, especially to research and development. In this context, the technology development efforts of indigenous firms have been pitifully small. Only two firms had more than five people (full-time equivalent) engaged in R & D (Table 6.7). This can be compared with small US start-up firms, which often have teams of twenty people or more in R & D for one to two years prior to launching their first product on the market — and this does not take into account the difference in the quality of the R & D work between the two countries. The low level of technical skills in the indigenous sector was mentioned in discussing Table 6.10, and is partly due to this low level of R & D.

Large indigenous firms in other industries have had virtually no involvement in the electronics industry. This is in sharp contrast to the experience in other countries, where such firms have usually played a major role. However, they are generally competing profitably in low-risk non-traded activities (packaging, building materials, etc.),[39] and the nature of the electronics industry is very different from these, so diversification into the industry is not very likely given their unfamiliarity with the sector and the higher risk involved. This is especially so when other lower-risk but highly profitable investments in areas more closely related to their existing activities are available to them, and in the absence of policy initiatives to change that situation.

To sum up: indigenous Irish firms have not pioneered new industry segments by entering with highly innovative products in the emergent phase, as the high-growth small firms have done in the United States. Neither have they had the scale or organisational resources to enter and successfully compete internationally at a later stage from a base in Ireland. A small number of firms with technical capability have had modest or reasonable success in specialised or niche areas but even these have generally not displayed the characteristics of rapid growth firms abroad. Given the origins of most of the firms, their organisational and technological characteristics, and the lack of a technology base in the country, it is not surprising that the indigenous firms have failed to overcome successfully the barriers to entry into international competition in electronics from a base in Ireland.[40] They have failed to overcome the obstacles of the small home market, peripheral location within Europe, and late involvement in the electronics industry. How these obstacles might be overcome is now considered.

OVERCOMING THE BARRIERS TO THE INDUSTRY'S DEVELOPMENT

It has been argued here that the electronics sector in Ireland has not developed a base of sufficient strength in the key competitive factors, in either the indigenous or the multi-national firms, which could lead to self-sustained growth and the continual improvement of its competitive position. We go on to consider how the barriers to the development of such an industry in Ireland might be overcome, especially those related to technology. Firstly, in the case of the multinational firms we consider how the forces acting against their locating research and development in Ireland might be counteracted, and whether this can be done sufficiently to bring about a base of the quality required for longer-term development. Secondly, in the case of the indigenous firms, we examine how the obstacles of a small home market, late involvement in the industry, and peripheral location might be overcome and a base of inter-nationally competitive firms created. We consider in turn small high-technology firms and larger firms as candidates for the latter.

Considering the *multinational firms* first, the larger European countries can try to influence these to locate production plants within their boundaries and to perform R & D, by the use of real or threatened trade barriers against suppliers from outside. They can also use access to public purchasing to greater effect as a lever, particularly in computers, tele-communications, and semiconductor components. These 'sticks' have been considerably more effective policy instruments for getting MNCs to do R & D than have 'carrots' such as financial inducements.[41] Small countries like Ireland can use neither of these 'sticks' to much effect since their total markets are so small. In any case, there is some evidence that the R & D functions set up under such duress are often merely tokens to give the appearance of satisfying the demands being made.[42]

The strength of the link with marketing also militates against the establishment of R & D in a peripheral location such as Ireland, given the strong attraction of the marketing function towards the large central markets. But the main disincentive to MNCs is the lack of an existing base of R & D in Ireland, and hence the critical lack of skilled and experienced researchers as well as an infrastructure of suppliers of the technical services and special components and materials which such facilities require; the role of these factors in R & D location was discussed earlier.

One approach to overcoming these disincentives is to offer sufficient financial inducements to the MNCs to get them to locate R & D in the country, on the grounds that there is some level of incentive above which MNCs will do this. The cost of such incentives obviously has to be weighed up against the prospective benefits. These are the extra growth of the subsidiary itself, its increased stability in the country, and the external effects listed earlier such as spin-offs; also the opportunity cost or alternative use of the funds has to be taken into account. A second approach is to build up the technical infrastructure on a large scale through a series or research activities in state or higher education institutes, in order to provide a supply of skilled research labour and contract research services. Other specialised technical services can be built up in conjunction with this, through state bodies or through providing incentives to private initiatives. For both of these approaches, the expenditures required to attract a significant amount of R & D by MNCs are likely to far outweigh the benefits which would result, given the experience of other peripheral locations in trying to attract firms' R & D facilities.[43]

A third approach is to try to identify those MNCs which are most likely to do R & D and whose R & D will have the greatest external effects. Both the expectations from the literature on the organisation of multinational firms and the evidence given here, indicate that those subsidiaries which are the sole producers within their corporation of their products are those most likely to perform R & D; also they tend to do more of their R & D on new products. MNCs which are organised into small, relatively autonomous, product divisions appear to be closest to this, so that the Irish subsidiary is relatively autonomous in terms of both R & D and marketing. These firms are generally in the more fragmented product groups such as instruments and industrial control equipment, which have a wide range of specialised products produced in relatively low volumes. Alternatively, if an MNC is producing standardised volume products but also produces some specialised items, for example specialised printers, then it may be possible that the Irish subsidiary be given responsibility for R & D and perhaps marketing for these specialised products. In fact, some of the Irish MNCs who perform R & D do it in this way. Another type of MNC likely to do R & D is one which has to modify its products to European technical standards or modifies them to customers' requirements,[44] although the R & D in these cases is of lesser quality.

The external effect of firms spinning off is also most likely to occur in Ireland in product areas which are fragmented, containing many specialised niches, and where a specialised technical capability is often the key factor in competition, especially for the smaller start-up firms. Hence spin-offs are most likely to occur in Ireland from the same firms which have just been identified as being most likely to do R & D.

It would not be a major task to identify in greater detail than done here those product groups within the electronics idustry which have the characteristics outlined above. It would be possible to target firms in those groups for priority attraction, using a combination of special financial incentives and the building up of infrastructure in those specialised areas instead of across most of the electronics field. However, while an increased amount of R & D can be built up in the multinational sector by the use of such selective measures, it is highly unlikely in this case as in the previous two approaches, that it would take place on a sufficient scale or quality to have the major development effect on the industry which the larger indigenous firms in other countries have had, without huge expenditures of state funds.

Given the forces acting against the location of R & D in general in peripheral locations like Ireland, it is unlikely that R & D facilities of multinational firms can be attracted to Ireland on a significant scale in other industries either. The latter contention is supported by the very low level of R & D by multinational firms in Ireland in all sectors.[45]

In the case of *the indigenous electronics sector,* the most frequently-promoted idea for its development in Ireland is that of a high rate of technology-based entrepreneurial firms starting up and growing rapidly. This is based on the idea of re-creating the US experience of Silicon Valley in California, particularly, and also Route 128 outside Boston. None of the characteristics of those cases have been repeated in Ireland to date.

The particular conditions needed for such a process to occur are so rarely present that it has happened in very few places in the world. The two cases mentioned are by far the most significant ones, and the few other locations that have displayed such a dynamic phenomenon have done so on a much smaller scale.[46] Earlier parts of the chapter have dealt with the circumstances needed for this phenomenon to take place. Two conditions in particular are required for it to happen on a sizeable scale: a substantial base of advanced electronics R & D to provide a supply of technically-based founders for the new firms, and, on the demand side, customers who will purchase the initially expensive new products. We consider each of these in turn.

There are two main sources of supply of founders for technology-based start up firms. Firstly, the R & D facilities of the most advanced firms, and secondly, higher education or state research institutions. The first has been by far the main source in the United States,[47] but does not exist in Ireland except on a very small scale. It has been argued here that they are unlikely to be attracted on a sufficient scale or quality to provide the necessary supply of skilled founders.

The main country where firms have been started from the higher education sector has also been the United States, by a wide margin. Even there, only a small number of institutions have been involved to any degree, principally MIT in Boston and Stanford University in California, and about eight others on a much lesser scale.[48] Even in the two most successful cases the process has been very slow in developing, taking decades to have a significant economic effect on the locality. The amount of electronics research taking place in the Irish higher education sector is small by comparison with the successful universities abroad and it would be very expensive indeed to boost this to an amount which might supply start-up personnel on a scale which could have an impact on the industry in the country, especially when the other obstacles to these firms' development in Ireland are taken into account. Also, such a process would take a long time to have an impact, even if it were successful.

'Science parks' and 'innovation centres' are special mechanisms which have been used, particularly in the United States, to encourage start-up firms linked to universities. Science parks are used to attract firms to universities in the hope that interaction will occur, leading to the growth of spin-off firms by people from either the firms or the universities. A recent review of the results to date in the US found that 'while a few parks have succeeded in attracting outside companies . . . the secondary spin-out effect has been generally dis-appointing'.[49] Innovation centres are purpose-built units on campuses which provide facilities such as workshops and administrative assistance to selected start-ups. These have also had very limited success to date, although they have been in operation only since 1979.[50] Neither of these mechanisms are likely to overcome to any significant degree the general obstacles to the development of such firms in Ireland.

On the demand side, there is a lack of sophisticated purchases of new advanced products in Ireland. In particular, the military and space markets, as well as advanced large corporations, that perform this function in the large developed countries are not present here. Public purchasing in tele-communictions has provided an initial market for indigenous electronics firms in Ireland but to date the products involved have not been of the highly advanced type. There is considerable scope in telecommunications and in other large public purchasing areas (e.g. health care, education and public administration) for providing a protected market during the initial learning stages for firms which develop new products. If this were to be successful, it would require a conscious and much more sophisticated approach to using this market for industrial development purpose than is the case at present. It would also have to avoid the standard problem of protected markets whereby the supplier firms become dependent on that market and do not use it as a springboard for penetrating other markets. This has happened in electronics in the UK especially, and in France to some extent.[51] In Ireland it has also happened to some firms in telecommunications, the main area of public purchasing in electronics, although there has also been the notable case of Ireland's currently most successful indigenous firm where it was used to good advantage to build up capabilities which were subsequently used to penetrate export markets.

Because the two basic conditions for the founding and development of new technology-based firms are missing in Ireland — the supply of people with the technical background for starting firms and a local demand for their advanced products — changes in the capital markets such as the provision of venture or risk capital would not have a major effect on the position. The shortage of suitable projects to fund is likely to continue. For the same reason, changes in the taxation system to encourage such firms are unlikely to have a significant impact.

Instead of entering at the emergent phase of segments on the basis of significant technological innovations, small firms can enter at a later stage by taking the basic technology and applying it to specialised needs in market niches. Several small Irish firms have taken this route, as outlined earlier. However, it is unlikely that a sufficient number of these firms will start up, for two reasons. Firstly, it is difficult for individual firms to grow rapidly on the basis of a succession of small niche markets because of the specialised expertise required for each niche. Secondly, for the same reasons the rate of establishment of such firms is not likely to be great in Ireland because of an insufficient supply of a range of such expertise across many specialised areas.

For all the reasons outlined here, it is unlikely that small firms can generate much employment or income within the next ten years in Ireland. This process will become much more difficult as the industry matures and competition increases. Consequently, the long time for the process to bear fruit, even if it were to do so, would make public investments aimed at this area even less effective in the future.

Given the obstacles which indigenous firms in Ireland face in competing internationally in the electronics industry, firms of a much larger scale are needed to overcome these and to provide a base for the subsequent development of the industry, as in other countries. Yet the small Irish firms are not growing to the size required, with one or two possible exceptions. Firms of adequate scale are unlikely to come about through 'normal' market processes in Ireland because of the barriers mentioned here. The development of an electronics industry — and more especially its rapid development — in small late developing countries such as Ireland almost certainly requires intervention in the structure of the industry to bring about firms of the scale required.

Large or medium-sized firms can be established in a variety of ways, all of which have been tried in other countries: mergers, joint ventures, 'national champions' (selecting individual firms and concentrating resources in support of these), and the creation of new firms (getting large firms in other sectors to diversify into the industry, or direct creation of firms by the state and/or private interests). Because of the fragmented nature of the indigenous sector in Ireland, with many small firms making different products, mergers and joint ventures among these firms are unlikely to bear much fruit. One is led to conclude, therefore, that the promotion of national champions and the creation of new firms are the only avenues to large firms in existing Irish circumstances.

It would appear that to get large firms in other sectors, either from non-traded industries or from outside the industrial sector, to diversify into electronics would require reducing the 'carrots' or incentives that are available to them in other activities and possibly the introduction of 'sticks' as well.[52] The latter may be necessary because of these firms' unwillingness to bear risks, and because of their lack of involvement in internationally traded industries, which results in a perception that the risks involved are higher than if they were more familiar with these industries and knew how to compete in them. The use of both carrots and sticks together can have dramatic results in cases where indigenous industry is largely engaged in non-traded activities; perhaps the most spectacularly successful example has been South Korea after such measures were taken in the early 1960s.[53]

The promotion of national champions in electronics has been tried in countries such as France, Japan, and South Korea. The creation of new firms has been tried in France, Sweden, Finland, the UK and South Korea, for example. Some of the latter have been highly successful and others a failure, usually due to mistakes in the original conception of the project. The direct creation of new firms is essentially the same process used by large corporations diversifying into new product areas by building from scratch: putting together the necessary finance and organisational structure, and employing management experienced in the area concerned, bringing them in from abroad where necessary.[54] It requires careful planning in an industry such as electronics if it is to be successful. Numerous methods of structural intervention have been tried in other countries and provide a large store of information on what might and might not succeed under Irish conditions.

Large or medium size can enable firms in late developing countries gradually to overcome their lack of technology. There are a number of options open to them, which may be tried in any combination. They have the resources to establish their own R & D facilities on an adequate scale, to buy in highly skilled expertise from abroad, and to buy into small high technology firms abroad and transfer technology back home. They can also use their strength in production or marketing as a negotiating strength in transferring technology from abroad through technology licensing or joint venture arrangements with foreign firms. Small firms lack these strengths and so find it difficult to find interested partners abroad. Licensing has played a major role in technology acquisition by other late developing countries. However, it has been little used by Irish industry, largely because the indigenous firms in traded industries do not have the necessary financial, production or marketing resources to pursue this strategy.[55] In other countries, larger companies competing on an international scale have also been the main mechanism in most industries for transferring advanced techniques into the country, as well as for developing new ones. These techniques have then been disseminated to other firms. This wider role of the larger firms has been important in virtually all countries, but particularly so in late developing ones as technology transfer is particularly important for those.

Intervention in the industry structure to build large firms (by Irish standards) in a reasonably short space of time would have the very important benefit of creating an environment within which the learning of important skills can take place. It was pointed out earlier that the electronics industry as presently constituted in Ireland does very little R & D and marketing. As a result, skills are not being developed in these areas, which are the most important for competition in many parts of the industry.

Comparing this situation with other countries, it may be said that this has been the single greatest failure in the development of the industry to date in Ireland, and it is difficult to see the industry progressing without it being remedied.

Large indigenous firms can break through this barrier to the industry's development by putting into place substantial R & D and international marketing activities. An important by-product of carrying on both of these activities is the learning effect both for individuals and organisations. In other words, two things are being produced simultaneously: the product which is sold on the market, and the increase in skills and organisational capabilities which benefits the firm subsequently. The firm can then go on to develop and market more complex products which have a greater return, and is also in a better position to ward off competitive threats which arise due to future changes in technology.[56] These learning processes in the fields of technology and international marketing have been central to the development of industry in general in late industrialising countries, leading to a continual improvement of their international competitive position. It is argued here that the mechanisms by which this learning occurs merit great attention.[57]

Other firms also benefit where some of the skilled people leave the original firms and go to other firms, bringing with them the skills which they have learned. This training function has been legendary in the case of Fairchild supplying people to the semiconductor industry in the United States for example.[58] The more advanced large firms have played a similar crucial role in countries such as South Korea. The failure to put the learning mechanisms outlined here into place in Ireland means that other countries where this is occurring are continually improving their competitive position relative to Ireland.

CONCLUSIONS

In this chapter we have considered the processes by which an electronics industry base, capable of self-sustained growth, can be built up in the particular conditions existing in Ireland. Special attention was paid to the role of technology in developing this base. It was argued that the crucial conditions in Ireland are that the country is industrialising relatively late, is on the periphery of Europe, and has a small home market. Three approaches to building such an electronics industry under these conditions were discussed. *Firstly,* the approach which relies mainly on attracting multinational firms was found to be inadequate for building the type of base required, despite their contribution to employment to date. It is significant that the three other countries in the world which have tried this approach, Scotland, Singapore and Puerto Rico, have also failed to develop a base of the quality required. *Secondly,* the 'Silicon Valley' process whereby many high-technology firms start up, enter new industry segments which are in the emergent phase, and grow rapidly, was found not to be a feasible proposition under Irish conditions. It has occurred in only a very few locations worldwide under specific conditons which are unlikely to be even approached in Ireland in the foreseeable future.

In considering the *third* approach, it was argued that the standard option for overcoming the barriers to late industrial development (especially those related to technology) — protecting the home market to provide an environment where an 'infant industry' can learn and where domestic firms can build up their scale before competing against existing large sophisticated firms abroad — is not available to small countries. Their home markets are too small for most industries. We argued that measures which lie outside the standard prescriptions are necessary under these circumstances, and that much can be learned from the measures adopted in other countries facing comparable obstacles. Especially in industries such as electronics where technologies are changing rapidly, it appears that to provide the necessary learning environment for building individual and organisational capabilities requires intervention by the state in the structure of the domestic industry, in small late industrialising countries. This intervention is needed to bring about a base of indigenous firms with sufficient scale and resources to compete internationally from a peripheral location, and which can provide the learning environment required. The experience of the electronics industry in other countries as well as in Ireland supports this analysis.

The same arguments apply to other industries where technological and organisational experience are important factors in competition. This applies to most of the growing industries identified at the beginning of this chapter as being crucial to the development of indigenous industry in Ireland, including software and engineering products with even a moderate degree of complexity. If Ireland is to build up a sustainable position in the industries which are growing internationally, then the question of the structure of industry and its effect on the development processes will require far greater attention than it has received to date.

Appendix

Data gathering in Science Policy Research Centre, University College, Dublin, Study of the Irish Electronics Industry, 1981

Initially, a list of firms in the industry was compiled using lists from State agencies, business directories, and diverse sources such as trade journals and newspapers. Basic data on nationality of ownership, year of establishment, employment, and products was gathered for all the firms, from the same sources, supplemented by telephone enquiries to the firms. The firms were divided into multinational subsidiaries and Irish companies and a stratified sample of each was chosen for detailed interviews; stratification was by employment size, age, product group, and by whether the firms performed R & D or not. Outline information supplied by the National Board for Science and Technology on R & D performance by firms was used to select a majority of R & D performers for the sample, including all those with the largest R & D efforts. Twenty-one of the 74 multinationals were interviewed, covering 60 per cent of employment in these firms. Sixteen of the 35 indigenous firms were included, containing 79 per cent of employment in the latter.

The origins of all the indigenous firms were investigated using a variety of means including telephone interviews with firms and discussions with personnel from the Industrial Development Authority. Those firms which originated as spin-offs from the electronics industry in Ireland (i.e. where the founders had left other electronics firms to start their present firm) were interviewed on the circumstances surrounding the process.

Hence, the issues discussed in the chapter were based on data from the following proportions of the industry.

Issues	*Coverage*
Employment, growth rates, size of R & D efforts, spin-offs.	All electronics firms
Factors related to R & D performance, marketing, technical skills, use of Irish technology services.	Interview sample
Markets served.	Interview sample, supplemented by information on many other firms from diverse sources.

NOTES AND REFERENCES

1. The author would like to thank the editors and a referee for comments on an earlier draft. The initial research work on the industry in Ireland, carried out at the Science Policy Research Centre, University College Dublin, was funded by the National Board for Science and Technology. None of these are of course answerable for the views expressed here.

2. Irish indigenous employment by industry from Industrial Development Authority, *Annual Report 1982* (Dublin, Industrial Development Authority, 1983); the types of products produced within these broad industry categories are discussed in Telesis Consultancy Group, *A Review of Industrial Policy* (Dublin, National Economic and Social Council [Report No. 64], 1982). Data on developing countries from *Yearbook of Industrial Statistics 1980,* (New York, United Nations, 1982). Growth rates by industry from *ibid.;* the world food market appears to have reached a plateau after reasonable growth rates during the 1960s and 1970s.

3. PA Consulting Group, *Exports to Britain: Scope for Improvement,* Report to Coras Trachtala, summarised in *Export Review,* vol. 2, no. 3 (1983); Telesis Consultancy Group, *op. cit.*

4. Natural resource-based industries, especially food and timber processing, appear to have considerable potential in Ireland, but are not included since their development depends to a considerable degree on the supply of raw materials, and this involves issues well outside the topics discussed in this chapter. Cf. Telesis Consultancy Group, *op. cit.*

5. E.g. Sen, A., 'Followers Strategy for Technological Development', *The Developing Economies,* vol. 17, no. 4 (1979), pp. 506-28.

6. Due to the nature of the market for technology itself, it is usually more advantageous for a firm which makes a new development to exploit this directly itself through its own production than simply licensing it to others. Von Hippel, E., 'Appropriability of Innovation Benefit as a Predictor of the Source of Innovation', *Research Policy,* vol. 11, no. 2 (1982), pp. 95-115. This is particularly true at the earlier stages of an industry's life cycle, whereas at later stages it usually becomes more profitable for these firms to sell the technology to others. The reasons for this are complex and the situation varies by industry and according to a firm's position in its industry; particularly important is the difference in a firm's ability to appropriate the economic benefits of its technology developments at the various stages of the life cycle. Cf. Ford, D., & Ryan, C., 'Taking Technology to Market', *Harvard Business Review,* vol. 59, No. 3 (1981), pp. 117-26; Shvartz, L., Horesh, R., & Raz, B., 'Trade in Technology: Management Decisions and Pricing', *Technological Forecasting and Social Change,* vol. 23, no. 2 (1983), pp. 173-84.

6a. The concepts addressed in this section are discussed by the following authors, among others: "appropriability" and "response time": Von Hippel, E., op. cit.; "technological opportunity": Mowery, D., and Rosenberg, N., 'The influence of market demand upon innovation: a critical review of some recent studies,' *Research Policy*, vol. 8, no. 2 (1979), pp. 103-53; "cumulative" technologies: Nelson, R. and Winter, S., *An Evolutionary Theory of Economic Growth* (Cambridge, Mass., Belknap Harvard, 1982).

7. Freeman, C., *The Economics of Industrial Innovation* (London, Frances Pinter, 1982), Table 1.3a.

8. E.g.: Teubal, M., 'The R & D Performance through Time of Young, High-technology Firms', *Research Policy*, vol. 11, no. 6 (1982), pp. 336-46; Dosi, G., *Technical Change and Survival: Europe's Semiconductor Industry* (Industrial Adjustment and Policy Series, No. II, Brighton, Sussex European Research Centre, 1981).

9. Porter, M., *Competitive Strategy: Techniques for Analysing Industries and Competitors* (New York, The Free Press, 1980); Abernathy, W., and Utterback, J., 'Patterns of Industrial Innovation', *Technology Review*, no. 80 (1978), pp. 40-49; Klein, B., *Dynamic Competition* (Cambridge, Mass., Harvard University Press, 1977). There are some similarities in this presentation to the 'product cycle' model associated with R. Vernon and S. Hirsch. The conclusions drawn here for small developed countries in particular are different from those of Hirsch, the only one of those authors to consider small countries; he does not consider the strategy option outlined here for these countries. Vernon, R., 'International Trade and Investment in the Product Cycle', *Quarterly Journal of Economics,* vol. 80, no. 2 (1966), pp. 190-207; Hirsch, S., *Location of Industry and International Competiveness* (London, Oxford University Press, 1967).

10. This option is discussed at greater length in the National Board for Science and Technology discussion document, *Technology and Irish Industrial Policy,* 1983, in the writing of which the author participated.

11. The general evolutionary picture outlined here does not hold true in its entirety for all industries or industry segments. More detailed analyses have to be carried out when applying this picture to individual industries or segments, with greater attention to the underlying forces which shape the overall picture — in particular, the specific nature of technical change in the industry. Some examples are given in Walker, W., *Industrial Innovation and International Trading Performance* (Greenwich, Conn., JAI Press, 1979), Ch. 2.

12. Kristensen, P., and Levinsen, J., *The Small Country Squeeze* (Lund, Research Policy Institute, 1979).

13. Malecki, E., 'Science, Technology, and Regional Economic Development: Review and Prospects', *Research Policy*, vol. 10, no. 4 (1981), pp. 312-34; Hekman, J., 'Can New England Hold onto It's High Technology Industry?', *New England Economic Review* (March-April 1980), pp. 35-44.

14. Cf. the references in note 13; also Malecki, E., 'Corporate Organisation of R & D and the Location of Technological Activities', *Regional Studies,* vol. 14, no. 3 (1980), pp. 219-34.
15. OECD, *Impact of Multinational Enterprises on National Scientific and Technical Capacities: Analytical Report* (Paris, OECD, 1980), mimeo.
16. Cable, V., and Clarke, J., *British Electronics and Competition with Newly Industrialising Countries* (London, Overseas Development Institute, 1981). They appear to considerably underestimate the electronics exports from Malaysia, however.
17. Lim, L., *Multinational Firms and Manufacturing for Export in Less-Developed Countries: The Case of the Electronics Industry in Malaysia and Singapore,* Ph.D. Dissertation, University of Michigan, 1978; 'Electronics Industry in Korea', *Korea Exchange Bank Monthly Review,* vol. 11, no. 9 (Sept. 1977). pp. 1-13.
18. Kim, L., 'Stages of Development of Industrial Technology in a Developing Country: a Model', *Research Policy,* vol. 9 no. 3 (1980) pp. 254-77; Wong Chiu Yan, 'Hong Kong Electronics: Taking Giant Steps', *Hong Kong Trader,* no. 6 (1981), pp. 77-80.
19. 1970 figure from 'Electronics Industry in Korea', *op. cit.,* p. 6.; 1979 figure from Kim, W., 'Challenge to US Domination — The Promises of Technology for Newly Industrialising Countries', paper to Financial Times World Electronics Conference, Monte Carlo, 5-7 May 1980.
20. 'Taiwan's Spur to Technology' *Electronic Business* (January 1982), p. 114; Graim, T., 'Taiwan Begins Output of Bipolar and Custom Integrated Circuits', *Electronic Business* (January 1982), p. 30; Neff, R., 'Hong Kong Prepares to Change', *Electronics* (July 14, 1982), pp. 124-26.
21. Center for Policy Alternatives, *National Support for Science and Technology: an Examination of Foreign Experience* (Boston, Massachusetts Institute of Technology, 1976).
22. Data for Europe from *Mackintosh Electronics Year Book 1981* (Luton, Machintosh Publications, 1981). Other countries from a wide variety of trade literature.
23. SRI International, *The Electronics Industry in Denmark* (Menlo Park, Cal., SRI International, 1978).
24. Labour costs per hour, including social charges, were 2.41 times higher in Denmark than Ireland in 1979. Dresdner Bank, *Economic Quarterly* (November1980), quoted in *Report of the Committee on Costs and Competitiveness* (Dublin, Stationery Office, 1981), p. 53.
25. SRI International, *op. cit.*
26. Manners, D., 'Finns Swimming in Trade Ties', *Electronics Weekly* (November 11, 1981); Barnes, H., 'Electronics: Big Companies Increase Share', *Financial Times,* Survey on Finland, June 16, 1982; SRI International, *op. cit.*
27. O'Brien, R., Cogan, D.J., Kelly, J., Lawless, E., Onyenadum, E., and Wrynn, J., *The Irish Electronics Industry,* Report to the National Board for Science and Technology by the Science Policy Research Centre (University College Dublin, 1981).

28. Dataproducts and Teradyne data from *Business Week International,* June 20, 1983; Samsung data from L. Kraar, 'Make Way for the New Japans', *Fortune,* August 10, 1981.

29. Science Council Working Group on Industrial Policies, *Multinationals and Industrial Strategy: The Role of World Product Mandates* (Ottawa, Science Council of Canada, 1980).

30. Computed from US Department of Commerce, *op. cit.*

31. A more detailed explanation of the differences in skill profile between four of these countries is given in Cogan, D.J., and O'Brien, R., 'The Irish Electronics Sector: Technical Manpower as an Indicator of Structure and Sophistication', *Journal of Irish Business and Administrative Research,* vol. 5, no. 1 (1983), pp. 3-11.

32. Discussed in greater detail in Cogan, D.J., and Onyenadum, E., 'Spin-off Companies in the Irish Electronics Industry', *Journal of Irish Business and Administrative Research,* vol. 3, no. 2 (1981), pp. 3-15.

33. Unpublished research by E. Onyenadum, Faculty of Commerce, UCD.

34. Lim, *op. cit.*

35. A major empirical study of university-industry relationships found that: 'Contrary to some expectations, *innovation is not a major industrial motivation for university-industry interactions.* Industry rarely looks to the university for technological innovations that result directly in new products or processes. . . . if a company must go outside its own organisation for such innovation it is unlikely to go to a university' (emphasis in the original). National Science Foundation, *University-Industry Research Relationships: Myths, Realities and Potentials* (Washington, National Science Foundation, 1982), p. 20.

36. Telesis Consultancy Group, *op. cit.*

37. Booz, Allen & Hamilton, *The Electronics Industry in Scotland* (Glasgow, Scottish Development Agency, 1978).

38. E.g. Cooper, A., *The Founding of New Technologically-Based Firms* (Wisconsin, Center for Venture Management, 1971).

39. See Eoin O'Malley's contribution to this book, and Telesis Consultancy Group, *op. cit.*

40. These findings on the indigenous electronics sector are supported by other research: Landy, P., *Competing in the Global Electronics Industry: The Challenge for Indigenous Irish Firms,* MBS Thesis, University College Dublin, 1982. Landy's study also found that the strategic planning by indigenous firms in the key areas of marketing and R & D were grossly inadequate for competing internationally in electronics. His conclusions were pessimistic on the future for indigenous firms under current policies. The author has benefited from numerous discussions with Landy about the indigenous electronics sector in Ireland.

41. OECD, *op. cit.*

42. Sciberras, E., *Multinational Electronics Companies and National Economic Policies* (Greenwich, Connecticut, JAI Press, 1977).

43. E.g. Malecki, E., 'Science, Technology and Regional Economic Development', *op. cit.*

44. O'Brien et al., op. cit.

45. Data by industry supplied by the National Board for Science and Technology from their 1979 national R & D survey.

46. E.g. Phoenix in Arizona, Boulder in Colorado, Ottawa in Canada, and Berkshire in the UK.

47. Cooper, *op. cit.;* research by A. Bruno, Santa Clara University, reported in Malone, M., 'Successful High-Tech Startups Require more than Innovation,' *Electronic Business* (April 1981), pp. 100-02; Bullock, M., *Academic Enterprise, Industrial Innovation, and the Development of High Technology Financing in the United States* (London, Brand Brothers, 1983).

48. Bullock, *op. cit.*

49. Bullock, *op. cit.,* p. 9.

50. Bullock, *ibid.*

51. Sciberras, E., *op. cit.;* Sciberras, E., Swords-Isherwood, N., and Senker, P., *Competition, Technical Change and Manpower in Electronic Capital Equipment: A Study of the U.K. Minicomputer Industry,* (Brighton, Science Policy Research Unit, Sussex University, 1978); Zysman, J., *Political Strategies for Industrial Order: State, Market and Industry in France* (Berkeley, Cal., University of California Press, 1977).

52. The Telesis Report argued that both measures are necessary to get these firms to move into traded industries in general. Cf. Telesis Consulting Group, *op. cit.*

53. Cf. Jones, L., and Sakong, I., *Government, Business, and Entrepeneurship in Economic Development: The Korean Case* (Cambridge, Mass., Harvard University Press, 1980).

54. The Telesis Report contains some ideas on how new firms could be created in internationally traded industries; they overlap with those in this paper. Cf. Telesis Consultancy Group, *op. cit.,* pp. 232-34. An example of new firm creation in a sector of electronics identified as having strategic national importance, is the creation of the Finnish firm Micronas: Manners, D., 'Finns Plan their own IC Strategy', *Electronics Weekly* (4 Nov. 1981). Further elaboration of methods of new firm creation is given in the National Board for Science and Technology discussion document, *Formulating Strategy in a Technology-Intensive Sector,* 1983, in which the author participated.

55. Empirical support for this view is given in a study of licensing by indigenous firms in Ireland: Cashell, J., *The Transfer of Technology into Ireland and Company Diversification through Technology Licensing and Joint Venturing,* MBA Thesis, UCD, 1983.

56. Teubal, M., *op. cit.;* Nelson, R., and Winter, S., op. cit. (see note 6a), pp. 255-262. It can be seen that 'learning' is being used in this chapter to cover a much broader range of activities than the more well-known notion confined to the area of production, associated with K. Arrow.

57. Cf., for example, Westphal, L., Rhee, Y., and Pursell, G., *Korean Industrial Competence: Where it Came From,* World Bank Staff Working Paper no. 469 (Washington, D.C., World Bank, 1981); Westphal, L., *Empirical Justification for Infant Industry Protection,* World Bank Staff Working Paper no. 445 (Washington D.C., World Bank, 1981).

58. Golding, A., *The Semiconductor Industry in Britain and the United States: a Case Study in Innovation, Growth and Diffusion of Technology,* Ph.D Thesis, University of Sussex, 1971.

Index

257